RICHARD
AND SABINA

RICHARD AND SABINA

*A Biography of the
Rev. Richard Wurmbrand
and His Wife Sabina*

Jack Cole

Copyright © 2000 by Jack Cole.

Library of Congress Number: 00-192227
ISBN #:   Softcover   1-59109-472-0

All rights reserved. No part of this book may be reproduced or transmitted in any form or by any means, electronic or mechanical, including photocopying, recording, or by any information storage and retrieval system, without permission in writing from the copyright owner.

This book was printed in the United States of America.

CONTENTS

ACKNOWLEDGEMENTS 9
PROLOGUE 11

CHAPTER 1
Richard smells the flowers 13
CHAPTER 2
Congress of Cults 17
CHAPTER 3
Richard imprisoned 23
CHAPTER 4
Torture 30
CHAPTER 5
Solitary Confinement 35
CHAPTER 6
Room Four 47
CHAPTER 7
Communist Reeducation 63
CHAPTER 8
Richard freed after $8^{1/2}$ years imprisonment 74
CHAPTER 9
Sabina 86
CHAPTER 10
Her life story 105
CHAPTER 11
Three years of Slave Labor 110
CHAPTER 12
Sabina released 127
CHAPTER 13
Underground Church 136

CHAPTER 14
　Sabina struggles to exist 152
CHAPTER 15
　Richard rearrested 161
CHAPTER 16
　Religious Disharmony 178
CHAPTER 17
　Brainwashed 182
CHAPTER 18
　Richard's Poem 206
CHAPTER 19
　Conversion to Christianity 211
CHAPTER 20
　Richard Ordained 233
CHAPTER 21
　Flight to America 241
CHAPTER 22
　Worldwide Preaching 250
CHAPTER 23
　Voice of the Martyrs 260
CHAPTER 24
　Richard's Lullaby 270
CHAPTER 25
　Triumphant Return 273

EPILOGUE 276
CHRONOLOGY 282
BIBLIOGRAPHY 289

To Beverly

my beloved daughter and literary manager

whose faith in me kept the fires lit.

ACKNOWLEDGEMENTS

First thanks goes to my son Christopher for introducing me to the Wurmbrands about 1993 and thanks to his wife Maya who entertained me and the Wurmbrands at her home before she was my daughter-in-law. Maya was also the go-between frequently during the five years of writing. She is Romanian and the Wurmbrands consider her the "daughter of their heart." In fact, Richard gave her away when she married my son. I'm especially indebted to Ellen Oblander of California. She faithfully edited line by line my manuscript as I sent her chapter after chapter. I'm indebted to The Voice of the Martyrs for supplying me with all of the books written by Richard and Sabina. Thanks to Fern Bradley, my son Tom's wife, for reading my manuscript and suggesting a chronology for those not yet born during much of this history. Lastly, I'm indebted to my family, especially my wife Lynn and daughter Leslie, for tolerating me all the years I spent pounding away at my word processor, and to son Bob for guiding me through the maze of computers at Lehigh University's libraries. There are many others such as Chris's friends who sent me items of interest about the Wurmbrands, the Bethlehem Public Library for finding out-of-print books, and those who unfortunately shall remain unnamed.

PROLOGUE

I met the Reverend Richard Wurmbrand six days after he had had a "little stroke." He said in his rich Romanian accent, "My doctor said I should stop traveling and rest. I told him if twenty-five strokes of the torturer's whip didn't stop me, why should one little stroke?"

Richard was imprisoned fourteen years by the Communist government in various Romanian prisons because of his refusal to renounce his Christian faith and because of his intense efforts to propagate the faith.

The Communist government in Bucharest convened a Congress of Cults which was attended by bishops, priests, pastors, and rabbis. One after another they got up and declared communism and their religions compatible and pledged allegiance to the government. Richard's wife Sabina urged him to defend Jesus. "If I do," he said, "you'll be without a husband."

Sabina replied, "I don't want a coward for a husband." Richard got up and spoke, pledging his allegiance to Jesus. This was the beginning of years of harassment.

Three of his fourteen years in prison were spent in solitary confinement thirty feet below ground in a dank dungeon. The only breaks in silence were the screams of those being tortured. During these years Richard composed 356 sermons which he memorized by putting them into poetry. Memory was his only tool. He had no pen or paper.

Prison was nothing new to him. He and Sabina and their families had suffered severely under Nazi rule of Romania.

When not in prison, Richard was active in the underground church. Even while in prison he converted many to Christianity, including guards and torturers. His driving philosophy was: hate the sin but love the sinner.

Richard was not always a saint. Although born a Jew, his early years were atheistic. He wanted to believe in a God but couldn't. He spent his youth and early adulthood drinking, womanizing, and gambling. His conversion to Christianity was followed shortly by Sabina's conversion.

He gives much credit to Sabina for his direction in life. Sabina had a difficult life of her own. While waiting for his release from prison, never knowing if he was alive or dead, she spent three years as a slave laborer helping to build the Danube Canal.

Richard was bought from the communist government for $10,000 by a Norwegian Christian mission. Since that time he has devoted his life to easing the plight of Christians throughout the world persecuted because of their faith.

CHAPTER 1

Richard stood in front of Jilava prison. The space around him seemed vast. He squinted in the bright sunlight. It was a warm June day and a gentle breeze played around his face. He sniffed as if smelling a precious perfume and breathed a deep sigh. A symphony of birds broke the silence. He was free.

When Khrushchev came to power he denounced Stalin as a murderer and tyrant. An amnesty followed and many prisoners were released. Richard wondered if he would be one of them. The thought saddened him. He wondered what use he would be as a free man. His son Mihai had grown up and would hardly remember him. Sabina was accustomed to going her own way. The church had other pastors who made less trouble.

Early one morning a guard shouted, "Interrogation at once. Move!" Richard started to gather his things while the guard continued to bellow. They hurried through the corridors and across the yard. One after another the steel gates were unlocked as they climbed the steps. Then he was outside. A clerk handed him a slip of paper which contained a court order saying he was free under the amnesty.

Richard was alarmed. While he stupidly stared at the paper he said, "I've done only eight and a half years and my sentence is for twenty. I've got twelve years yet to serve."

The clerk said, "You must leave at once. Don't argue. Get out."

"But look at me." Richard's ragged shirt was gray with dirt. His trousers had patches on patches. His boots looked like Charlie Chaplin's. "I'll be arrested by the first policeman."

"We have no clothes for you. Get out of here." With that the clerk went into the prison and locked the gates behind him.

Jilava is three miles from Bucharest. He heaved his bundle onto his shoulder and set off across the fields. He waded through the deep grass. He touched the rough bark of the trees. He stopped to gaze at a flower or a budding leaf.

An old country couple came toward him. "You come from *there*?" they asked. From his pocket the man took a leu, a coin worth about a penny, and gave it to Richard. He almost laughed. No one had ever given him a leu before. He asked for their address so that he could repay it. "No, no, keep it," they urged, using the word "thou" as people do in Romania when speaking to children and beggars.

He continued on. Another woman stopped him. "You come from *there*?" She inquired about a priest in prison. He had not met him but explained that he was also a pastor. They sat on a wall by the roadside and talked about Christ. This made him so happy that he forgot he was on his way home. When he started to leave, she handed him a leu for the tram fare. "But I have a leu already."

"Then take it for our Lord's sake."

He walked on until he reached a tram stop on the outskirts of the capital. People crowded around him, knowing at once where he had come from. They inquired about relatives. They all had someone in prison. When he boarded the tram they would not let him pay. Several offered him their seat. He sat with his bundle on his knees. Just as the car started there were shouts from outside, "Stop! Stop!" Richard's heart pounded. The tram jerked to a halt as a militiaman's motorcycle swerved in front. Richard knew they had come to take him back. The driver turned and shouted, "Someone is standing on the steps."

Next to Richard sat a woman with a basket of fresh strawberries. He stared at them. "Haven't you had any this year?" she asked.

"Not for eight years," he replied.

"Go on, take some," she said and filled his hands with them. He stuffed his mouth like a child.

At last he stood in front of his own front door and hesitated. He was a fearful sight in his filth and rags. He opened the door. There were several young people. Among them was a gawky young man who stared at Richard and burst out, "Father." It was his son Mihai who was nine when he left and was now eighteen.

Then Sabina came forward. Her fine-boned face was thinner but her hair was still black. Richard thought she was more beautiful than ever. She put her arms around him and with great effort Richard said, "Before we kiss I must say something. Don't think I've simply come from misery to happiness. I've come from the joy of being with Christ in prison to the joy of being with him in my family. I'm not coming from strangers to my own, but from my own in prison to my own at home." Sabina sobbed and they kissed. Later, Richard sang softly a little song he had made for her years before in prison to sing if they ever met again.

Mihai informed his dad that the place was full of visitors who would not leave without seeing him. Members of his church had been telephoning all over Bucharest. The doorbell rang continuously. Old friends brought new ones. Every time he was introduced, he was conscious of his absurd trousers held up by string. It was near midnight when everyone had gone. Sabina urged Richard to eat something but he felt no hunger. He said, "Today we have had happiness enough. Let's make tomorrow a day of fasting in thankfulness, with Holy Communion before supper."

He turned to Mihai. Three of the visitors, one a philosophy professor from the university whom Richard had not met before, told him that Mihai had brought them to faith in Christ. Richard was extremely happy. He had feared that Mihai, left without parents, would be lost. He put his arm around Mihai and told him he had nearly forgotten the Bible but he had four things always in mind: there is a God, Christ is our Savior, there is eternal life, and love is the best of ways.

In his clean, soft bed that night, he couldn't sleep. He sat up and opened the Bible. He couldn't find the Book of Daniel. His eye fell on a line in the Epistles of St. John. "I have no greater joy than to hear that my children walk in truth." Richard had this joy. He went into Mihai's room to make sure he was really there.

It was two weeks before he could sleep regularly. As an ex-prisoner, everyone wanted to help him, in the streets, the shops, everywhere, and the stream of visitors began again.

CHAPTER 2

In the summer of 1944, when Hitler's Germany was collapsing, one million Soviet troops invaded Romania. As the first columns approached Bucharest, Richard and Sabina took a tram to meet them. It was the last day of August, a hot sunny day.

Richard, who had been a wartime pastor, had known many Russians in Romanian prison camps. In spite of their having been drilled in atheism for twenty-five years, he found them instinctively religious. He had said to Sabina, "We must go out and meet them. To speak to Russians about Christ is heaven on earth."

They got off at the suburban crossroads. There they saw a group of red flags, carried by local Communists who had come out of hiding to greet the "Glorious Red Army." They looked at the Wurmbrands uncertainly; most locals were keeping out of the way.

As roaring motorcycles and tanks approached, welcoming Communists fell into line and raised the red flags. At the conclusion of the welcoming speech, they presented the traditional gifts to strangers, a loaf of bread and a handful of salt.

A young sergeant caught Sabina's eye. "Well, sweetheart," he said, "what have you to offer?"

Sabina, the only woman present, said, "I've brought you the Holy Bible." She handed it up to him in the towering tank.

"Bread, salt, and Bibles. All we want is a drink. Thanks anyway." He laughed as he pushed his helmet back.

From the tram on the way home, Richard and Sabina saw soldiers looting shops of wine-casks, chickens, hams, sausages. Although Bucharest was a sad shell of its former self, to the Russians it was wealth beyond belief.

When they got off the tram, Richard tried to speak to some of them but the only response was, "Where can we find vodka?" They went home to make other plans.

The people of Romania had suffered under Nazi rule. They now hoped the Russians would settle down and be friends and that there would be peace.

The local Communists still pretended democracy in spite of the fact they were ruled from Moscow. Richard knew this was done to dupe the western powers. This hypocrisy ended when the Soviet Minister Vishinsky marched into the palace and ordered King Michael to disband the army and police force and to appoint trusted Communists to key posts.

The government called for every religious faith to send a large delegation to a meeting in the Parliament building. It was called a Congress of Cults. Richard believed the same thing was happening in Romania as had happened in Russia. The church would be lulled into acceptance and then clobbered. He proved to be right.

When the day for the Congress of Cults arrived, Richard and Sabina climbed Parliament Hill. The delegates were crowded into the galleries and on the floor of the huge hall. Attending were Moslem, Jew, Protestant, Orthodox, and Catholic. There were 4000 bishops, pastors, priests, rabbis, and mullahs.

Red flags hung everywhere. Although Stalin was president of the World Atheists Organization, the delegates applauded when it was announced that he was patron of the Congress. Although dedicated to the destruction of religion, the Communists were welcomed by the delegates. One after another the church leaders got up and said they were glad to cooperate with them.

Sabina knew that Richard was boiling inside and said to him, "Will you not wash this shame from the face of Christ?"

Richard replied, "If I speak, you will lose a husband."

Sabina said, "I don't need a coward for a husband."

Richard requested permission to speak. The Communists were delighted. Here was a prominent pastor, a representative of the World Council of Churches and of other foreign missions who was going to make propaganda for them. The program was being broadcast over radio.

Richard got up to speak. He said, "When the children of God meet, the angels also gather to hear about the wisdom of God. It is the duty of all present not to praise earthly powers that come and go, but to glorify God the Creator and Christ the Savior who died for us on the Cross."

Suddenly the Minister of Cults, Burducea, jumped to his feet. He shouted, "Your right to speak is withdrawn."

Richard ignored him and went on. Burducea bellowed, "Cut that microphone." The Congress shouted Burducea down.

Richard, Sabina, and Mihai

They chanted rhythmically, "The Pastor! The Pastor!" Richard had been elevated from "a pastor" to "The Pastor."

The uproar lasted many minutes. The shouting and applause went on long after the microphone wires had been cut and Richard had left the podium. That ended the Congress for the day.

When Richard and Sabina reached home, they found his mother terrified. She had heard everything on the radio and thought she would never see them again. "What will happen now?" she asked.

Richard replied, "Mother, I have a powerful Savior. He'll do what's best for me."

No immediate official move was made. Soon, Communist hecklers were sent to break up the pastor's church meetings. Week after week rough-looking youths pushed their way into the back of the church to whistle, jeer, and interrupt.

Richard and Sabina worked out street-preaching tactics. Many people were afraid to go into church. This way the Wurmbrands could reach them. With a small group as a nucleus, they would meet on a street corner to sing hymns. Since this procedure was totally unknown in Romania, a crowd always gathered. Then a short and emphatic message would be delivered.

One afternoon outside the great Malaxa factory there was a protest meeting against the Communist take-over. Sabina spoke to the workers about salvation. Next day, police opened fire on a crowd at the factory. Many workers were shot.

A reign of terror began in 1947. Rigged elections put the Communists in complete control. Leaders of the opposition, police chiefs, and civil servants were liquidated. Catholic bishops, clergy, monks, and nuns were arrested while religious broadcasts were made as usual to the West. Tens of thousands of ordinary citizens were sent to jails and labor camps. Some joined the freedom fighters in the mountains. Jews who had not yet escaped were trapped by the closing of borders..

Richard got his first warning. He was working in the mission when a plain-clothes man walked in. He introduced himself as

Inspector Riosanu. "I've come to give you a tip," he said. "There's a big fat file on you at police HQ. I've seen it. Someone has informed against you lately. You've been talking to a lot of Russian friends, haven't you? I thought we might come to an agreement." He said for a sum of money he would destroy the report.

The Wurmbrands and the inspector agreed on an amount and the sum was paid. The inspector started to tell them the name of the informer but they refused to hear it. Riosanu shrugged and left.

Shortly after this, Richard was taken in for questioning. He still had some influential friends and after three weeks his release was obtained.

More and more of the Wurmbrands' friends and helpers were arrested. With bribes and threats the Communists put certain church leaders to work for them. The obstinate ones were sent to prison.

In December of 1947, after the United States and Britain recognized the Kremlin's puppet, Groza, King Michael was forced to abdicate.

Richard was struggling with his conscience. It wasn't too late to leave Romania. Although it grew more difficult every day, thousands were still buying their way out.

One day he said to Sabina, "Under Nazi rule we were never imprisoned for more than two or three weeks at a time. With the Communists it can last for years. And they may take you, too. And who will look after Mihai?"

Then an odd thing happened. An alcoholic who had become a pastor after Richard converted him, came to visit. He reminded him of his conversion and several times he repeated, "What struck me most in what you said then was a verse: 'Escape for thy life; look not behind thee.' The angel's words to Lot."

When he had left, Richard said to Sabina, "Don't you think that may have been a message from God? Why should he come to see us after so long a time and repeat over and over, 'Escape for thy life'? Wasn't it a warning I must save my life by fleeing?"

Sabina said, "Escape for what life?" She opened the Bible to where Jesus says: "Whoever will save his life shall lose it and whosoever will lose his life for my sake shall find it."

Sabina asked, "If you leave now, will you ever be able again to preach about this text?" That night they spoke no more about leaving.

A few days later, Richard said, "If we go to the West, won't we be able to do more for the church in Romania? If we stay I'll follow the others into prison. It'll be the end of our life together. I'll be tortured, perhaps killed. And if you're imprisoned too, it's the end of the mission. Mihai will be brought up on the streets—a Communist. What good will it do anyone?"

Sabina said quietly, "I think we must stay."

They began to hold meetings in private homes around Bucharest because it was safer than in churches. One night at the home of a rich man who had lost everything except his house (he soon lost this too) they held a prayer meeting. About fifty had gathered for an all-night vigil. Toward midnight a kneeling woman cried aloud, "And you, the one who thinks of leaving, remember that the Good Shepherd did not desert his flock. He stayed to the last." The Wurmbrands knew she had no knowledge of Richard's struggle.

At dawn, the Wurmbrands walked home in the cold. It was January and snow was falling. They agreed they could not leave Romania. Their friends rejoiced when they told them, "We are here to stay."

Fourteen years later, when Richard came home from prison, the praying woman who had shouted the message met him at the station with flowers. Richard said to her, "I don't regret taking your advice. I'm thankful for it."

CHAPTER 3

February 29, 1948 was a beautiful Sunday. Richard was walking to his church, his official church. He had been serving as pastor to a church known to the Communists and also as a pastor to the underground church, which met secretly.

A black Ford van stopped in front of him. Two men jumped out and forced him into it. A third man sitting beside the driver kept him covered with a pistol. They sped through the evening traffic to a street called Calea Rahova. They drove between steel gates which clanged behind them. They were at the headquarters of the Communist Secret Police.

Richard's papers, belongings, tie, and shoelaces were taken from him. "From now on," said the official on duty, "you are Vasile Georgescu." They did not want even the guards to know whom they were guarding. Richard realized that, like many others, he was to disappear without a trace. In fact, at a later date, people were sent to tell Sabina they had attended his burial at prison.

Richard was placed in a cell with a small window high in the concrete wall. There were two plank beds and the usual bucket in the corner.

Through the small window he could see a corner of the yard. As he looked, a priest was let in through the gates. He passed through a door. Richard knew that he was an informer who had come to report on the members of his congregation.

In order to keep their places of worship from being closed, priests, pastors, and rabbis had to cooperate with the Communists. Those who refused were jailed. Interrogators told the clergy, "As a Christian you must promise to tell us the whole truth about everything."

Richard had prepared himself for interrogation. He knew that in the eyes of the Party, his connections with Western church missions and with the World Council of Churches were treasonable. He knew that no matter what he said he would be found guilty. He had studied the lives of Christians who had faced pain and temptations to surrender and thought how he could adapt their experiences. He decided that under torture he would incriminate himself, but never betray friends who had helped him spread the gospel. He would confuse and mislead interrogators as much as possible.

Richard decided his first task was to warn colleagues and to let Sabina know where he was. He suborned a guard, with the help of $2000 over the next few weeks, to act as intermediary. This stopped when everything the Wurmbrands owned was seized. The guard brought word that the Swedish Ambassador had protested about Richard's disappearance. The Foreign Minister, Mrs. Ana Pauker, had replied that nothing was known of his whereabouts since he had secretly left the country some time ago.

A few days after his arrival at Calea Rahova, the door of Richard's cell opened and in walked Comrade Patrascanu, the man who had brought Communism to power in Romania.

Richard assumed he had come to interrogate him. The door was locked behind him and Richard noted Patrascanu's tie and shoestrings had been removed. The new prisoner had made the mistake of asking an official if there was any truth to the rumor that prisoners were being tortured and had let it be known he was disturbed if it were true.

At ten that evening, after Richard and his cellmate had gone to bed, the cell was entered and Richard was called by his new name. He was told to dress. Black goggles were placed over his eyes and he was led down a long corridor to a room in which he was placed in a chair. The goggles were removed. He sat before a table with a harsh accusing light shining in his eyes. When his eyes had adjusted to the glare, he recognized a man called Moravetz, a former police inspector, who had betrayed secrets to the Communists.

"Ah," said Moravetz, "Vasile Georgescu. You'll find paper and pen on that desk. Take your chair over there and write about your activities and your life. As a priest you have heard many confessions. We've brought you here to confess to us."

Richard wrote about his life up to the time of his conversion. He explained how while an atheist his eyes had been opened to the truth. After an hour, Moravetz took the paper and said that was enough for that night.

During the week Patrascanu shared his cell, Richard discussed the Bible and Christian belief. Patrascanu countered with his beliefs but at times seemed interested. One morning Patrascanu was taken from the cell and Richard never saw him again.

Several days passed without Richard being interrogated. The Communists rely on the shock of arrest to make a prisoner talk. First they let him "ripen." The interrogator doesn't say what he wants but speaks suggestively to create anxiety and guilt. While the prisoner is trying to determine the reason for his arrest, tension is built up by constantly postponing trial and by playing tape-recorded sounds of a firing squad and screams from other prisoners. Exhaustion finally forces him to accept his guilt. The interrogator becomes sympathetic and offers better things if the prisoner admits he deserves punishment and tells all.

In a few days, Appel, the man who had escorted him from his cell for the first interview, returned and the first of Richard's innumerable interrogations began.

He was taken to a room not far from his cell and offered a chair and a toffee. One of Appel's colleagues took notes. Appel checked Richard's written statement and commented that a man's thinking was decided by his class; not being of proletarian origin, Richard was bound to have reactionary views. Richard pointed out that none of the great Party thinkers were "workers" in that sense. Marx was a lawyer's son, Engels' father was a man of property, and Lenin came from nobility.

Appel broke in, "What were your connections with Mr. Teodorescu?" Since that was a common name, Richard asked him which one he meant. Appel did not answer but started discussing the Bible. From time to time, he mentioned the names of people who had helped in distributing Richard's books to Soviet soldiers or in handling relief for the World Council of Churches. He was always polite and appeared to be more interested in Richard's reactions to sudden questions than in his answers. Richard was returned to his cell.

His next inquisitor was Vasilu, a little man who talked out the corner of his mouth. He asked Richard to write down the names of everyone he knew, where he had met them, and what his relations with them were. Vasilu snapped, "Don't pick and choose. I said everyone."

Richard listed the names of his assistants and parishioners already known to the Communists. To this he added the names of Communist members of Parliament and every fellow-traveler and informer he could think of.

The next question was to tell what he had done against the State. "What am I accused of?" Richard asked.

Vasilu slapped the table. "You know what you've done. Get it off your chest. Start by telling us about your contacts with your Orthodox colleague, Father Grigoriu, and what you think of him. Just keep writing."

It was the custom to ask clergymen about one another to stoke sectarian rivalries. The prisoner would be told to sign with a nickname. After he had made several statements signed with different names, he would be asked to denounce a friend. If he refused he was warned that everyone would be told that he was an informer who had already given statements under false names. Richard said the threat was enough to make many real informers.

During the long solitary waits between interrogations, fresh questions were prepared and Richard tried to remember what he had said before and what he had concealed. The inquisitors came in pairs and if one left the room, the other didn't speak until he returned. One inquisitor, however, when alone with Richard, showed him statements made against him. Several were made by men he trusted. Sadly he realized the pressure that had been used on them.

Richard was greatly relieved one day when a barber shaving him, whispered that Sabina was well and carrying on the work of the underground church. He had thought Sabina might have been arrested and their son Mihai left to starve or to rely on the charity of neighbors. The news put him in good heart and he was prepared to spout as many chapters from his spiritual biography as the interrogators desired. On other matters he would reveal as little as possible.

Interrogations continued month after month. The endpoint was when the prisoner was convinced of his criminal guilt. Only then could Communist ideals be implanted and take root. The prisoner must succumb to the belief that he was entirely and endlessly in the Party's power and had surrendered every fragment of his past.

It was being said in Romania that life consisted of the four "autos": the "automobile" which took you to the Secret Police; the forced "autocriticism"; the "autobiography" which they made you write; and the "autopsy."

Richard knew it was just a matter of time until he faced torture. He resolved to commit suicide rather than betray others. He felt his duty to protect his friends was higher than life and that God would understand.

The problem was securing the means of suicide. Guards checked constantly for instruments of death. One morning when the doctor was making his rounds, Richard told him he hadn't slept for weeks and was unable to remember all the details the interrogators needed. The doctor ordered a nightly sleeping pill. He concealed the pill under his tongue when the guard looked into his mouth to see if he had swallowed it. He tore open a few stitches of the pallet Patrascanu had used and daily hid the pills in the straw. By the end of the month he had accumulated thirty.

Richard had fits of black depression at the thought of the pills. It was summer. From the world outside he heard a girl singing, a tram-car grinding around the corner, mothers calling their sons. He asked God why he was being forced to put an end to a life dedicated to His service. One evening as he looked through the narrow window he could see the first star appear in the darkening sky. The thought came to his mind that God had sent this light to him, a light that had begun its journey billions of years ago.

Next morning a guard came in and took the spare pallet containing the pills. Richard was upset, but then he laughed and felt a sudden calm. He knew then, that God would give him the strength to bear the suffering ahead.

At the next interrogation, he was told that the Secret Police had been patient but that now it was time for results. Colonel Dulgheru, the grand inquisitor, sat at his desk. "You've been playing with us," he said.

Dulgheru began to question Richard about a Red Army man who had been caught smuggling Bibles into Russia. Richard knew he had to weigh every word he said because he had baptized the Red Army man in Bucharest and had enlisted him in their mission.

Dulgheru sensed he was onto something important and in the following weeks Richard was worn down by a variety of means. The beds were removed from his cell and he had barely an hour's sleep a night balanced on a chair. Every thirty seconds the spyhole in the door gave a metallic click and the eye of a guard appeared. When he dozed, the guard came in and kicked him awake. Richard lost all sense of time. Once he awoke to see the cell door ajar. A woman's voice was sobbing. She began to scream. Richard knew it was his wife. "No, no! Please don't beat me. Not again. I can't bear it."

There was a sound of a whip hitting flesh. The screams rose to an appalling pitch. Every muscle in his body became rigid. The voice began to subside and became the voice of a stranger. The moaning faded into silence. Richard was drained, trembling, and drenched with sweat. Later, he learned it was a tape-recording and that every prisoner who heard it thought the victim was his wife or sweetheart.

Dulgheru, being all-powerful in the prisons, could dispense with notes and witnesses and often came alone to Richard's cell at night to continue interrogation. One critical session dragged on for hours. He asked about Richard's contact with the Church of England Mission. When Richard told him he had visited Westminster Abbey, Dulgheru became incensed. "Do you know," he said venomously, "that I can order your execution now, tonight, as a counterrevolutionary?"

Richard said, "Colonel, here you have the opportunity for an experiment. You say you can have me shot. I know you can. So put your hand here on my heart. If it beats rapidly, showing that I am afraid, then know there is no God and no eternal life. But if it beats calmly, as if to say, 'I go to the one I love,' then you must think again. There is a God and an eternal life."

Dulgheru struck Richard across the face. "You fool, Georgescu," he said. "Can't you see you're completely at my mercy and that your Savior or whatever you call him, isn't going to open any prison doors? You'll never see Westminster Abbey."

Richard said, "His name is Jesus Christ, and if He wishes He can release me, and I shall see Westminster Abbey too."

Dulgheru struggled for breath in his rage. He shouted, "Tomorrow you'll meet Comrade Brinzaru."

Richard was aware that Major Brinzaru presided over the torture chamber.

CHAPTER 4

Richard finds it difficult to talk about his tortures. Such discussion is followed by sleepless nights. He did manage to reveal the following.

Brinzaru, the torturer, was a heartless man. The Russian poet of the day, Voznesensky, had written, "In these days of untold suffering, one is lucky indeed to have no heart." Brinzaru was one of the lucky ones.

The guard told Richard that Brinzaru had worked before the war for a prominent politician who had treated him as one of the family. After the Communist take-over which elevated him up the ranks of the Secret Police, a young prisoner was brought to him for questioning. It was the politician's son, who had tried to start a patriotic movement. Brinzaru told him, "I used to hold you on my knee when you were a baby." He then tortured the lad and executed him with his own hands.

Brinzaru introduced Richard to his arsenal of weapons. "Are there any you fancy?" he asked. "We like to be democratic here." He displayed his own favorite, a long, black, rubber truncheon. He showed Richard the label. It was inscribed, "MADE IN U.S.A."

For some reason, Brinzaru didn't beat Richard. That night he looked through the spyhole to watch him. "Still there, Georgescu? What's Jesus doing tonight?"

Richard replied, "He's praying for you."

Next day Brinzaru returned. He made Richard stand facing a wall with his hands raised above his head so that his fingertips just touched the wall. The guard was instructed to keep him there.

He stood for hours, long after he had lost feeling in his arms, and his legs trembled and began to swell. When he collapsed on the floor, he was given a crust and a sip of water and made to stand again. The guards worked shifts. Some would force him into ridiculous or obscene postures. This went on for days and nights, with an occasional short break.

During these long days, Richard thought of various Bible passages referring to walls. He was saddened by a verse from Isaiah: God says that Israel's wrongdoings put a wall between Him and the people. Richard's interpretation was that the failures of Christianity had allowed a Communist triumph and thus this wall. He thought of the Jewish spies who returned from Canaan to report that the cities were walled. If the walls of Jericho fell, so could this wall at the will of God. When pain was overwhelming, he comforted himself with a phrase from the Song of Songs: "My beloved is like a roe or a young hart; behold, he stands behind our wall." He imagined that Jesus stood behind his wall, giving him strength.

Occasionally, Major Brinzaru looked in to ask Richard if he was ready to cooperate. Once, when he had collapsed on the floor, the major said, "Get up. We've decided to let you see Westminster Abbey, after all. You start now."

The guard ordered Richard to walk. He tried to pull his shoes on but his feet were too swollen. He was required to walk around and around in his cell in his torn socks. Each time the spyhole clicked, the guard shouted, "Faster,. faster. Or do you want a beating?" Richard's head spun. He bumped into a wall. His eyes stung with sweat. He was ordered to walk in the opposite direction. He stumbled and fell. As he struggled to get up, the guard charged in and cracked him on the elbow with a club. Because of the agonizing pain, he fell again. "Get up and keep moving. This is the manège." It was also called the training ring.

Hours went by before Richard got a cup of water or anything to eat. Stabbing hot knives ran up his legs. Stiff joints, cracked muscles, and lacerated feet would not support his weight. He clung to the walls. When he could no longer stand, he went on all fours.

Richard doesn't know how many days and nights he spent in the manège. He prayed for the guards as he moved. Again he thought of the Song of Songs, which tells of the holy dance of the Bride of Christ in honor of her Bridegroom. He determined to move with as much grace as if it were a dance of divine love, for Jesus. He felt as if he really was dancing with grace.

After he had been without sleep for a month, a guard fixed a pair of blacked-out goggles over his eyes and led him to a new interview office, a large, bare room. Behind a table sat three or four figures whom he saw only dimly because of the blinding lights. He stood before them handcuffed and in bare feet wearing only a filthy, torn shirt. He was familiar with the oft-repeated questions to which he gave the same replies. One of the inquisitors, a woman, said shrilly, "If you don't answer properly, we'll have you stretched on the rack."

Richard said, "In St. Paul's Epistle to the Ephesians it is written we must strive to reach the measure of the stature of Christ. If you stretch me on the rack, you'll be helping me to fulfill my purpose." The woman banged the table and a discussion followed behind the dazzling reflectors. His ready answer had deflected a blow; at least he wasn't "racked."

He was taken to another cell. After a hood was pulled over his head, he was ordered to squat and to place his arms around his knees. Then a metal bar was thrust between his elbows and his knees. He was lifted onto trestles, so that he hung head down with his feet in the air. His head was held while the soles of his feet were flogged. The blows were like explosions. Some fell on his thighs and the base of his spine. He fainted and was revived by being drenched in cold water. He was told that if he gave just one of the names they wanted, the torture would stop. When they took him down from the spit, he had to be carried to his cell.

Every time he was taken to this room, he wore the black goggles which were sometimes left on while he was beaten.

Richard explained that when one sees a blow coming, one tenses himself to receive it. But blindfolded, not knowing where or when it will fall, the fear is redoubled.

He described other tortures. After a few strokes with Brinzaru's nylon whip, Richard would lose consciousness. A knife was held to his throat while Brinzaru urged him to talk. Two men held him down as the blade pierced his skin. He fainted and woke to find his chest covered with blood. Water was poured down a funnel into his throat until his stomach felt as if it would burst. Then the guards kicked and stepped on him. He was left in a cell with two wolf dogs trained to leap forward, snarling at the slightest movement, but not to bite. Some bread would be placed nearby but he dared not touch it, lest their teeth snap inches from his face. At one time he was branded with a red-hot iron.

As a result, Richard signed all the confessions about himself that they wanted. He confessed he was an adulterer and at the same time a homosexual; that he had sold the church bells and pocketed the money (although his church had no bells); that under cover of work for the World Council of Churches he had spied with the object of overthrowing the régime by treachery; that he had infiltrated the Party organization under false pretenses and revealed its secrets.

When Brinzaru read these confessions he asked, "What are the names of those you passed the secrets to?" He was pleased when Richard gave him a list of names and addresses.

When Brinzaru had the names checked and learned they were men who had gone West or who had died, Richard received another flogging. He pointed out that while the names were being checked he had had time to gain some strength.

Richard said waiting was the worst torture: listening to screams and weeping, knowing your turn was coming. He said God helped him never to say a word to harm another. Fortunately, he lost consciousness easily, but his interrogators wanted him alive because he could be a further source of information. A doctor was present at torture sessions to check that the patient wasn't about to die.

Richard kept in mind the fact that Jesus could have come to earth as a king, but instead chose to be condemned as a criminal and to be whipped. He felt joy in sharing Jesus' pain with Him.

Jesus often said he would be scourged, mocked, and crucified. Richard used to think mockery, compared to scourging and crucifixion, was nothing. That was before his mouth was forced open so that others could spit or urinate in it.

Many Party men felt what they did was justified. Colonel Dulgheru was one of these. He said, "It is in the vital interest of society that men should be maltreated if they withhold information needed to protect it." Later on, when he saw Richard reduced to a wreck, weeping from nervous fatigue, he said, "Why don't you give in? It's all so futile. You're only flesh and you'll break in the end." Richard thought differently. He knew if he had been just flesh, he couldn't have resisted. The Communists, relying on the instinct of self-preservation, thought a man would do anything to avoid extinction. Richard knew they were wrong. Believing Christians knew that to die wasn't the end of life but its fulfillment; not extinction, but the promise of eternity.

CHAPTER 5

One day, after having been in Calea Rahova prison for seven months, a plate of savory goulash with four whole slices of bread appeared. Before he had a chance to eat it, the guard reappeared and ordered him to gather his things and follow him. Joining a group of other prisoners, he was trucked to the Ministry of the Interior, a splendid building much admired by tourists who do not know it is built over an extensive prison with a labyrinth of corridors and hundreds of helpless inmates.

Richard's cell was thirty feet underground. From the ceiling a light bulb shone on bare walls, an iron bedstead with three planks, and a straw pallet. Air entered through a pipe high in the wall. There was no bucket, meaning he would have to wait for the guard to take him to the latrine. This form of torture often forced Richard to use the dish from which he ate.

The silence was complete. The guards wore felt-soled shoes. Occasionally there was the far-off sound of a prisoner pounding on his door or screaming. The cell allowed only three paces in each direction. Richard lay down and stared at the bulb which burned all night. Since he could not sleep, he prayed. In this cell, he spent the next three years in solitary confinement, with nothing to read, no writing materials, with nothing but his thoughts.

Richard's mind went back to one of his favorite books, *The Pateric*, concerning fourth-century saints who formed desert monasteries when the Church was persecuted. It contained a passage in which an elder defined "silence" for a brother. He said, "Silence is to sit alone in your cell in wisdom and fear of God, shielding the heart from the burning arrows of thought. Silence like this brings to birth the good . . .. He who keeps silent is the one who sings, `My heart is ready to praise Thee, O Lord!'"

As days passed into weeks his only visitor was the guard, who brought wedges of black bread and watery soup, and never spoke a word. Richard realized that in this silence he was coming closer to God. He could spend night after night in prayer, spiritual exercise and praise. He knew now that he was not play-acting, believing that he believed.

He worked out a routine which he used for the next two years. He stayed awake all night, starting his program when the 10 p.m. bell signaled time to sleep. He began with a prayer, often with tears of thankfulness. Next, he preached a sermon as he would in church, beginning with "beloved brethren" and ending with "amen." Every night he talked to his wife and son. Richard believes that his thoughts reached Sabina, who made notations in her Bible: "Today I saw Richard and he spoke to me." While many marriages were destroyed by prison, theirs held firm and was fortified.

Richard knew that Sabina would undergo intense pressure to divorce him. If she refused, and carried on her Underground Church work, she would almost certainly be arrested. Ten-year-old Mihai would be left alone. Richard lay down on his pallet and hugged it as if it were his son. Once he leapt up and smashed his fists on the steel door, shouting, "Give me back my boy!" The guards ran in to hold him down and gave him an injection which made him unconscious for hours. When he awoke he thought he might be going mad as had happened to many others.

In the first days, Richard spent much time searching his soul. He found it was a mistake. Love, goodness, and beauty are shy creatures that hide themselves when they know they are being observed. Now he knew the quiet "yes" of his heart was enough when he put the question, "Do you love Jesus?"

Each night he spent an hour living in the minds of his adversaries. Imagining himself in the place of Colonel Dulgheru, he found a thousand excuses for him. In this way he could love him and the other torturers. Then he considered his own faults from Dulgheru's point of view and found a new comprehension of himself.

In his empty cell Richard managed to have amusement. He told himself jokes and invented new ones. He played chess with himself, using pieces made from bread: Black versus Less-Black, whitened with chalk from the wall. He divided his mind so that Black should not know Less-Black's next move, and vice-versa, and since he didn't lose a game in two years, he felt he could claim to be a master.

Alone in his cell, cold, hungry, and in rags, he danced for joy every night. He had boyhood memories of watching dancing dervishes. He was moved by their ecstasy, the grave beauty of the Muslim worshippers, and their grace of movement as they called out to Allah. Later he learned that many other sects—Jews, Pentecostals, early Christians, and Bible people such as David and Miriam also danced for God. He remembered the words of Jesus, "Blessed are you when men come to hate you, when they exclude you from their company and reproach you and cast out your name as evil on account of the Son of Man. Rejoice in that day and leap for joy."

When the guard peered through the spyhole and saw Richard leaping about his cell, he assumed the prisoner was going mad. He immediately left and returned with a hunk of bread, some cheese, and sugar. Richard recalled the verse in St. Luke: "Rejoice in that day and leap for joy—for behold your reward is great." It was a very large piece of bread; more than a week's ration.

From then on, Richard rarely allowed a night to pass without dancing, although he was never again rewarded. He composed songs and sang them softly to himself while he danced to his own music. The guards became accustomed to it. They had seen many strange things in these sunken cells. Richard didn't mind if his captors thought him mad, for he had discovered a beauty in Christ which he had not known before.

Richard in his Bucharest pulpit

Sometimes he saw visions. Once while dancing he heard his name called, and the cell was flooded with light. He interpreted this as a sign that he must work with Jesus and the saints to build a bridge between good and evil: a bridge of tears, prayers, and self-sacrifice for sinners to cross over and join the blessed.

Another night he became aware of a great throng of angels moving slowly through the darkness toward his bed. As they approached they sang a song of love. He couldn't believe that the guards did not hear this marvelous, passionate music that was so real to him.

He was aware that prisoners in solitary often have visions. He felt that the soul uses the body for its own purposes. These visions helped to sustain his life. He didn't consider them hallucinations.

One night he heard a faint tapping on the wall beside his bed. He assumed a new prisoner had arrived in the adjacent cell and was signaling to him. He tapped back and provoked a flurry of fresh taps. Soon he realized his neighbor was using a simple code: A—one tap; B—two taps; etc. "Who are you?" was the neighbor's first message.

"A pastor," he replied.

They developed a less cumbersome system: one tap for the

first five letters of the alphabet, two taps for the second five, and so on. Thus F was two taps followed by one tap. This still did not satisfy his new friend, who knew the Morse Code, which he taught to Richard.

After learning his friend's name, Richard asked him, "Are you a Christian?"

The answer came after a long pause, "I can not claim to be so."

Richard learned he was a radioengineer awaiting trial on a capital charge. He was fifty-two and in poor health. He had lapsed from faith some years before, having married an unbeliever. He was in deep depression. Richard spoke to him through the wall every night, growing fluent in the use of Morse.

One night the engineer tapped, "I should like to confess my sins." It was a confession broken by many pauses: "I was seven I kicked a boy because he was a Jew. He cursed me 'May your mother not be able to see you...when she dies' Mother was dying when they arrested me."

When the man had unburdened himself, he said he felt happier than he had for years. Richard taught him Bible verses. They exchanged jokes and tapped out the movements of chess games. Richard preached about Christ. When the guard caught him at it, he was transferred to another cell, to a new neighbor, and began again. In time, many prisoners learned the Morse Code. A few times Richard was betrayed by an informer. Because of this he avoided politics and stuck to religion.

Prisoners were forced by solitary confinement to delve into deeply-buried happenings. Old betrayals and dishonesties popped up. All confessions Richard heard in Morse began: "When I was a boy," "When I was at school" memory of old transgressions. These stood before the sanctuary of God's peace. Richard said, "There remains the gate of tears and it was through this gate that we prisoners had to pass."

On a Good Friday morning, Richard scratched "Jesus" on his cell wall. The guard was angry and said, "You're for the carcer." He took Richard down the corridor to a cupboard built into the wall.

The closet was just tall enough to stand in and was twenty inches square. It had a few small airholes and a hole for serving food. This was the carcer.

The guard shoved Richard in and closed the door. When Richard tried to move he discovered it was lined with sharp spikes on all sides. After a surge of panic, he managed to stand still.

His legs began to ache and soon every muscle seemed to hurt. His feet, still sore from the *manège*, became swollen. When he collapsed, his body was lacerated in several places by the spikes. He was taken out for a short rest and then put back. He tried repeating over and over, "Jesus, dear bridegroom of my soul, I love you." Soon this became meaningless. He had ceased to think.

Richard spent two days and nights in the carcer. Some were kept in it for a week or more, but the doctor had warned that Richard's condition was delicate. He was in a borderland between the living and the dead.

He began having hallucinations. He stared at his tin cup of water to convince himself he wasn't in Hell, because there is no water in Hell. Then his cup turned into a helmet. He saw a table laden with delicious food. The table stretched out far beyond his cell. From a distance, Sabina approached carrying a platter piled high with smoking sausages. Richard snarled at her, "Is that all? How small they are."

Sometimes his cell expanded into a library with shelves full of books of all sorts: famous novels, poetry, biographies, religious and scientific works. At other times, thousands of faces turned eagerly toward him, waiting for him to speak. There were questions and answers, cheers and counter-cheers. A sea of faces stretched into infinity.

Richard was troubled by dreams of violence against those who had imprisoned him. He was tormented by erotic fantasies. Thirty-nine when first imprisoned, he was healthy and active. He felt that his recurrent TB caused increased sexual desire. Lying awake, he had hot sweaty dreams of sensual pleasure with women and girls. Then came visions of perversions and exaggerations of the act of love. Frustration and the sense of sin caused him horrible suffering.

He found a way of shaking off such hallucinations by treating them as hostile intruders, like the tuberculosis bacteria weakening his body. He claimed credit for resisting them. By regarding the hallucinations as enemies, he could plan how to destroy them. He didn't try to drive them out.

In real life if he surrendered to them, the costs were considerable: misery to other families and his own, Sabina would have to divorce him, Mihai's future would be wrecked, and his parishioners would lose faith. He would then have to answer to God for the harm he had caused.

One day, the latrines being blocked, Richard was taken to the toilet used by the guards. There was a mirror on the wall over the washbowl. Richard saw himself for the first time in two years. He had been young and healthy on entering jail. He had been considered handsome. Now as he looked at himself, he laughed a sad laughter. If those who had admired and loved him could see the fearful old man in the mirror, they would be appalled. Richard learned from this that what is really fine in us is invisible to the eye. He realized he would become uglier still, a skeleton and a skull. This strengthened his faith and his desire to keep to the spiritual life.

In the toilet was a torn newspaper. Richard had not seen one for two years. It contained the news that Premier Groza had decided to wipe out the wealthy. He looked for Patrascanu's name among the Ministers of the Chamber. It was not there.

On the way back to his cell, he heard a woman weeping and crying out in a crazed way. Her shrieks seemed to come from a level below him. A few days later, he learned the woman was the wife of a former Prime Minister, Ion Gigurtu. He discovered this through the usual Morse wall tapping.

Shortly after this, Richard's interrogations resumed. They were usually conducted by Lieutenant Grecu, a tough, intelligent, and self-assured young man who believed he was making a better world.

Again, he questioned Richard about the famine relief which he had undertaken for the Scandinavian church mission: did he still deny the funds were used for spying? Richard argued that Norway is famous for its democratic spirit and Sweden had had a socialist government for forty years.

"Nonsense," Grecu retorted, "They're as Fascist as the rest."

At their next meeting, Grecu said he had checked and thought Richard might be right. Then he inquired about the distribution of the Gospel in Russian.

Richard suggested a director of the Bible Society, Emile Klein, might be behind it. Asked why he had made repeated visits to the town of Iasi, Richard said he had a standing invitation to visit the Patriarch.

Next morning he was called again to the office of Grecu who sat at his desk with a rubber truncheon in his hand. "Your story was lies," he shouted. "Emile Klein died before you were arrested. We've checked the dates of your trips to Iasi. Patriarch Justinian was hardly ever there."

Pushing back his chair, Grecu said, "Enough! Here's some paper. We know you've communicated in code with other prisoners. We must know exactly what each of them said. We want to know your other breaches of prison rules. You have half an hour. Tell the truth. If you don't" He snapped the truncheon and left the room.

Richard had trouble starting to write. It was the first he had held a pen in two years. He admitted he had broken rules. He had tapped the Gospel message through the walls. He had hoarded pills to kill himself. He had made a knife from a piece of tin. He had communicated with other prisoners but didn't know their names. He didn't mention he had received confessions and converted men through Morse code. He wrote, "I have never spoken against the Communists. I am a disciple of Christ who taught us to love our enemies. I understand them and pray for their conversion so that they will become my brothers in the faith. I can give no statement about what others said to me, for a priest of God can never be a witness for the prosecution. My calling is to defend, not to accuse."

Grecu returned swinging his truncheon. He had been beating prisoners. He picked up Richard's "Declaration" and began to read. After awhile, he put the truncheon aside. When he came to the end, he looked at Richard with troubled eyes. He said, "Mr. Wurmbrand (he had never called Richard `Mr.' before), why do you say you love me? This is one of your Christian commandments that no one can keep. I couldn't love someone who shut me up for years, who starved and beat me."

Richard said, "It's not a matter of keeping a commandment. When I became a Christian it was as if I had been reborn, with a new character that was full of love. Just as only water can flow from a spring, so only love can come from a loving heart."

For two hours they talked about Christianity and its relation to the Marxist doctrines on which Grecu had been brought up. He was surprised when Richard said Marx's first work was a commentary on St. John's Gospel. Nor did he know that Marx, in his foreword to *Das Kapital*, wrote that Christianity, especially in its Protestant form, is "the ideal religion for the renewal of lives made wretched by sin." Richard said since his life had been made wretched by sin, he was simply following Marx's advice in becoming a Protestant Christian.

After this meeting, Grecu called Richard to his office almost daily for an hour or two. There were long discussions about Christianity. Richard stressed its democratic and revolutionary early spirit.

Repeatedly, Grecu said, "I was brought up an atheist and I'll always be an atheist." Richard knew he had to be a Marxist with the Marxist Grecu and speak the language he understood.

He told him, "Atheism is a holy word for Christians. Our forefathers, when they were thrown to the wild beasts because of their faith, were called atheists by Nero and Caligula."

Grecu smiled. Richard continued, "Lieutenant, one of my ancestors was a rabbi of the seventeenth century. He met an atheist and said, `I envy you, dear brother. Your spiritual life must be so much stronger than my own. When I see a man in trouble, I often say, "God will help him," and pass on. Since you don't believe in God, you have to take on His burdens and help everyone you meet.'"

Richard continued, "Christians don't criticize the Party for atheism, but for producing the wrong kind of atheists. There are two kinds: those who say, 'There is no God, so I can do all the evil I like,' and those who reason, 'Since there is no God, I must do all the good that God would do if He existed.' When Jesus saw men hungry, sick, and distressed, He took the whole responsibility on Himself. That is how they discovered that Jesus was God. Lieutenant, if you can become this sort of atheist, loving and serving everyone, men will soon discover that you have become a son of God, and you will discover the Godhead in you."

The words went to Grecu's heart. He began to think and to love Jesus. Two weeks later, Grecu confessed to Richard. They became brethren. After that, he bravely helped prisoners as best he could, through difficulties and dangers. He still gave lip-service to the Party and played an outward role. One day he disappeared and no one knew what became of him. The guards thought he had been arrested.

Richard met other secret believers among the Secret Police, and some still went about their duties. During his second year of confinement, one of these divided souls was put in his cell. All the time he was with Richard, his hands were chained behind his back. Richard had to feed and do everything for him.

He, Dionisiu, was a young sculptor, full of new ideas. Having no money to buy bread, he took a post with the Secret Police which obliged him to beat prisoners. At the same time he took great risks to warn the prisoners of informers. When he found himself under suspicion, he decided to flee the country. When close to freedom, he returned and gave himself up. Such split personalities were common under Communism.

For ten nights, all through the night, Richard taught Dionisiu about the Bible. His sense of guilt was expelled. When he was removed from Richard's cell, he said, "If one of the fifteen priests in my little town had stopped to talk to me when I was younger, I would have found Jesus long ago."

Interrogations did not cease with Grecu's departure. Richard feels that God granted him the gift of being able to forget the names of all those for whom he could cause trouble. Although he mentally composed more than 300 poems in solitary, totaling some 100,000 words, and wrote them all down after his release, he could make his mind blank during interrogations.

A new method was tried on Richard. On the pretext that his tuberculosis had worsened (his coughing was almost continuous), the doctors ordered a new drug: a yellow capsule that brought long periods of sleep filled with delightful dreams. When he awoke, he was given another. He remained unconscious for several days, awakened only by guards bringing meals that had become light and wholesome.

Richard's recollection of the resumed questioning is hazy. He believes the drug didn't make him betray his friends, because when he was put on trial, he was tried alone. No grand trial of the men behind the World Council of Churches' "spy net" ever took place. The drug, which was used on Cardinal Mindszenty, some Trotskyists, and many others, weakened will-power until the victim went into a delirium of self-accusation. Later, Richard heard men who were on the drug banging on cell doors, demanding to see the political officer so that they could make new confessions. He feels that by God's grace, he was saved from treachery.

Richard became still weaker after the drugging and one day collapsed. Although he could rise from bed only with great effort, his mind remained lucid. Alone in his cold, dark cell, he went through an intense struggle with the Devil. He couldn't think of one argument proving Christ was the Messiah. His joy and serenity were gone. Slowly he composed a long poem which he feels may shock those who never experienced his struggle. It was his salvation. He felt he had defeated Satan. (The poem, in English and in free verse, is found elsewhere in this book).

After nearly three years of solitary confinement, Richard was close to death. He continually spat blood. Colonel Dulgheru taunted, "We're not murderers like the Nazis. We want you to live and suffer."

A specialist was called. Anxious to avoid infection, he made his diagnosis through a spy-hole in the cell door. Orders were given for Richard's transfer to a prison hospital.

CHAPTER 6

Richard was carried from his dungeon cell to the yard of the Ministry of the Interior. Here he saw moonlight and stars again. Lying in the ambulance, he caught familiar glimpses of Bucharest. They were moving in the direction of Richard's house and for a moment he thought he was being taken home to die. Near his home the ambulance turned and began to climb a hill on the outskirts of the city. He knew then they were going to Vacaresti, one of the great monasteries of Bucharest which had been converted into a jail.

A sheet was wrapped around his head before the guards lifted him out of the ambulance. Gripping him under the arms, they half-carried him across the courtyard, up some stairs, and along a balcony. When the sheet was removed, Richard found himself in a narrow, bare cell. An officer instructed a guard, "No one is allowed to see this man except the doctor accompanied by you." He realized his existence was to remain a secret.

When the officer had gone, the guard asked Richard what he had done. He said, "I am a pastor and a child of God."

The guard bent over him and whispered, "Praise be to the Lord. I'm one of Jesus' soldiers." He was a secret member of "The Army of the Lord" a revivalist movement which had branched off from the Orthodox Church. In spite of being persecuted by Communists and clergy alike, it had spread rapidly through the villages, gathering hundreds of thousands of followers.

The guard's name was Tachici. They exchanged Bible verses and Tachici helped Richard as much as he dared. Warders had been sentenced to twelve years for giving an apple or a cigarette to a prisoner.

Richard was too weak to leave his bed and often he lay in his feces. For a short spell in the morning he could think clearly and then he would lapse into delirium. There was a small window through which he could see the sky. In the morning he was awakened by a strange sound—the song of birds.

Richard told Tachici, "Martin Luther, when walking in the woods, used to raise his hat to the birds and say, 'Good morning, theologians. You wake and sing, but I, old fool, know less than you and worry over everything, instead of simply trusting in the heavenly Father's care.'"

An old man's voice came from the adjacent cell one morning. "I'm Leonte Filipescu. Who are you?"

Richard recognized the name of one of Romania's first socialists, a brilliant man whom the Party had used and then discarded. "Fight your illness," he called. "Don't give in. We'll all be free in two weeks' time."

"How do you know?" Richard asked.

"The Americans are driving the Communists back in Korea. They'll be here in two weeks."

Richard said, "Even if they meet no opposition, it will take them more than a fortnight to reach Romania."

"Bosh! Distance is nothing to them. They have supersonic jets."

Richard didn't argue. He knew that prisoners lived on their illusions. If the daily gruel was a little thicker, it implied that an American ultimatum had frightened Russia. If a prisoner was knocked down by a warder, it meant the Communists were making the most of their last days of power.

No man could bear to think he would spend the next ten or twenty years in prison. Filipescu was still hopeful of early release when he was moved, a month later, to another prison hospital where he and Richard were to meet again.

Filipescu's cell was then occupied by Radu Mironovici, a leader of the Fascist Iron Guard, who claimed to be a fervent Christian but was always spouting hatred of the Jews.

Richard called to Radu, "When you take Holy Communion in your Orthodox church, are the bread and wine transformed into the actual body and blood of Jesus?" Radu answered in the affirmative.

"Jesus was a Jew," Richard said. "If the wine becomes His blood, then that blood is Jewish, isn't it?" Radu reluctantly supposed it was. Richard continued, "If eating His body and drinking His blood gives eternal life, how then can you hate Jews?

Richard begged Radu to see that it was absurd for a follower of Jesus to hate Jews, just as it was absurd for Communists to be anti-Semitic, since they believed in a Jew called Karl Marx.

Radu was moved to a distant cell but he told Tachici, "A part of my life which was false has fallen away. I was a Christian who was too proud to follow Christ."

One day when Richard was running a high fever and was feeling sick and faint, the guards wrapped a sheet around his head and led him down a corridor. When the sheet was removed, he found himself in a large room with barred windows. Four men and a woman sat facing him behind a table. He knew this was his trial and that they were his judges.

"A lawyer has been nominated to defend you," said the president of the court. "He has waived your right to call witnesses. You may sit down."

Guards held Richard in a chair while he was given an injection. When the waves of nausea and dizziness cleared, the prosecutor had already commenced. He was saying that Richard stood for the same criminal ideology in Romania as Josef Broz Tito did in Yugoslavia. Richard thought he must be delirious. At the time of his arrest, Marshal Tito was held up as a model Communist. He didn't know Tito had since been revealed as a deviationist and traitor.

Richard was accused of spy work through the Scandinavian church missions and the World Council of Churches, spreading imperialist ideology under cover of religion, infiltrating the Party under the same pretense, with the real purpose of destroying it, and so on. As the prosecutor's voice continued, he started to slip from the chair. Proceedings were delayed while he received another injection.

"Have you anything to say?" asked the president. To Richard, his voice seemed far away and the room was growing dark. Only one thing came into his confused brain.

"I love God," he said.

Richard heard his sentence: twenty years' hard labor. The trial had taken ten minutes. The sheet was wrapped around his head again.

Two days later, Tachici whispered to Richard, "You're leaving. God be with you." He and another guard carried him to the main gate. Again, he had a view of Bucharest, the last time he would see it for six years. Regulation chains weighing fifty pounds were hammered into place around his ankles. He was lifted into a truck in which were already some forty men and a few women. All were chained. Near Richard, a girl began to weep. He tried to comfort her.

"You don't remember me?" she sobbed. "I was one of your congregation." She told him poverty had forced her into theft. Now she had to serve three months. "I'm so ashamed. I was in your church and now you're a martyr and I'm a thief."

"I'm a sinner too, saved by the grace of God. Believe in Christ and your sins will be forgiven."

She kissed his hand and promised that on her release she would let his family know that she had seen him.

At a railway siding, they were loaded into a special coach for transporting prisoners. The windows were small and opaque. Leaving the plain and going into the Carpathian foothills, they decided that since they all had tuberculosis, they must be bound for Tirgul-Ocna where there was a sanatorium for TB prisoners. It had an excellent reputation before the Communists took over.

The two-hundred-mile journey took a day and a night. Richard was laid on the back of a cart with six other men unable to walk.

The other prisoners hauled them to a big building at the edge of town. As he was carried in he saw a familiar face. It was Dr. Aldea, an ex-Fascist who had been converted and had become a family friend. After Richard had been helped to a bed in the quarantine room, Dr. Aldea examined him.

"I'm a prisoner myself," he said, "but they let me work as a doctor. There are no nurses and only one physician. We must look after each other as best we can."

After the examination, Aldea said, "I won't deceive you. There is nothing we can do. You may have about two weeks to live. Try to eat what they give you although it is not good. Otherwise" He touched Richard's shoulder and moved on.

During the next few days, two men who had been in the cart with Richard died. He heard another of them pleading with Aldea, "I swear I'm better. Don't let them put me in Room Four."

Richard asked the man who brought his watery gruel what happened in Room Four. He replied, "That's where you go when they know there is no hope."

Richard tried to eat the gruel but could not. He was fed with a spoon but the food wouldn't stay down. Dr. Aldea said, "I'm sorry. They insist. You must go to Room Four."

Richard rejoined his cart companions.

In Room Four, prisoners crossed themselves as they passed the foot of Richard's bed. He lay most of the time in a coma. When he groaned, others turned him on his side or gave him water.

There was little Dr. Aldea could do. He yearned for modern drugs. He had heard of a new American discovery, streptomycin, which was said to be doing wonders against tuberculosis. The Party said this was Western propaganda.

Four men who had gone to Room Four with Richard died in the next two weeks. He slept at night in snatches. Often he was awakened by stabs of agony. To ease his pain, other prisoners turned him an average of forty times a night. Pus was running from a dozen sores. He spat blood constantly and he knew from the pain in his spine that it too was infected with tuberculosis.

Richard questioned his guardian angel, "What kind of guardian are you who can't keep me from this suffering nor from un-Christian thoughts?" There was a flash of dazzling light that seemed to last a thousandth of a second. He saw a being who was many-armed like Krishna and heard a voice.

"I can not do all I should for you. I too am a convert." He remembered vaguely that Orthodox mystics spoke of isolated cases where black angels have been brought back to God's service even though their conversion could not restore them completely. Richard felt the vision offered some explanation for things through which he had passed and was comforted.

Sabina

Richard survived the first crisis. Dr. Aldea was puzzled as he clung to life. Though he received no medication, the fever subsided and his mind became clearer. He began to look around and take stock of his surroundings.

There were twelve beds in the room, close together, and some small tables. The windows were open and Richard could watch men working in a small vegetable patch. Beyond that were high walls and barbed wire. It was very quiet. Alarm bells and warders were absent because of their fear of infection. Through neglect and indifference, Tirgul-Ocna was one of the less rigorous prisons. Scarcely anything was done for the prisoners. They even wore the clothes in which they were arrested.

Food was brought to the political prisoner section by common-law criminals and left at the door. The patients got their own and carried some to the bed-ridden. The usual fare was watery cabbage soup, a few haricot beans or a gruel of barley or maize.

A few prisoners who were well enough did the gardening outside the building. The rest lay on their plank beds and gossiped the hours away. In Room Four things were different because no one ever left it alive. It was known as the "death room."

In the thirty months Richard lay in this room, scores of men died and their places were taken by others. He noted a remarkable fact: not one died an atheist. Fascists, Communists, saints, murderers, thieves, priests, rich landowners, and the poorest peasants were crowded together in one small cell. Yet none of them died without making peace with God and man. Many entered Room Four as firm unbelievers. Richard saw their unbelief collapse in the face of death.

Filipescu denied God. Richard suggested to him he was denying only his primitive conception of the word, not the realities of love, righteousness, and eternity. He replied, "I believe in Jesus Christ and love Him as the greatest of human beings but I cannot think of Him as God."

Filipescu's condition was growing steadily worse. He died within two weeks after a series of hemorrhages. He spoke his last words to Richard. "I love Jesus." He was thrown naked into a common grave that the prisoners had dug.

The Abbot Iscu of Tismana crossed himself and said, "We must be grateful he came to God at the end."

Bucur disagreed, "Nothing of the sort. He told us he couldn't think of Christ as God."

Richard said, "Filipescu will have found out the truth by now in the other world, for he loved Jesus who will never reject anyone. I believe in the Godhead of Jesus, and also in His love for those who cannot see it."

Prisoners from other wards often came to Room Four to spend the night helping the dying and offering comfort.

At Easter, a friend brought something wrapped in a twist of paper for Gafencu, a former Iron Guard trooper. His friend said, "It's been smuggled in." Gafencu unwrapped it and found two lumps of sugar. Richard said it was the first sugar any of them had seen in years, and their wasted bodies craved it.

Gafencu slowly wrapped it again, saying, "I shall not eat it yet. Someone might need it more than I during the day." He put the present beside his bed and there it stayed.

A few days later, Richard's fever increased and he became very weak. The sugar was passed from bed to bed until it came to rest on his. Richard left the sugar untouched in case someone needed it more than he. For two years the sugar went from man to man but was always resisted.

Soteris was a Communist guerrilla who had fled to Romania at the end of the Greek civil war. He had been arrested by his comrades for fighting poorly. As long as he could hope for life, he was proud of his atheism. As death approached he cried out for help from God. He was quieted by the priest's promise of heavenly forgiveness. Soteris also refused the lumps of sugar. His body was prepared for burial by a prisoner known as "The Professor" who often came to Room Four to help. His name was Popp.

Since Richard had no strength to wash himself, the task was taken on by Professor Popp. Like Richard, Popp was adept at telling stories and jokes. This sustained the prisoners who lay all day with only their miseries to think about. Richard often talked for hours on end although ill and dizzy with hunger. He felt it was as important as bread.

Gafencu had spent his entire adult life in prison. Jailed when he was nineteen, he had never known a girl, and when others discussed sex, he asked, "What is it like?"

As an Iron Guard he, of course, was anti-Semitic. He had left this behind him. He shocked his visiting Fascist friends when he said, "I'd like to see the country run entirely by Jews."

Gafencu had been in Room Four one year. In all that time he had been unable to lie down because of back pain. Every day he had a little less control over his body. As the end approached, his friends gathered around his bed with tears in their eyes.

His last words were, "The spirit of God wishes us jealously for Himself." The others knelt and prayed.

Richard said, "Jesus tells us that if a seed does not fall into the earth and die, it cannot bring forth fruit, and that as a seed is reborn in a beautiful flower, so man dies and his mortal body is renewed in a spiritual body. His heart which has come to be filled with the ideals of Christianity will surely bear fruit."

Gafencu was wrapped in his sheet and carried to the mortuary. During the night he was buried in a common grave by criminal convicts.

The two lumps of sugar remained in Room Four.

Informing had spread like a disease. One could be denounced for speaking of God or for praying aloud, even for learning or teaching a foreign language. The informer might be friend, son, father, wife, or husband because of the tremendous pressure to inform. The informer was more of a menace to "free" men than to those already behind bars. In Room Four the prisoners exercised more free speech than was heard anywhere else in Romania, since none of them were going to live.

A new system of "re-educating" prisoners was inaugurated, not with books but by beating. The tutors were usually turncoat

Iron Guards who had been formed into an organization of prisoners with Communist convictions (PCC). After a visit by re-education leader Formagiu, the new system was started at Tirgul-Ocna.

Before this, the prisoners were tormented most of the day, but they knew that sooner or later the guards would go to eat or sleep. Now the PCC moved in with them and had the power to beat and bully as they pleased. They all carried rubber truncheons. They had been hand-picked from the worst and most violent prisoners. For every fifty prisoners there were ten to twenty PCCs living with them. Those who declared themselves ready to become Communists had to prove their conversion by converting others in the same way.

Cruelty was under medical supervision to ensure that prisoners didn't die. Doctors were often PCCs themselves. A Dr. Turcu, after examining a cellmate, would advise a pause, give an injection, and tell the re-educators when to resume.

When Turcu decided the victim had reached his limit, he was thrown back into his cell until the next day.

A wave of madness swept Tirgul-Ocna. Tuberculosis patients were stripped, laid on the stone floors, and drenched with buckets of freezing water. Starving men with hands tied behind their backs were forced to lap up pig swill from the floor. Men were forced by PCC bullies to swallow excrement and drink urine. Some were made to perform sexual perversions. Richard hadn't thought such mockery of body and soul was possible.

Those who clung to their faith were treated the worst. Christians were tied for four days to crosses, and each day the crosses were laid on the floor so that other prisoners could defecate on their faces and bodies. Then the crosses were put up again so that the "filthy savior" could be mocked.

These things were done with the encouragement of the prison administration on orders from Bucharest. Turcanu, Formagiu, and other torture specialists went from prison to prison, recruiting PCCs and whipping up fervor. Party leaders, including men from the Central Committee, such as Constantin Doncea and the Under-secretary of the Interior Ministry, Marin Jianu, came to watch the sport.

The re-education system, imported from Russia, brought incredible results. Victims blurted secrets they had kept during months of interrogation. They denounced friends, wives, parents. Thousands more arrests were made.

Re-education was claiming new victims every day. It was decided that, unless something was done, all the prisoners would be either converted or killed. A rumor reached Room Four that a protest was being planned by the Communist prisoners. Christians debated what should be done. Some felt it was time to "turn the other cheek" and others were undecided.

Richard said, "Jesus is usually portrayed as meek and mild, but he was a fighter, too. He drove the merchants from the temple with a whip." It was decided to work with the rebels.

It was the custom of the town of Tirgul-Ocna to relax once a week with a football match in a stadium near the prison. A Labor Day game was to be played on May 1, and the whole town would be there. The signal for the demonstration was to be the smashing of a window.

Soon after the game began, the window was smashed and the whole prison broke into bedlam. More windows were smashed, plates and mugs were thrown out, and chairs were shattered. There was a steady chant, "Help us. Help us." Others shouted, "We are tortured. Your fathers, brothers, and sons are being killed." The game stopped, the crowd was on its feet, and hundreds gathered in front of the prison wall.

Guards began lashing out with clubs. The crowds in the street were driven away by troops with rifle butts.

News of the revolt spread rapidly through the country. There were no reprisals, only a stiffening of the régime.

Dr. Aldea decided Richard needed a pneumothorax, and with his permission performed it. Richard said it was relatively painless and he fell asleep after it was done. When he awoke, he was happily surprised to find Professor Popp, who had been away for months in Jilava prison, sitting at his bedside. The professor had suffered terribly under the re-education system. The two talked for hours.

Slowly, the scandal of re-education was coming into the light of day. Those in high places were alarmed. Another reversal of Party fortunes was imminent and they thought they might soon face the same treatment. The leading re-educators were interrogated by the Secret Police and several of them, including Turcanu, were sentenced to death.

The re-education scandal was used as a weapon against the Ministry of the Interior, headed by Georgescu. In the political purge of 1952, the triumvirate which had ruled Romania since the Communist take-over was overthrown. Other Ministers were made scapegoats for the catastrophic inflation and the disasters caused by collectivization.

Many of those who came to help in Room Four were farmers who had rebelled against forcible collectivization of their land. They told many tales of horror. Romania's prisons were full of them. Thousands of farmers had been put before firing squads. Because they lacked organization, their rebellions could always be stamped out.

Winter came on, with heavy snowstorms. Icicles hung from the roof. Hoarfrost painted the windowpanes. It was being claimed that this was the coldest winter in a hundred years. There was no heating, but the prisoners in Room Four had two or three blankets each, because every time a man died, his bedclothes were taken by another occupant. Then there was a check and the men were left with a single blanket. Often there was no bread. The soup, made of carrots too rotten to be sold, became still thinner.

On Christmas Eve, prison conversation became more serious. Richard spoke of Christ, while all the time his feet and hands were cold as steel, his teeth chattered, and an icy lump of hunger in his stomach seemed to spread through his body until only his heart was alive. When he was unable to continue, a simple farming lad, Aristar, took up where Richard had left off. He had never been to school, yet he talked so naturally, describing the scene of the nativity as if it had happened in his own barn recently, that there were tears in the eyes of all who listened.

Someone began to sing in the prison that night. At first, the voice barely came through Richard's thoughts of home, of Sabina, of Mihai. Gradually the voice swelled in the crisp air until it echoed through the corridors. Everybody stopped and listened. There was silence when it ceased. The guards, huddled around a stove in their quarters, didn't stir all evening. The prisoners started to tell stories. When Richard was asked to tell a story, thinking of the song just finished, he told an old Jewish legend:

King Saul of Israel brought David, the shepherd, to his court. David loved music and was delighted when he saw a harp of great beauty in the palace. Saul said, "I paid much for that instrument, but I was deceived. It gives forth only ugly sounds."

David took it up and drew from it music so exquisite that every man was moved. The harp seemed to laugh and sing and weep. King Saul asked, "How is it that all the musicians I called brought discord from this harp and only you could bring out music?"

David replied, "Before me, each man tried to play his own song on these strings. But I sang to the harp its own song. I recalled how it had been a young tree, with birds that chirped in its branches and limbs green with leaves that blossomed in the sun. I reminded it of the day when men came to cut it down, and you heard it weep under my fingers. I explained that this was not the end. Its death as a tree meant the start of a new life in which it would glorify God as a harp, and you heard how it rejoiced under my hands. So when the Messiah comes, many will try to sing on their harps their own songs, and their tunes will be harsh. We must sing on His harp His own song, the song of His life, passions, joys, sufferings, death, and resurrection. Only then will the music be true."

It was a song like this that Richard and his cellmates heard that Christmas Eve in Room Four of Tirgul-Ocna.

Aristar died in February. They had to dig through deep snow and rock-hard ground to bury him in the prison yard alongside

Abbot Iscu, Gafencu, Bucur, and a score of others he had known in Room Four.

Aristar's bed was taken over by Avram Radonovici, who had been a music critic in Bucharest. He knew long passages from the scores of Bach, Beethoven, and Mozart and could hum them for hours. Richard enjoyed it as much as a symphony concert. Later, he found Avram had brought a more precious gift with him.

Because of the tuberculosis of his spine, Avram was encased in a plaster body cast when he arrived. As the prisoners watched, he put his hand under his cast and extracted a small, tattered book. None of the prisoners had seen a book of any kind for many years. Avram lay there quietly turning the pages, until he became conscious of the eager eyes fixed on him.

Richard said, "What is it and where did you get it?"

"It's the Gospel according to St. John. I hid it in my cast when the police came for me. Would you like to borrow it?"

Richard took the little book in his hands as if it were a live bird. No life-saving drug could have been more precious to him.

The Gospel went from hand to hand. It was difficult to pass it on. Many learned the Gospel by heart. They discussed it every day among themselves. Because of informers, they had to be careful which prisoners were let in on the secret.

Avram's Gospel helped to bring many to Christ, among them Professor Popp, who, by being near many living Christians, had come steadily closer to faith. He had one final problem.

"I've tried to pray again," said the professor, "but between reciting the Orthodox formulas I learned as a boy and demanding favors of the Almighty to which I have no claim, there is nothing much to say. Like the king in *Hamlet*, my words fly up and my thoughts remain below."

Richard told him of a man who kept a chair by his bedside so that Jesus could sit in it while he prayed.

The professor asked, "Is that how you pray?"

Richard said, "I like to think that Jesus stands near me while I talk to him." This satisfied Professor Popp and he became a Christian. Richard and the professor became very close and often read the thoughts in each other's mind.

A thaw came in March. Through his chilblained hands, his feet wrapped in rags, his face stiff with cold, Richard felt life start again.

News galvanized the prison. Stalin is dead! No tears were shed, as everyone speculated excitedly on what it would mean.

A few days later, they heard train whistles blowing and bells tolling to mark Stalin's funeral in Moscow. The prison echoed with laughter and curses. The guards looked surly and the officers were nervous. No one knew what might happen next.

After weeks of uncertainty, a high official came from the Legal Department, and the prisoners believed he had come to study prison conditions. No one spoke as he went from cell to cell asking for complaints. Most thought it was a trick. When he reached Room Four, Richard said, "I have something to say, but I won't start unless you promise to hear me to the end."

"That's what I've come for," said the official politely.

Richard said, "Prosecutor, you had a renowned predecessor in history called Pontius Pilate. He was asked to handle the trial of a man he knew to be innocent. 'Never mind,' said Pilate to himself. 'Am I to risk my career for a Jew and a carpenter?'

"Although two thousand years have passed, this betrayal of justice has not been forgotten. In any church you enter throughout the world you hear it said in the Creed that Jesus was crucified under Pontius Pilate."

The others in Room Four were looking worried for Richard.

He continued, "Look into your heart and you'll see that we are the victims of injustice. Even if we're guilty in the Party's eyes, we were to purge our crimes in prison, but this is a long-drawn-out death sentence. Before you make your report, look at our food, the lack of heating and simple medicine, and the dirt and disease. Ask about some of the barbarities we've suffered. Then write the truth. Don't wash your hands of helpless men as Pilate did."

The prosecutor looked at Richard somberly, turned on his heel, and left without a word. The news that he had heard Richard out spread through the prison and encouraged others to speak. Before he left, the prisoners heard there had been angry words in the commandant's office. Later that day the guards became polite, almost apologetic. A week later the commandant was dismissed.

Richard began to get out of bed and walk a few paces each day. Dr. Aldea brought the official doctor to see him. Aldea said, "We can't make you out. Your lungs are like a sieve, the spinal vertebrae are diseased. You've had practically no treatment. You're neither better nor worse. We're going to move you out of Room Four."

Richard's friends were happy. They took courage from the fact that after two and a half years he was the first man to leave the cell alive.

"How's it done, Pastor?" said one jokingly. "Why doesn't that old body of yours obey doctor's orders and die?"

Richard said, "I expect you could find a medical reason if you tried. But I believe it is a miracle of God and an answer to prayer."

He knew that many people, prisoners he had met as well as his congregation, prayed for him, but not for many years did he learn how many thousands around the world had joined them in prayer.

CHAPTER 7

Gheorghiu-Dej, his rivals eclipsed, was now Romania's dictator. He admitted freely that grave mistakes had been committed, and among the gravest was the Danube-Black Sea Canal project. After three years in which millions of dollars had been wasted and thousands of lives lost, only five of its planned forty miles had been completed. Engineers and camp administrators were accused of sabotage and three were sentenced to death, two summarily executed. Others were sentenced from fifteen years to life. Before the canal was started, engineers were shot for saying the Danube could not supply enough water for the project. A new survey showed that this was true. The canal was abandoned.

While they were talking about the fiasco, Professor Popp took Richard aside. He said, "I have been keeping something from you since my return to Tirgul-Ocna. Dr. Aldea thought it might be too much of a shock for you in your poor condition. Your wife is now in prison, and she had been a laborer at the canal."

Popp had pieced facts together from various prisoners who had worked there. Sabina had been arrested two years after Richard. She had been leading the women in the church as a deaconess. She had been told what to preach but that was not her style. and she was arrested. At the canal she had to shovel earth into a wheelbarrow and push it great distances. If she failed her quota, she was denied bread.

Sabina ate grass, rats, snakes, dogs, anything available. She was tiny and fragile. A favorite sport of the guards was to throw her into the freezing Danube and fish her out again. At the collapse of the canal project, she was sent to a state farm where pigs were bred.

The professor said a prisoner from Vacaresti had spoken with Sabina in the hospital there. "She has been very ill," said Popp, "but she will live. The women around her told her you were dead. She refused to believe it."

This news devastated Richard and almost shattered his self-control. He tried to pray. His mind was burdened with a black gloom. He spoke to no one for days. One morning in the prison yard, he saw a very dignified old priest, his white beard blowing in the cold wind. Father Suroianu had come to confess the prisoners.

There was such an aura of holiness around him that Richard felt an impulse to tell the Father the whole truth. Although he was not a believer in sacramental confession, he revealed to the priest his sense of despair and sins that he had never told before. The more he confessed, the more the Father looked at him not with contempt but with love.

Suroianu had more reason to mourn than any of the prisoners. Tragedy had engulfed his whole family. A crippled daughter had been deprived of her husband,,who was in prison with Richard. Another daughter and her husband had been sentenced to twenty years. One of his sons had died in prison. Another son had turned against him. His grandchildren had been driven out of school or had lost their jobs because of their parents' "anti-Party activities." In spite of all his misfortune, Father Suroianu spent his days en-couraging and cheering others. He always greeted people with "Rejoice".

Richard asked him, "How can you always 'rejoice'?"

"It's a grave sin not to do so," he said. "There's always a good reason to rejoice. There is a God in heaven and in my heart. I had a piece of bread this morning. The sun is shining. Many here love me. Every day you do not rejoice is a day lost. You will never have that day again."

For a few months after Stalin's death, monthly parcels from

home were permitted. On the postcards they were given, Richard requested food, cigarettes, and "Doctor Filon's old clothes."

Richard didn't smoke but gave them to other men. The request for Dr. Filon's clothes puzzled his family. The doctor was small, Richard was large. Richard hoped that they would guess that what he really wanted from the doctor was streptomycin. He was not allowed to ask for it in his parcels.

Besides tuberculosis, Richard was tormented with a toothache, which plagued all the prisoners. The lack of food and dental care caused teeth to decay rapidly, and many were broken in beatings. With fifty-pound chains around his ankles, he couldn't even walk to ease the pain.

He tried to ease the pain by talking to a new young man named Josif, who previously had become angry when Richard preached. He sat beside Josif and asked him why he had been upset when he spoke.

Josif said, "I hate God. If you go on I'll call the guards." His eyes filled with tears. "Leave me alone."

Josif's good nature always broke through. A day later he was telling Richard of his hopes of meeting his sister in Germany and going on together to join relatives in America.

"You must start to learn English," Richard said.

"I'd love to, but who will teach me?"

"I will give you lessons if you wish."

"Could you? Really?" Josif was overjoyed and proved to be a bright pupil in spite of no books, paper, or pencil. Richard had him repeat passages from books and from the Bible, passages that Richard knew by heart.

Josif wasn't the only prisoner who threatened to report Richard. The real danger was the hidden informer. Often such men used the pretense of patriotism to serve their purpose, especially with the young.

The partisans who held out for years in the mountains of Romania inspired many youngsters to form their own anti-Communist groups. When discovered, boys and girls of seventeen and eighteen were arrested and herded into jail. There was even a fourteen-year-old at Tirgul-Ocna. They loved to hear the stories told by Armeanu, a former intelligence colonel.

General Stavrat, who had known Armeanu before, said, "I don't trust that man. We must keep an eye on him."

Richard, General Stavrat, and Josif listened to Armeanu's conversations with the young prisoners, who trusted him. They were giving him names and places.

When Richard found Armeanu alone, he struck up a conversation with him. Armeanu asked Richard why he was in prison. Richard took a desperate chance and said, "For spying." He added, "I know I can speak freely to a nationalist like you. I'm only a minor dog in the organization."

Richard dropped further hints and allowed Armeanu to wheedle names and addresses of his "contacts." He saw a look of cunning triumph in Armeanu's face, who thought he had information that would secure his release.

Next day, Stavrat saw Armeanu whispering to the guard. Immediately afterwards, Armeanu was called for a medical inspection, a frequent pretext for consulting informers. Then Richard was sent for by the political officer, who probably imagined an extra star on his shoulder already. Without any attempt to shield Armeanu, the officer demanded the full story of the great international spy-network.

Richard said, "I invented the whole thing. I wanted to check my suspicions about Armeanu. Now I know."

The officer stared at Richard in disbelief. Then he burst out laughing.

When confronted, Armeanu tried to bluster, but he was an outcast from that day forward.

At last, one of Richard's parcels contained 100 grams of streptomycin. His family had deciphered his code. Richard thought of the men he had left behind in Room Four. He asked General Stavrat to offer it to the most serious case there.

"That would be Sultaniuc, the Iron Guard Fascist," said

Stavrat with distaste. He tried to persuade Richard to use it himself, without success.

When Stavrat came back from Room Four, he said, "When I told him who it was from, he said he wouldn't take anything from an opponent of the Iron Guard."

Richard asked Josif to act as go-between. "Tell Sultaniuc the general was mistaken. Say it's a gift from Graniceru, who is also an Iron Guard."

Josif was unsuccessful. "Sultaniuc won't accept the medicine unless you swear on your oath that it doesn't come from you."

"Why not?" Richard said. "I've given him the drug, and I can give him an oath to go with it."

There was much discussion concerning the right to lie, especially by the clergy. Richard said, "I have no qualms about saying the first thing that comes into my head, so long as it misleads those who are trying to trap my friends. I respect truth but I'd lie to save a friend."

When they were alone, Josif asked Richard, "What do you call a lie, then?"

"Why should you expect a definition from me? Your own conscience, if guided by the Holy Spirit, will tell you in every circumstance of life what to say and what to leave unsaid. You don't think the oath you carried to Sultaniuc about the streptomycin was a lie, do you?"

"Oh no," said Josif, smiling sweetly, "that was an act of love."

Richard's toothache was relieved by good news. The letter raised his spirits to the skies; it said Sabina was free. She was still confined to Bucharest, but Mihai would soon be permitted to visit him.

Richard hadn't seen Mihai since he was nine, and now he was fifteen. He worried day and night about their meeting. At last, he was led into a large hall where he had to sit in a box with a window blocked by three iron bars, so small that the visitor sitting opposite would see only a small part of his face. When the guard shouted, "Mihai Wurmbrand," Mihai came and sat down before his dad.

He was pale, thin, and hollow-cheeked, with the beginnings of a moustache.

Mihai said with a rush, in case he was cut off, "Mother says even if you die in prison, you must not be sad because we'll all meet in paradise."

Richard didn't know whether to laugh or cry. Pulling himself together, he said, "How is she? Have you food at home?"

"She's well again. And we have food. Our Father is very rich."

The listening guards grinned because they thought Richard's wife had re-married.

Mihai replied to Richard's questions with verses of the Bible, so that he received little family news. Mihai told him he had left a parcel with the guards at the gate.

Richard received the parcel next day, in excess of his allowance, because Mihai had addressed it to Richard Wurmbrand instead of his prison name, Vasile Georgescu. Shortly afterwards, restrictions were fully restored: no visits, no parcels, no letters.

Josif's sentence had only weeks to run. Already he was planning for the future. He told Richard, "My sister in Germany will work for a permit for us to go to America. I'll perfect my English and learn a trade."

Josif hated his disfigured face. One evening Richard told him about Helen Keller; how she overcame her many disabilities and helped others. Josif was fascinated. He also told him how things which were considered bad, such as mold, had been used to make penicillin.

Seeing him shivering with the cold, Richard took the woolen jacket his relatives had sent, tore the lining out for himself, then persuaded Josif to take it. The young man's conversion began on that day. Yet he needed something else to bring it to fruition.

It happened during the distribution of the bread rations, which were laid in rows on the table each morning. Some were larger, some were smaller. The men quarreled over whose turn it was to get first choice. When a surly prisoner called Trailescu tried to cheat Richard, Josif was watching.

Richard told Trailescu, "Take mine too. I know how hungry you are." He shrugged and stuffed the bread into his mouth.

While reciting New Testament verses in English that evening, Josif said, "I wonder what Jesus was like to know as a man."

Richard told him about a pastor in Room Four who would give away everything he had—his bread, his medicine, his coat. One day a prisoner asked the pastor what Jesus was like. The pastor replied, "Jesus is like me." The prisoner said, "If Christ was like you, then I love Him."

Richard said, "To me, that is what it means to be a Christian. To believe in Him is not such a great thing. To become like Him is truly great."

Thoughtfully, Josif replied, "If Jesus is like you, then I love Him too." Next day, Josif worked in Room Four as he often did now. That evening he said, "I want to be a Christian more than anything."

Richard baptized him with a little water from a tin mug. The bitterness had left Josif's heart completely. On the day of his departure, he embraced Richard. There were tears in his eyes as he said, "You've helped me as though you were my own father. Now I can stand by myself, with God."

Years later they met again. Josif was a Christian and was proud to bear the scar he once hated.

The prison administrators soon got over their fright at Stalin's death. Because of serious trouble in the slave-camps of Siberia, they were determined to show no weakness. Old restrictions were revived and new ones created. The windows were closed and painted over. The prisoners could open them only an inch at night when the guards weren't looking. In summer the heat and stench were horrible.

A new batch of prisoners came in, and one of them who had been badly beaten asked for Richard. He went with Professor Popp along the passage.

It was their old acquaintance, Boris, the old trade unionist. He had been in several prisons since re-education ended. He lay on the stone floor where the guards had thrown him. Richard and

Popp eased him onto a plank bed. His grubby shirt was stuck to him with congealed blood. Slowly and painfully they soaked it off, revealing a back criss-crossed with lash strokes, both fresh and old. It was his reward for cooperating with the re-educators.

Boris clutched Richard's arm. "I met someone you know. Patrascanu gave me a message for you."

Boris said that Patrascanu, the former Communist Minister of Justice and former cell-mate of Richard, was feared by the Party bosses. After six years in jail, he had been given a rushed trial and a death sentence. Refusing to die under severe torture, he was taken out and shot.

The message Patrascanu gave Boris for Richard was this:

"If you meet Wurmbrand again, tell him he was right about Communism."

Sex was an abiding torment to everyone in jail. Prisoners sat gazing at nothing, their heads filled with sexual fantasies, including every kind of perversion. They tried to find relief in endless talk and often baited Richard with provocative questions.

Married men, thinking of what their wives were doing, suffered most of all. A good half had already been divorced in their absence; the pressure to divorce counterrevolutionaries was strong, and wives who had left their imprisoned husbands for other men had no reason to resist it.

Emil, a farmer, trembled with anger as he told how he had returned after a previous sentence. "My dog scented me from halfway down the street. She tore her chain from the fence and rushed to greet me, and when I bent down she jumped up to lick my face. Then I went into the house and found my wife in bed with another man."

Emil looked at Richard and asked, "Which of the two was the dog?"

The Communist Party worked deliberately to corrode morality. Was Christian teaching in sexual matters respected? Some Christian prisoners tried to find out by asking a simple question: "Have you always obeyed the basic rule of the Christian church in remaining chaste in word, thought, and deed before marriage, and faithful thereafter?" Of 300 prisoners, all at least nominal Christians, two men answered yes. One was saintly old Father Suroianu and the other a fifteen-year-old boy.

Prisons are supposed to encourage homosexuality, but Richard saw no evidence of this, perhaps because of the illness, the exhaustion, the overcrowding.

He and Popp took turns looking after Boris, who lay in Room Four, coughing weakly. Dr. Aldea, whom Boris had beaten when he was cooperating with re-education, said, "If he eats he may last ten days. He's filled with remorse over that beating he gave me. It harms him to see me."

Richard asked if Boris could be moved into his cell. Aldea arranged it, and Boris was carried to the bed next to his so that he could nurse him through the last week of his life.

He withered away under their eyes. His hair was reduced to a few strands. His cheeks were sunken. He sweated feverishly as Richard sponged him down day after day. Boris murmured, "All over soon. A priest once told me, 'You'll rot in hell.' So be it."

"What made him speak like that?" Richard asked.

"I was cursing God for my sufferings. He said I'd be punished for eternity."

There was much discussion about eternal punishment. To lighten the situation, Richard told a story: "It is said that when Hitler went to hell he looked about until he found Mussolini. 'What's it like down here?' he asked. Mussolini replied, 'Not so bad, but there's a lot of forced labor.' Then he began to sob. 'Come, Duce,' said Hitler, 'let's know the worst.' 'Well, then, it's this—Stalin's in charge of the working party.'"

Boris smiled. "I'd certainly hate to find my old boss Ana Pauker down below."

Boris' old prejudices fell away one by one. Instead of becoming cheerful he grew depressed. "I feel I've wasted my life. I thought myself clever. I've misled a great many people in the last fifty years. If your God exists, He won't want me in heaven. So down I go to join that old sow Pauker. I'm really scared now."

Often when Boris couldn't sleep he asked Richard to talk to him. "Who's going to pray for me when I'm gone?" he asked. He thought Lutherans forbade prayer for the dead. Richard explained to him that Luther simply didn't want people to suppose that, however much they sinned, they might pay a priest to pray them out of purgatory.

"If I were you, I wouldn't waste prayers on me." He laughed and brought on a fit of coughing.

Richard sat with Boris a long time. For some hours Boris was silent. Richard thought he was asleep. Suddenly he murmured, "What can it be like?"

"What?" Richard asked.

"The judgement of God. Does He sit on a throne and say hell or heaven as souls come before Him?" Richard told him of his idea of the judgement.

During the night Boris had a hemorrhage and Richard had a difficult time with him. Then he fell into a coma. He lay quietly, his eyes staring at the ceiling for an hour. His pulse was weak but still present. Suddenly he pulled his hand away and half sat up. He gave a cry, "Lord God, forgive me."

When dawn came, Richard began to wash the body to prepare it for burial. While this was being done, someone informed the Orthodox bishop in a cell down the corridor that a man had died. He came and began the ritual while Richard went on with his work. The bishop berated him for showing no respect.

Angered, Richard said, "Where were you when this man was dying all last week? Did you hold a cup to his mouth when he was thirsty? Why do you come only now to perform a ceremony which meant nothing to him?"

The ritual seemed such a hollow thing compared to that simple cry from the depths of his heart, "Lord God, forgive me."

Spring of 1955 brought signs of a political thaw. A number of commandants were arrested for "sabotage." Many of the slave workers who had been victims of the "saboteurs" came to Tirgul-Ocna. Beds had to be found for them, and Richard was among a group who were ordered in early June to prepare for transfer to another jail.

Dr. Aldea said, "You're not fit to move, but there is nothing we can do. Take care of yourself. If you get any more streptomycin, don't give it away."

Richard said good-bye to his friends amid many tears. "We'll meet again; I know it," said Professor Popp.

Richard heard his name shouted and joined a line of men in the yard. They were a bizarre gathering, with shaven heads, suits of many patches, and clutching a bundle of rags. Some could hardly walk. Those serving long sentences were ordered to march a step forward and sit on the ground while their ankles were chained.

The political officer stood over the blacksmith as he moved from man to man. When Richard's turn came, the officer smiled unpleasantly. "Ah, Vasile Georgescu. Surely you have something to say about being put in irons."

Richard looked up and replied, "Yes, Lieutenant, I can answer you in song."

"Oh, please. I'm sure we'd all like to hear you."

Richard sang the opening words of the Republic's anthem, "Broken chains are left behind us . . ." The blacksmith's hammer finished the task in a few more blows. "You sing that broken chains are left behind, but this régime has put more people in chains than any other."

Before the lieutenant found a reply, the guards announced the arrival of transport. The prisoners were taken to the station and herded into cars. They lay for hours before the train began to creak and rattle across country. Through holes in the tiny painted windows, they glimpsed forests and mountains. It was a warm, beautiful day.

CHAPTER 8

It was a 200-mile journey across the plains from Bucharest, but it took almost two days and nights before the walls of notorious Craiova Prison came into sight.

Chains were struck off in the stone-flagged courtyard. The prisoners were goaded with blows along filthy dark passages. They were thrust, in small groups, into cells along a gallery. Loud protests came from within the cells:

"There's no room in here. We're suffocating already." The guards squeezed the new arrivals in forcibly, like rush hour on the subway.

A push on Richard's spine sent him stumbling forward, and the door slammed behind him. The stench made him nauseous. At first he could see nothing. As he groped about his hand came in contact with a naked, sweating body. As his eyes adjusted to the dim light from a ceiling bulb, he saw rows of bunks rising in tiers, packed with men who lay gasping for breath. More men, half-naked, sat on the floor or leaned against the walls. Richard's stay in this cell for the next two months was broken only by journeys to the stinking sump outside, carrying lavatory pails.

He told the prisoners he was a pastor and said a brief prayer. A few swore at him but many listened quietly. Someone called his name from an upper bunk hidden in the darkness. "I recognize your voice," he said. "I heard your speech at the Congress of Cults many years ago."

Richard asked him who he was. He replied, "We'll speak tomorrow."

The long night ended at 5:00 a.m. when a guard beat on a dangling piece of railway line with an iron bar. The man from the upper bunk came down to shake Richard's hand. He said, "It's a good thing I recognize your voice. I wouldn't know you by sight. The Party has had its revenge for your protest, I see. How thin you are."

He was Nassim, who had represented the small Muslim community at the 1945 Congress of Cults.

Friendship between the two developed while Richard was trying to eat the vile greasy soup in which shreds of rotten cabbage and unwashed offal floated in a scum. Considering it a duty to eat, he emptied his dish.

"How can you?" asked Nassim, whose stomach had revolted.

"It's a Christian secret," Richard said. "I think of St. Paul's words, 'Rejoice with those that rejoice.' Then I remember friends in America who are now eating grilled chicken, and I thank God with them as I take the first mouthful of soup. Next, I rejoice with friends in England who may be eating roast beef. And I get down another spoonful. By way of many friendly countries, I rejoice with those that rejoice, and stay alive."

Richard and Nassim shared a bunk through the hot, stuffy nights. He felt lucky not to be on the floor. "You lie very still," said Nassim. "Does St. Paul help you now?"

Richard replied, "Yes, for now I rejoice with those in the West by thinking of their comfortable homes, the books they have, the holidays they can plan, the music they hear, and the love they have for their families. And I remember the second part of the verse, from the Epistle to the Romans, 'And weep with those that weep.' I am sure that in the West many thousands think of us and try to help us with their prayers."

Because all men in prison feel a need to assert themselves, like to argue, and flare up at a word, Richard found, in the terrible conditions at Craiova, almost insuperable difficulties. When he preached, he had to raise his voice over groans and pretended snores. The prisoners were desperately bored. They had no inner resources and they longed for their familiar distractions. Richard found his sermons turned into discussions and then into quarrels. Anyone who could tell a story, particularly a crime story, was sure of an audience. Richard told them thrillers of his own invention in which the Christian message played a central but inconspicuous part.

"Pastor," said a forester called Radion, "I've heard many crime stories, but none like yours, which always end with the criminal, the victim, and the policeman all going to church together."

Richard said, "When we understand how criminals had become what they were, we can pity them. From pity comes love, and love among mankind is the chief aim of Christianity. We condemn men, but how rarely we offer the love which might save them from crime."

Richard addressing annual meeting of The Voice of the Martyrs

Richard could have spoken twenty-four hours a day without exhausting the demand for stories. He began to draw on classics with a Christian viewpoint.

Many prisoners told of their personal tragedies. Before long they knew each other intimately. It was a nervous, highly-charged atmosphere. No one could bear contradiction. All sense of proportion or logic was lost.

The food at Craiova was the worst that Richard had encountered anywhere. Then one day the guards brought in a canister of onion soup, another of stew with real meat, white mashed potatoes, fresh carrots, two rolls for each man, and a big basket of apples.

What did it mean? The prisoners hoped for new wonders. During the afternoon, half-a-dozen well-dressed women were being led toward the gate by the commandant. They were, said a guard, a delegation of "democratic women" from the West, leaving after an hour, with comments on the excellence of the food.

The meals were even worse during the following week. Later, Richard heard that the visitors' eye-witness reports on Romania's model prisons were circulated in Britain, France, and the United States.

There were several of these guided tours at that time. When the Russian leadership changes hands there is usually a brief thaw. After a hidden struggle among Stalin's successors, Marshal Bulganin emerged as Chairman of the Council of Ministers.

Calescu said that the rise to power of this former War Minister means "the Americans will have to fight at last." Prison rumor supported his opinion. President Eisenhower's "very words" on the question were quoted: "I have only to do up the last button on my uniform and the captives of Eastern Europe will be free."

The spring brought news, this time official. The Russians had promised to withdraw their troops from Austria, and the first summit meeting between East and West after ten years of cold warfare was to take place in Geneva.

Soon, peaceful co-existence was all the rage. "Why shouldn't the West live harmoniously with the Communist East?" demanded Constantinescu.

Richard said, "I'm no politician, but I know the Church, at least, can never make peace with atheism."

"You hate atheists, then?" said Constantinescu.

Richard replied, "I hate atheism, but I love atheists, just as I hate blindness, but love the blind. Since atheism is a form of spiritual blindness, it must be fought."

A newcomer to Craiova, the engineer Glodeanu said he had heard BBC broadcasts which took the line that the Western powers should no longer try to interfere in the internal affairs of the Communist bloc.

Richard objected, "If I start to knock a hole in a boat which we are sharing, and say, 'Don't interfere. This is my side of the boat,' will you agree? No. The hole in my side will drown us all. The Communists have seized whole countries and have tried to poison youth with hatred. Their plan to overturn the established order all over the world is not an internal affair."

Constantinescu insisted there had been industrial, and even cultural, progress under Communism.

Richard replied, "A visitor to Egypt in ancient times would have been amazed by Pharaoh's monuments. They were the work of slaves, whom God sent Moses to free. In Russia and the satellites today, slave labor is building the houses, factories, and schools, in which is being taught hatred of everything Western."

"The Communists say they plan for the future," said Constantinescu. "A generation or two may be sacrificed, but the basis is being laid for the future good of mankind."

Richard said, "To make future generations happy, men must be good themselves. Communist leaders are constantly denouncing one another as the worst of criminals. The most powerful men in the Soviet Union have been murdered by their own comrades. What Communist can be happy, knowing he may fall in the next Party purge?"

"There is good in them," Constantinescu objected. "No man is entirely bad. Communists are men who keep something of God's image."

Richard replied, "I agree. There was even good in Hitler. He improved the lot of most Germans. He made his country the strongest in Europe. But he murdered millions. He gained the world for Germany, and destroyed its soul, even before his defeat. Communist successes have also been made at the expense of the soul, by crushing man's most vital element, his personality."

"I still say there's been progress," said Constantinescu.

"For my part, I admire no progress that is bought with tears and blood, however impressive it may look from outside."

Richard could make no impression on the apologist's resolve to take Soviet gestures at their face value. Leaning out from his bunk, he snatched Constantinescu's pillow, the small, lumpy bundle of personal things he used as a head-rest. His skull hit the wall. He was furious.

"Why can't you co-exist peacefully with me?" Richard asked. "Now that I've stolen all you have, I'm ready to be friends." Richard restored his property.

According to Richard, Constantinescu was a victim of wishful thinking about Communism. Men trained in the school of Lenin and Stalin see goodwill as weakness to be exploited. For their own good the West must work for their defeat. Love is not a universal panacea. Communist rulers are criminals on an international scale, and only when the criminal is vanquished does he repent; only then can he be brought to Christ. Richard was sure the fate of the West was either to destroy Communism or be destroyed by it.

Some of the worst excesses in the prison system were diminished because of a desire to show Communism in a better light before the summit meeting. At Salcia, where punishment had included hanging prisoners by the heels and plunging women in icy water for hours, the whole staff was arrested. Official evidence said fifty-eight people had died in the competitions between brigade leaders to see who could work to death the most prisoners. Salcia survivors who came to Craiova said there had been at least 800 deaths.

In a show of judicial indignation, the Salcia staff were given long sentences. This purge had a chastening effect in other jails. Beatings stopped. Guards became carefully polite. Punishments became mild.

Again the reforms were short-lived. Soon beatings and insults became routine. A year or so later, when the trials had been forgotten abroad, the mass-murderers were reinstated, with promotions.

During this shake-up in the jails, Richard was moved several times. These nightmare journeys have merged into one in his mind. He would close his eyes and see a frieze of stubble-chinned, shaven-headed convicts jogging gently with the movement of the train. They always wore fifty-pound chains, which chafed them through their clothes and made sores that took months to heal in their undernourished state.

At Poarta-Alba, where political and common criminals were kept together, there were many thieves. Once Richard dozed off while a group were playing with home-made dice. He was awakened by a tickle on his foot. He sat up, rubbing his eyes, to find a prisoner unlacing one of his shoes. The other was already off. "What are you doing with my shoes?" he demanded.

"I've just won them at dice," he said grinning. He was offended when Richard refused to give them up.

One evening, when most prisoners were outside, the door crashed open and the guards flung in a pickpocket, known to everyone as "Fingers." He rolled on the floor gasping and groaning as Richard helped him to his bunk. Soaking a rag in water, Richard began to wash the blood from his swollen mouth. It seemed he had been pilfering from the kitchen.

"You're not a bad sort, Pastor," Fingers said. "When I get out and make my next good haul, I won't forget your share."

Richard said, "I hope you will find a better means of making a living."

Fingers laughed. "They're wasting their time beating me. I love my work. I'll never give it up."

Richard put his arm around his shoulder and said, "Thank you. You've taught me a great lesson."

"What do you mean?" Fingers asked.

"If beatings don't persuade you to give up your ways, why should I listen to those who want me to change mine? I must put at least as much thought into winning a soul as you do into pulling off your next coup. The more I listen to the stories you and your friends tell, the more I learn."

With a pained grin, he said, "You're joking, Pastor."

"No. For example, you work at night, and if you fail the first night, you try again the next. So I, as a pastor, should spend my night in prayer, and if I don't get what I want, I shouldn't give up. You steal from others, but there is honesty among thieves. We Christians should be as united among ourselves. Although you risk your liberty and lives for money, as soon as you get it you throw it right and left. We shouldn't overvalue money either. You thieves don't let punishment deter you. Neither should we shrink from suffering. Just as you hazard everything, so too should we, knowing there is a paradise to win."

The prison at Poarta-Alba consisted of the remains of the labor camp beside the canal project on which Sabina had been forced to work. Richard knew that somehow she was living in Bucharest. No hour passed without his thinking of her. The prisoners lived in long, bare huts which held fifty men each. All around were vegetable patches which Sabina must have known. This melancholy comfort was taken away from him when he was told to prepare for another move.

Fingers came to say good bye. With him was an associate called Calapod, a villainous bandit. He slapped Richard on the back, shouting, "So this is the Holy Reverend who likes thieves and robbers."

"Mr. Calapod," Richard said, "Jesus didn't mind comparing himself to a thief. He promised, 'I will come as a thief in the night.' Just as those whom you have robbed never knew you were coming, so one night Jesus will come for your soul, and you will not be ready."

Weeks in the dank chill of Craiova and Poarta-Alba, along with journeys in chain-gangs, worsened Richard's tuberculosis. He arrived at his next prison at Gherla, in the Transylvanian mountains, in such poor condition he was put into one of a group of cells known as "the hospital." The doctor, a young woman called Marina, said this was her first post. Other patients told Richard that on Dr. Marina's first day she had turned pale as she made her rounds. Nothing in her training had prepared her for the dirt, the hunger, the lack of simple medicines and equipment, the ruthless cruelty.

Marina was a tall, fragile girl with fair hair framing an exhausted face. After examining Richard, she said, "You need good food and plenty of fresh air."

Richard couldn't help laughing. "But don't you know where we are, Dr. Marina?"

With tears in her eyes, she said, "That's what I learned in medical school."

Some days later, high-ranking officers came on a visit. Dr. Marina challenged them in the gallery outside the cells. "Comrades, these men haven't been sentenced to death. The state pays me to keep them alive, just as it pays you to keep them safe. I only ask for conditions which will allow me to do my job."

A man's voice said, "So you side with convicted outlaws."

"They may be outlaws to you, Comrade Inspector. To me they are patients."

Conditions didn't improve. Instead, the prisoners got news which was worth more than all the drugs in the pharmacopoeia, especially to Richard. Before the summit meeting in Geneva, visits by relatives were to be allowed.

Excitement was high. The prisoners were all nervous. Some had been ten or twelve years without news of their families. Richard hadn't seen Sabina for eight years.

The big day came. When Richard's name was called he was marched into an echoing hall and made to stand behind a table. Some twenty yards further on, he saw Sabina, behind another table. The commandant, flanked by officers and guards, stood near the wall between Richard and Sabina, as if ready to umpire a tennis match.

Richard gazed at Sabina. It seemed to him that in the years of her suffering she had achieved a peace and beauty such as he had never seen before. She stood with folded hands, smiling.

Richard called, "Are you well at home?"

"Yes, we are all well at home, thank God."

The commandant broke in, "You are not allowed to mention God here."

"Is my mother still alive?" Richard asked.

"Praise God, she is alive."

"I have told you that you are not allowed to mention God."

Sabina asked, "How is your health?"

"I am in the prison hospital"

The commandant interrupted again, "You are not allowed to say where you are in prison."

Richard tried again, "About my trial, is there hope of an appeal?"

The commandant, "You are not allowed to discuss your trial."

So it went on until Richard said, "Go home, Sabina, dear. They won't let us speak."

Sabina had brought a basket of food and of clothes. She wasn't allowed to give so much as an apple.

That evening, Dr. Marina stopped at the foot of Richard's bed. "Oh dear," she said, "I thought your wife's visit would do you so much good."

Richard and the doctor became friends. She told him she had been taught nothing about religion and supposed herself to be an atheist. "Isn't everyone these days?"

One day, when alone with Marina and another Christian prisoner in a little cubicle which served as her surgery, Richard mentioned it was the day of Pentecost.

"What is that?" she asked.

Richard waited until the guard on orderly duty left and then replied, "It's the day on which God gave us the Ten Commandments, thousands of years ago."

Richard heard the guard returning and said, "It hurts me here, doctor, when I cough."

When the guard moved on, Richard continued, "Pentecost is also the day on which the Holy Spirit came to the Apostles."

Again the guard's footsteps and Richard added hastily, "And at night the pain in my back is terrible."

Dr. Marina bit her lips to keep from laughing. Richard went on with his interrupted sermon while she examined him. At last, she burst into laughter. "Do stop," she gasped, holding a handkerchief to her mouth as the guard appeared again. "Tell me later."

Richard told her the story of the Gospel in the weeks that followed. When he and others at Gherla had brought Dr. Marina to Christ, she took even greater risks to help them.

Years later, in another prison, he heard she had died of rheumatic heart disease and overwork.

Richard was moved back to Vacaresti, the prison-hospital where he had spent a month after his solitary confinement in the dungeon cell beneath the Ministry of the Interior. It was more crowded than ever. Tuberculosis patients had to share rooms and exchange infections with sufferers with other diseases.

Richard's next journey was by road, in a truck labeled "State Food Trust." Security vans often bore such labels so that people would not know how many were on the move, and also for fear of rescue attempts.

The new prison was called Jilava, which means "wet place" in Romanian. To enter it, the truck drove down a steep ramp and they sank below the earth into darkness, more than thirty feet below the ground. It had been designed as a fortress, surrounded by trenches. Strangers could pass by unaware of its existence. Sheep grazed above it. Jilava was intended to hold 500 troops but now held 2000 prisoners.

The meal was announced by a shout from the corridor. Richard took his rotten-carrot soup over to a neighbor's bunk and they talked. He was a young radio engineer who had sent information to the West for a patriotic group. He said he had been brought to Christ through his knowledge of Morse. "It happened five or six years ago. I was interrogated in the cells of the Ministry of the Interior and, while I was there, an unknown pastor next door tapped Bible verses to me through the wall."

When he mentioned the position of his cell, Richard said, "I was that pastor." The two of them built up a nucleus of Christians who spread their influence throughout the prison.

Richard was sent for interrogation to Bucharest. Shields were placed over his eyes before he was taken by car to the city. At Secret Police headquarters he was questioned by a uniformed colonel who seemed more interested in learning Richard's attitude to the régime rather than getting information.

The place was crowded and "secret" prisoners were sharing cells. Richard was put with Vasile Turcanu, the chief "re-educator" who had been sentenced to death by the régime which had once given him license to kill.

While at Secret Police H.Q., Richard learned that Stalin had been denounced as a murderer and tyrant by his successor, Khrushchev. The first reports of how Beria and six of his top men were executed on Christmas Eve, 1953, along with thousands of lesser Soviet secret agents, had just been published. The process of discrediting Stalin had begun in Romania. When Richard took this news back to Jilava, it threw the cell into an uproar. Everyone was delighted and hoped it would hasten their own release.

The weeks passed at Jilava. It seemed the denunciation of Stalin did herald another thaw. Many prisoners were being released. Richard wondered if he would be one of them.

CHAPTER 9

Sabina, Richard's wife, has her own brave story. Born a Jewess, she became a Christian shortly after Richard's conversion. Before this, like her husband, she enjoyed the good life: partying, drinking, dining, with little thought for the welfare of others.

She suffered greatly under the Nazi rule of Romania. Her parents, brother, three sisters, and many friends and relatives were wiped out by the German soldiers during the Holocaust. In spite of this, she sheltered, at great risk, Nazi soldiers during the Russian occupation of Romania. Like Richard, she diligently practiced the Christian principle:

"Love your enemies."

It was Sabina who encouraged Richard to defend Jesus at the Congress of Cults, and it was she who convinced him to stay in Romania, rather than flee to the West. All ninety pounds of her radiated fiery courage.

At the age of seventeen, Sabina went to Paris to study at the Sorbonne. She tells of an intimate part of her life while there. She had been brought up in a strictly Orthodox Jewish family in a small town, and now she found herself free of parental control in a large city.

When the first boy in her life on her first date wanted to kiss her, she rebuffed him. The boy said, "If you believe in God, wouldn't you say that the same God made the hands and the lips? And if I can touch your hand to mine, why is it wrong to touch your lips or to embrace you?"

Neither parents, teachers, nor rabbis had warned her of this question. She had no answer to it. The boy was very appealing. Sabina altered her convictions to suit the life of "gay Paris." An atheist is free to kiss and behave as she likes.

In her book, *The Pastor's Wife*, Sabina said, "His eyes and his hands were the brokers of sin. My eyes and my heart were his handmaiden. But conscience won't be stifled forever. The problem nagged. Why should a girl keep herself pure? What purpose does it serve? I didn't know. Many years later I learned the answer."

A pastor's wife doesn't usually discuss sexual questions, nor is she expected to experience such temptations herself. But pastors and their wives are human. In the past, Richard and Sabina had both led thoughtless, self-indulgent lives. They were converts, insecure about some things lifelong Christians took for granted. Sexuality is vital to human nature, and in their marriage the stresses it caused were sometimes great. Richard was so good, so handsome, and so brilliant that Sabina feared all the adulation he was given might turn his head. Many girls fell in love with him, and to one he was much attracted. Sabina saw that he was being torn in two. Quietly she tried to help him. Sin is often the result of occasion. It is a wife's duty to stay close to her husband in crises like these.

Richard said nothing. One day, as he played a Christian hymn on the piano, he came to the words, "I need you every hour." He wept. Sabina put her arms around him and said, "Richard, you're not an angel. Don't take it so hard. You're only a man. These things will pass." They did pass. When Sabina was left alone during his fourteen years of imprisonment, temptations came to her also. To some she nearly yielded in her loneliness. Then she understood him better.

The Wurmbrand family grew overnight from one son to four sons and three daughters. Thousands of orphaned Jewish children were returning from concentration camps. The Wurmbrands were glad to take six of them. The children, who had seen their relatives and friends killed, were thin and had haunted eyes.

Soon their hollow cheeks filled out and they began to laugh and play. The Russian soldiers, who hadn't seen their own families for years, loved them. They talked to Mihai and the children in the streets and put their hands on their heads. The children smiled, thanked them, and in turn gave them Gospels.

It was dangerous for adults to do so, but children were safe. Many soldiers who wouldn't otherwise have done so, became aware of God.

The church members went out almost nightly with posters to stick on walls, doors, sides of buses, and in railway waiting rooms. Each poster carried Bible verses or a Christian message. Although Sabina's friends were arrested for work among the Russians, Sabina wasn't betrayed.

On top of Soviet looting and extortions (war damage claims) had come drought and shriveling crops, leaving millions to exist on a starvation level. People made soup from leaves and roots of trees.

A section of the World Council of Churches sent food, clothes, and money. Sabina organized relief for the hungry. A canteen run by Pastor Solheim and Richard fed 200 each day in the church hall. Administrative work was heavy and the Communist government tried to sabotage the effort, but there were many volunteers.

When the Russians occupied Budapest, someone was needed to take money for relief work to the mission there. Richard couldn't leave Bucharest and no one else could take the responsibility. Sabina went.

In normal times it wasn't a long journey. But now the Red Army was seizing every train and car for its own use. At the stations there was unimaginable confusion and panic as swarms of hungry and displaced people tried to crowd into the few cars available. Sabina, the only woman in a train full of Russian soldiers, found a corner for herself. For days they rumbled across the country to Budapest.

When she arrived, German troops were still engaged in house to house combat. All was in ruins. There was no transport of any kind. Sabina walked past smoking ruins, unable to find any of the people she sought. The Germans had deported many who never returned. Others had been killed in the last days of street fighting. Finally she found Pastor Johnson, leader of the Norwegian mission, and Pastor Ungar, a Hebrew Christian who led the free church where Jews and other nationalities worshipped. She had arrived when the famine was at its worst. As people emerged from the cellars, food grew scarcer. A horse killed in the battle was cut up and eaten. The help she brought was most welcome.

From Budapest, Sabina went to Vienna. Normally a four-hour journey, it now took six days. She found a train about to leave early one morning. People were clinging to the doors and sitting on the roof. She heard her name called. Perched on top of a freight car was a group of girls, all Auschwitz refugees, who had stayed with the Wurmbrands in Bucharest. "We'll make room," they laughed. From Tuesday until Sunday they sat on the roof and finally reached Vienna.

This city was also starving and badly damaged. After many adventures, Sabina was able to contact friends and Christian leaders. When her work was completed she returned home to a thoroughly worried Richard.

On Sunday morning, February 29, 1948, Richard walked to church alone, followed by Sabina. When Sabina reached church, Richard hadn't arrived. She waited for him all that day. Then she telephoned all the hospitals. She visited emergency wards, thinking he might have had an accident. Finally she realized she must go to the Ministry of the Interior; that he had been arrested. Then began the years of searching.

Sabina learned that important prisoners were kept in cells in the Interior Ministries basement. So many women were seeking arrested husbands, sons, and fathers that an information office was opened to handle inquiries. A slogan decorated the otherwise bare wall: WE WILL BE RUTHLESS TO THE CLASS ENEMY.

A rumor spread that Richard had been taken to Moscow. Sabina refused to believe this. Evening after evening she made a meal and sat by the window, thinking, "He'll come tonight."

He didn't come. Sabina put her forehead against the pane and wept. She went to bed late but couldn't sleep. In the morning, Pastor Solheim went with her to ask the help of the Swedish Ambassador. Mr. Reuterswaerd said he would speak at once to the

Foreign Minister, Ana Pauker, who in turn had a ready answer: "Our information is that Pastor Wurmbrand has absconded from the country with a suitcase full of dollars entrusted to him for famine relief work. They say he is in Denmark."

The ambassador brought the case up with Prime Minister Groza, who repeated Pauker's version. He added with a jovial promise, "So Wurmbrand's supposed to be in our jails. If you can prove that, I'll release him." The Communists were sure of themselves. Once in the Secret Police cells, a man ceased to exist. The only hope left was bribery.

"You know Theohari Georgescu, the Cabinet Minister?" asked a friend of Sabina's school days. "His brother lives near us, and I've heard he can open prison doors for the right sum. I'll talk to his wife for you."

Georgescu was willing. Everything was to be kept absolutely secret. The price of his favors was high. Sabina met him in a squalid hovel on the outskirts of town. "I arrange things," he said. "A word to my brother and it's as good as done. Guarantee? You have my word."

With great difficulty Sabina found the sum he requested. She handed it over. Nothing happened.

It was not the first nor the last time Sabina was swindled in this way. There was nothing she could do. These professional tricksters were in a class of their own. Some were high-ranking officials.

After some months of wasted effort, a stranger came one evening to the door. The man was unshaven and reeked of brandy. He insisted they talk alone. "I've met your husband," he said. "I'm a ward clerk. Don't ask what prison. I take him his food. He said you'd pay me well for a bit of news."

"It depends how much," Sabina said.

"I'm risking my neck, you know." The sum he named was huge. He wouldn't bargain.

Pastor Solheim was as doubtful as Sabina. He said, "Bring me a few words in Wurmbrand's writing." He gave him a bar of chocolate from the famine relief stores. "Take this to Wurmbrand and bring back a message with his signature."

Two days later the ward clerk returned. He removed his cap and felt in the lining. He handed Sabina the wrapper from the chocolate bar. On it was written, "My dearest wife, I thank you for your sweetness. I'm well. Richard."

It was his handwriting.

"He's all right," said the man. "Some can't take solitary. He sends you his love."

Sabina agreed to pay the money if he would continue to carry messages. He said, "All right. I could get twelve years for this. You know, it's not just the cash."

He risked his freedom out of a divided love. He loved the money, loved the drink it bought, and he loved Richard, whom he sometimes slipped extra bread. He continued to bring verbal messages.

Sabina asked, "What do you do with this money we pay you?"

"Get drunk." He laughed. But she felt the Lord had touched his heart.

Pastor Solheim went with Sabina to the Swedish Embassy, where they were at once received by the ambassador. When he saw the scrap of paper with Richard's writing, he quickly drafted a note to the Premier, "You promised to release Pastor Wurmbrand if we could prove he is in a Romanian prison. I now have that proof in my hands."

Premier Groza passed the note on to Ana Pauker at the Foreign Ministry. She sent for Mr. von Reuterswaerd and stormed at him. If she said Wurmbrand had fled to Denmark, then so he had. She would not be insulted by the envoy of a minor power who was poking his nose into a purely domestic matter. She was not a liar.

The ambassador was declared *persona non qrata*. His superiors questioned the wisdom of his intervention. Von Reuterswaerd said his conscience obliged him to help a man whom he knew to be innocent. He was recalled to Stockholm and retired from the diplomatic service.

Next Pastor Solheim was obliged to leave the country. He had identified himself with the Wurmbrands and his mission station, as all good missionaries do.

The wife of a political prisoner could get no ration card. Neither could she get work. If she had no ration card, she didn't exist. Sabina didn't argue that the highest authorities in the land denied Richard was in prison. She asked them, "How am I and my son to live?"

Their response: "That's your business."

Mihai was now Sabina's only child. Before Richard's arrest, they had felt it was safest to send the six orphans where the new State of Israel was about to be born. The orphans joined a group of refugees aboard the Turkish steamer, Bulbul. The ship never arrived and was never found. It was assumed that it had hit a wartime mine. Sabina loved the children as her own and suffered much pain. Her Christian faith was put to a hard test. Then one day the peace of God entered her heart.

She came home late one evening after doing secret pastoral work for the church. She found her cousin, who was staying with her while waiting to leave for Israel, in an alarmed state. A suspicious visitor had called. He talked about putting more people in the flat, but he seemed mostly interested in how many exits the apartment had.

Sabina knew then that she should expect a police raid. She went to sleep with prayers for the safety of her family. At 5 a.m. there was a hammering on the door. "We know you're hiding arms here. Show us where they are."

The police tore the flat apart, emptying drawers on the floor and knocking over bookcases. "So you won't tell us where the arms are hidden."

"The only weapon we have in this house is here," said Sabina, picking up a Bible from under their feet.

"You're coming with us to make a full statement about those arms."

Sabina laid the Bible on the table and said, "Please allow us a few moments to pray and then I'll go with you."

As they led her out, she snatched up a parcel from the sideboard. It was a present from the day before, containing stockings and underwear. Sabina said it was the most important thing she took with her to prison.

She was pushed into the back of an Oldsmobile. Blacked-out

goggles were put over her eyes. Minutes later she was lifted out and swept across the pavement. The goggles came off, she was pushed, and a door slammed behind her. She found herself in a long, bare room crowded with women. The door kept opening to admit more. Sabina recognized the wife of a liberal politician, a society woman she had seen in the newspapers, an actress, and a lady-in-waiting from the Palace.

By evening several hundred women were crammed into the room. The round-up was on a national scale in observance of August 23rd Freedom Day, as the Communists called it.

As Sabina prayed for Mihai, who fortunately was in the country with friends, a woman leaped up and beat on the door with her fists. She screamed, "My children. My children." A woman beside her collapsed in hysterics. Another woman vomited. A single toilet overflowed. The door opened to admit more women.

Next morning, brass bands were heard. The Freedom Day parade was on. Thousands of boots tramped by. Slogans were chanted: AUGUST 23rd HAS BROUGHT US FREEDOM, DEATH TO THE THIEVES AND TRAITORS IN PRISON, BROKEN CHAINS REMAIN BEHIND US.

The hours dragged on. At last, guards brought black bread and watery soup in heavy metal cans. Next day, a sergeant began calling out names. Sabina's name was on the first list. Again blacked-out goggles. She was put in a van and taken to what she learned later was Secret Police headquarters, on Rahova Street.

She was pushed into a small cell after a woman guard determined that no friends of Sabina were there.

Except for a young medical student, Sabina's companions were peasant women. Terror was being used to enforce collectivization of farms. An unknown number of peasants had been summarily executed, and nearly 100,000 were serving jail sentences.

Several days later Sabina was moved into solitary confinement. Her cell contained only an iron cot. There was no bucket, the item most desired by prisoners. The guards let her out at 5 a.m., 3 p.m., and 10 p.m. regardless of her needs.

High in the wall was a small window with an iron grill. The cell was damp and chill, although it was August. Sabina was glad she had a light summer coat and woolen stockings she found in the package she grabbed as she was led from her apartment.

It was several claustrophobic days before they came. The cell door opened. "Turn your back." Goggles were snapped over her eyes and she was pulled by the arm through passages.

They stopped. The goggles came off. Blinded by sunshine, she was put in a chair by a big oak desk in a large room. Behind the desk sat two men wearing blue-tabbed uniforms of the Secret Police. One was a heavy-set major cultivating a moustache. The other was a young blond lieutenant who had been present at the raid of her flat. He reminded Sabina of someone. Then she remembered. He had an extraordinary resemblance to the boy she had loved so many years ago in Paris.

Sabina

Sabina expected to hear some charge against her. The major said, "You know, Mrs. Wurmbrand, what your offense against the state has been. Now you will write for us a detailed statement about it."

"What should I write? I don't know why you've brought me here."

"You know very well," he said. On a side table were pen and paper. Sabina wrote a few lines saying she had no idea why she had been arrested. The major glanced at the paper and asked for the next prisoner.

All the way back to the cell, the guard shouted and pushed her, blindfolded, into walls. When the door slammed behind her, she saw his eye through the small spyhole. "Now you'll sit and think until you write what the officer told you, or you'll get the treatment."

It was mental torture to soften the prisoner up for interrogation. Tape-recorded voices screaming. A firing-squad volley on loudspeakers in the corridors. The torture of a mother separated from her child.

The major and his assistant were waiting for Sabina the next day. He read a string of questions on a pad. Sabina realized their purpose was to extract information that could be used against Richard.

The major made a little speech about the blessings of Communism. They assured Sabina they were her friends. Richard's friends, too. They wished to release him after securing the information they needed. He asked what Richard had said to colleagues on this or that occasion. Sabina replied that they discussed religion, never politics.

The major smiled and referred to politics in the Bible. "If your husband is a Christian, he must have clear views about the government."

"My husband doesn't interest himself in politics."

"Yet he had an audience with King Michael before the king left the country. Why?"

"It wasn't secret. The king gave audiences to many people."

"How long did this audience last?"

"About two hours."

"And in all that time there was no reference to politics?"

"As I said, my husband isn't interested in politics."

"Well, what *did* he talk about?"

"About the Gospel."

"And what did the king say?"

"He was in favor of it."

The lieutenant gave a little snort and quickly put his hand over his mouth.

The major smiled. "Now, Mrs. Wurmbrand, You're an intelligent woman. I can't understand your attitude. You and your husband are Jews. We Communists saved you from the Nazis. You should be grateful. You should be on our side. Your husband is accused of counterrevolutionary activities.

He could be shot. His colleagues have spoken. They support the charge against him. They may be just trying to save themselves. Perhaps they are the real counterrevolutionaries. We can't judge unless you tell us everything people working with the mission used to say. Speak out. Denounce the real counterrevolutionaries and your husband will be free tomorrow."

The lieutenant said, "You could go home to your family."

Sabina said, "I know nothing."

Back in her cell, she wondered what they were doing to Richard. At one moment she was ready to say anything to be safe with him again; the next, she trembled. She wanted him to live and she wanted him to resist, and the two wishes struggled within her.

The major looked tired but in his eyes was a glint of triumph. The questioning this time centered on the Nazis. What Germans did she know? What were her connections with them? Was she aware people were being shot for harboring Nazis? Why had she hidden officers in her home?

Sabina said she hadn't hidden Nazis.

"You deny the charge then. We have a surprise for you." He pressed a buzzer under his desk. Guards brought in a man Sabina recognized at once. Stefanescu had been with them in 1945. He knew everything they had done for the Germans.

"Now, Stefanescu," said the major, "tell us how the Wurmbrands kept Nazis in their home. You know this woman?"

"No."

"What!"

"I've never seen her."

"You're lying."

"No, sir."

The major shouted and ranted. He put his face an inch from Stefanescu's and yelled at the top of his lungs. The major told the guards to take him away. He looked at Sabina with speculative eyes. Sabina thought he must be thinking:

It's absurd. A Jewess who lost all her family in Nazi pogroms, hiding Nazis in her cellar. Risking her husband's life as well as her own. He switched to asking her about her work in the Red Army.

Sabina managed to dodge the dangerous questions.

Lying awake in her cell later, she remembered the big gangly Red Army boys who'd once filled the flat. With what wonderful simplicity they had heard the word of God. One had danced around the room with joy when Richard told him that on the third day Christ had risen from the dead.

The day's events encouraged her. God had given her the strength and wit to fend off questions about printing Russian Gospels and receiving relief funds. Perhaps the worst was over.

A piece of plaster had worked loose from the wall. She picked it up and drew on the dark blanket a big cross in thankfulness.

The new interrogator was a large perspiring, bald-headed man. Sabina stood a long time in front of his desk while he read documents in a brown file. At last he began. The questions were all personal. Her family, friends, trips abroad. Days as a student in Paris. He was warm and friendly. Smooth.

"And now," he said, "we want you to write down your sexual history."

Sabina was slow to understand. He explained patiently.

"Your sexual history. You have one, I suppose? Your first experience. The first boy you went with. How he fondled you. How you returned his kisses.

What happened next? Did he possess you on the spot, and which spot? Or was that left to the next one who came along? Tell us about *his* embraces. Compare the two. Or three. Continue with your other lovers. We want a complete account, blow by blow, so to speak. Write it all down. We want every detail. I'm sure there are plenty."

Sabina tried to stay calm. "You have no right to ask such a thing. You may accuse me of being a counterrevolutionary or what you like, but this isn't a court of morals."

"This is whatever we choose to make it. The story is spread that you are some kind of saint. We think otherwise. We *know* otherwise. Now we mean to show you in your true colors."

"As a whore," said the lieutenant.

"I shall not do as you ask, of course."

"We'll see about that."

The interrogator fired obscene questions at Sabina. A stream of four-letter words poured out of his mouth. He pounded the desk as he spoke.

Sabina was soaked in sweat. Her head swam. She thought she might faint. She kept refusing to write. This went on for an hour.

"Time is on our side," said the interrogator. "Your husband has already confessed to being a traitor and a spy. You're on your way to the rubbish heap." He came around the desk and breathed in her face. "You won't leave this place without telling us the facts about your sex life."

Sabina was trembling convulsively. Back at her cell, the goggles were removed a moment before she was pushed into it. She saw the number of her cell above the door: *seven*. The holy number. The symbolism was reassuring to her.

She lay on her cot and sobbed, then grew calmer. "Get up." Mielu, meaning "lamb" in Romanian, who was the head guard and anything but a lamb, stood in the doorway. "Turn to face me. Anything to report?"

Sabina requested a spoon with which to eat her soup. The greasy soup arrived at noon. It was required to drink it all. Hunger-strikers were forcibly fed. Two guards would hold the prisoner while a third poured the soup into his mouth. Some prisoners preferred this because the soup was enriched with egg-yolk and sugar to keep the "patient's" strength up.

Every night in cell 7 Sabina recited verses from Exodus. She knew that, somewhere, Richard was doing the same. She knew that, like the deliverance of the children of Israel from Egypt, God would deliver them.

"Ready to answer my questions now? Are we to be edified by the sex-life of a saint?" The interrogator ran through his routine of obscene questions for twenty minutes. He lit a cigarette and walked out of the room. The lieutenant continued to read. Sabina stood there for three hours.

The interrogator returned and grilled Sabina for another hour. She was very tired. Exhaustion came in black waves. She found the strength to say, "I will not tell you what you want."

He grunted an obscenity. "Take her away," he said.

Days later, Sabina was moved back to a communal cell which was like an icebox. Winter was approaching. Her coat and wool stockings were the envy of the cell. She shared her riches with the others.

The door opened sharply. "You," said the guard. They had trouble pronouncing Sabina's German name, Wurmbrand. "Put the goggles on." Then the blind march down the corridors.

They entered a room full of men's voices. Then silence. She could feel them staring at her. "Take the goggles off." Bright lights dazzled her. The room was windowless and apparently underground. Behind a long table sat ten uniformed officers, including the three she'd already met.

"Do you know what has happened to your husband?"

"Don't you know? You should be telling me."

"Sit down," said the moustached major. "If you cooperate and answer all our questions, we may allow you to see him."

Sabina really believed they might. They had committed no crime. Perhaps Richard had been tried and acquitted. How naive she was in those days.

Batches of photographs were spread out on the desk, both men and women. A sergeant held them up one by one.

"Who's this?"

"You know this man?"

Of the lot, Sabina recognized one man. He was a dear friend, a Russian soldier baptized in the Wurmbrand home. She kept saying, "No, no, no," while shaking her head.

They shouted and bullied. It was a long session and Sabina became confused by the questions and blinding light. Her head whirled.

"We have methods of making you talk which you won't like. Don't try to be clever with us. It wastes our time. It wastes your life."

The repetition and insistence were maddening. Sabina's nerves were stretched to the breaking point. It was hours before they sent her back to her cell. She lay on the straw mattress and sobbed wildly and noisily for two hours. Her cell-mates began to weep too. The guard informed them they were not allowed to cry. He turned and closed the door.

The next interrogation was played with new tactics. The bald man was alone and smiling. "Mrs. Wurmbrand, you're only thirty-six years old. The best years of a woman's life are before you. Why are you so obstinate? Why do you refuse to cooperate with us? You could go free tomorrow if you'd give us the names of these traitors."

Sabina didn't answer.

"Let's talk sense. Every man has his price, every woman too. You're an honest woman. You can raise your price. Judas was a fool to sell his boss for thirty pieces of silver. He could have held out for 300. Tell us what you want. Freedom for you and your husband? A good parish for him? We'd look after your family. You could be very valuable to us. Well?"

When he had finished talking there was silence in the room. Sabina finally broke it. "Thanks, but I've sold myself already. The Son of God was tortured and gave his life for me. Through him I can reach heaven. Can you offer a higher price than that?"

He suddenly looked very tired. His voice was hoarse. He appeared frustrated. As he clenched his hairy fist, Sabina thought he intended to hit her. He sighed deeply.

In November, the prison director came to Sabina's cell. A small group of women were told to be ready to leave in ten minutes. No questions were allowed. They expected to be either freed or shot.

Sabina had been sentenced to twenty-four months of forced labor. When that time was served, a new sentence would be imposed. She was one of many thousands of prisoners who were classified as "administrative." They were sent without benefit of trial to the slave camps. At the time, she didn't know she had been sentenced.

The slaves were an essential part of the economy now. The camps had been established all over the country. "Saboteurs" who failed to fulfill work norms, gypsies, criminals, priests, prostitutes, wealthy bourgeois, everyone who failed to fit into the Communist world, were sent there for re-education. The camps were huge, with a permanent population of 200,000. They held men, women, and children. Ages ranged from twelve years to over seventy.

The State did what it liked and published what it liked. Nothing appeared in the newspapers about trials and sentences; only congratulations to the government in creating jobs for all, so unlike the West where millions were unemployed.

Prominent people in the West pointed to Romania as an example of a country which had satisfactorily solved its unemployment problems. Before partaking in this satisfactory solution, Sabina was moved to a transit prison, Jilava, the most feared jail in the country.

The truck dipped suddenly and went down a ramp. There was a clang of steel gates. The prisoners waited in silence for orders. "Take the goggles off."

Sabina found herself in a large underground room without windows. Uniformed women guards milled about. A squat muscular woman with ginger hair wagged a finger and warned, "I'm sergeant Aspra (means 'harsh' in Romanian), hard by name and hard by nature. Don't you forget it."

A clerk was entering names in a ledger. "All superfluous articles of clothing," said Aspra, "are deposited on joining this establishment. So get out of your clothes."

They took Sabina's summer coat but let her keep her thin dress and stockings, which were now full of holes. An inventory was made. Hours later, they tramped along dark passages. Sergeant Aspra unlocked a heavy iron-barred door. "This lot for Cell 4."

The cell was dark, lighted by a weak bulb hanging from the ceiling. Two long tiers of wooden bunks lined the sides of a high vaulted room. At the far end was a small window, painted over and barred.

"I'm Viorica, your room-chief," said a voice. "Give her the end place."

At the darkest end of the cell stood one lavatory bucket beside an open drain. Sabina's bunk was directly over it. The bucket was shared by fifty women, most of them with diarrhea from the foul food.

It was airless and suffocatingly hot on the top tier. Sweating women lay half-naked. Wherever Sabina looked she saw bodies with thin arms, sores, and torture marks.

Each day at 5 a.m. a dangling piece of iron rail was struck with an iron bar. This started the women's day. A queue formed for the bucket. Canteens clattered as they were filled with water for washing.

On her first morning at Jilava, Sabina heard someone singing hymns. She was told they were nuns. She was also told that if Aspra heard them, she would tie their hands behind their back for hours.

Here, the women had learned the tapping method of communication between cells. They were severely punished if discovered by the guards. By this method they learned there were 200 women living in the four cells of their wing. Elsewhere there were 3000 men. The fortress was intended for 600 men.

Idleness was the big problem, just sitting and waiting. Tempers flared up easily. When the soup and black bread arrived at 11 a.m., the women quarreled over who had the largest piece of bread. Guards would rush in, striking out with sticks while Aspra bellowed, "We're too good to you. If this goes on, you'll starve tomorrow."

When the guards had gone, the melee broke loose again. Aspra stormed in. "There will be no more food today or tomorrow either."

A big masterful woman looked at Sabina and said, "Who are you? Why are you here? You haven't said a word since you arrived."

Sabina told them her name and that she was a pastor's wife. A gray-haired peasant woman asked if she knew any Bible stories. Other women asked for stories to ease the boredom. The masculine woman became hostile. "You'll turn this place into a vicarage." She walked off full of rage.

Elena said, "Don't mind Elsa Gavriloiu. She's an old Party member and grateful to be here to be re-educated."

Sabina told the story of Joseph and how he had saved his brothers from the ravages of famine. She explained the meaning of the story as she went along. A few women listened. The rest of the women hummed and squawked. Sabina caught a warning glance from Viorica.

"Be careful," whispered the peasant woman. "If Aspra hears you talked of God in here, there'll be trouble."

Next morning, Viorica pointed a finger at Sabina and said, "I know who you are. I've been puzzling for hours. You're a preacher, wife of that Pastor Wurmbrand." She explained that her uncle, who had charge of an Orthodox church in Bucharest, had heard Richard's speech at the Congress of Cults.

She turned to Sabina. "I've been to your church. I thought the service was lovely."

Sabina was the heroine of the hour. Viorica found her a better bunk ten feet from the bucket and then paid her a state visit.

Sabina received her first dishful of *tertch*, maize boiled in water. When she tried to pour it into her mouth, it ran down her chin. Sour Mrs. Gavriloiu jeered, "Lap it up."

To lap seemed too animal-like. She gave away her morning *tertch*. Sabina thought, "Jesus was humbled to the utmost. Why should I not be?" The next time *tertch* was served, she lapped.

Sabina became known to everyone in Cell 4. Women came to her for French and German lessons. They used soap on the sole of a shoe on which to write. Fanny Marinescu, Sabina's best pupil, said, "All Mrs. Wurmbrand's lessons start with the words 'Dieu' or 'Gott.'" Sabina used every opportunity to spread the Gospel.

Sometimes Mrs. Ioanid, whose two daughters were also in prison, would climb up to Sabina's bunk to talk about her husband and children. She asked about Richard, who was known to many prisoners by name. She was interested in the fact that they were Jews converted to Christianity. She wanted to know how it happened. Sabina obliged with the following story:

CHAPTER 10

When they met, Richard was twenty-seven and Sabina was twenty-three.

Sabina had accompanied her uncle to visit the Wurmbrands. As they approached the house, Sabina saw an angry young man on the balcony. When he saw them he waved and came down. When introductions were over, Richard told Sabina why he had looked so cross.

"My mother is nagging me to get married. She has the very girl, an heiress with a family business, two houses, and a million dowry. I don't mind the business and the inheritance. It's the girl I don't like. When I saw you, the thought came into my mind that if I could have a girl like you I wouldn't care about the million."

Sabina didn't return to Paris. She took a job in Bucharest, and she and Richard met every evening. They found they had everything in common. Both of them had been poor as children and both were Jews who had put aside their religion.

Richard was an up-and-coming business man, using his keen wits to make good money. He enjoyed spending it, and they went to night clubs and theaters and didn't think too much about tomorrow. One evening he said, "I'm not an easy person. You would suffer a lot with me."

But they were too deeply in love to think of anything else. They had a religious wedding to please their parents.

Happiness lasted less than a year. Richard developed an annoying cough. The doctor diagnosed pulmonary tuberculosis. He had a lesion on one lung and must go into a sanatorium at once.

Sabina felt as if Richard had been sentenced to death. It seemed the worst tragedy of her life, a cruel and horrible trick being played on her at the moment of her greatest happiness.

When Richard entered the mountain sanatorium, Sabina went to live with his mother. Many nights she cried herself to sleep.

Every fortnight she went by train to visit him. The sanatorium was in a beautiful area, with great views across hills and valleys covered with green forests. Richard seemed almost content there. He said, "For the first time in my life, I'm resting."

He was thankful and grew better, but a strange change was coming over him. "I've been thinking about the past, all the people I've harmed, my mother, and many girls you don't know about. I've thought only about myself."

"Don't grieve about it," Sabina said. "I've also lived such a life. This is youth."

One day, she found him reading a book given to him by a woman patient. "It's about the Brothers Ratisbonne," he said. "They founded an order to convert Jews. Others have been praying for me while I wasted my life."

He talked about Jesus Christ. It was the greatest shock he could have given. In Sabina's Orthodox Jewish family it was forbidden to mention Christ's name. They had to look away when they passed a church. Sabina thought she had outgrown her strict Jewish upbringing. Yet it upset her terribly that Richard should think about such things

She knew the history of Christian persecution of her people. How Jews were forcibly baptized, and how they had killed their own children and then themselves rather than change their religion. How they were forced to listen to Catholic Masses and plugged their ears with wax to avoid hearing what they considered blasphemy.

And what she saw around her wasn't encouraging. The Orthodox and the Lutheran churches were strongly anti-Semitic. The biggest anti-Semite body in the country was called the "National

Christian Defense League." Its chief activity consisted of beating Jewish students and smashing Jewish shops.

Sabina couldn't see what might persuade Richard to turn Christian. As he grew slowly better, she tried to talk to him about the good times they'd have when he returned to Bucharest. He tried to tell her about his discovery of the New Testament. Before, they hadn't thought of having children. Now he was talking about how they should bring them up.

While Richard convalesced in a mountain village, an uncanny thing happened. An old carpenter passed the time of day with the Wurmbrands. When he heard Richard was a Jew, his eyes lit up with excitement. He said, "I asked God to grant me one favor at the end of my life. Because Christ was a Jew, I wanted to bring a Jew to him. Since there are none here, and I cannot leave the village, God must send me one. And here you are in answer to my prayer."

Richard was deeply moved, but Sabina's heart sank. Before they left the village, the carpenter gave him a worn Bible, saying, "My wife and I have prayed for hours, asking for your conversion."

Richard read and read the Bible. Sabina didn't know what to do. She was dismayed. Few Gentiles can guess how strong a hold anti-Christian feelings may have on a Jewish heart. Beside the historical reasons, there were personal ones. As a child, Sabina had to walk home from school past a corner where two bigger girls lay in wait to pull her hair "because you're a dirty little Jewess." And they were Christians. Then when she grew up, the Nazi persecution of Jews began.

Richard told Sabina that Jesus himself was a victim of injustice. Sabina couldn't bear to hear that forbidden name on his lips. "I don't need Him," she said. "You don't need Him. It isn't natural. We're Jews. It's another way of life."

When he spoke of being baptized, Sabina quite lost her head. "I'd rather die than see you become a Christian. If you need religion, you can practice your own Jewish faith."

For a time he did. He went to the synagogue, but even there he talked about Christ. One day he persuaded Sabina, frightened but curious, to look inside a church. "The fact is," he said, as he showed her around inside the church, "the Christian religion is simply our Jewish faith opened to all the nations of the earth. Jesus, his mother Mary, and half the saints were Jews. The commandments are from the Book of Moses, the psalms are from King David, and the Old Testament is full of prophecies about Christ."

With patient arguments over many nights, Richard wore down Sabina's objections. She read the New Testament and found she admired and loved Jesus. She felt empathy with Gandhi, who once said, "From Christianity give me Christ and you can keep all the rest." Sabina wanted nothing to do with His followers who had wronged her people.

Richard wouldn't hear of this. In time, Sabina's intellectual objections were overcome but the emotional ones were still there. And they grew stronger. For weeks more, this internal struggle raged within her.

One evening Richard came home from a prayer meeting at the Anglican Church Mission to the Jews. He took Sabina's hands in his and said, "I have surrendered my heart to Christ. Soon I will be baptized."

The news was more than Sabina could bear. She shut herself alone in her room for hours. She decided that on the day he was baptized, she would commit suicide.

When the day came and she was left alone, she locked her door and threw herself on the floor, racked with dry sobs. In her desperation she cried aloud, "Jesus, I can't come to you. I don't want Richard to be yours. I can't bear any more."

She lay there for a long time sobbing and then, slowly, she grew calmer. Something had changed within her.

Richard's baptism had taken place in another town. Sabina went with flowers to meet him at the station. He was elated. They sat up until late at night, discussing all that had happened. Sabina saw that she had been moving toward conversion without understanding the forces involved. But she was not yet prepared to call herself a Christian. She still yearned for the young fun life.

To humor her, Richard took her to a party one Sunday evening. Suddenly Sabina realized she was bored. The noise, drinks, smoke, and jokes grew worse. She asked Richard to take her home, but he kept her there under one pretext or another. On their way home, very late, she blurted out, "Richard, I'd like to be baptized at once."

Next day, Richard took her to the Anglican Mission, where she was baptized. Overflowing with happiness, she felt she had to share it. At work she told a close friend, a Jewess, of her baptism. "So now I've lost you," the friend said and turned away weeping.

The Wurmbrand's son, Mihai, was born in 1939. War clouds were already gathering over Romania. They were in Hitler's orbit and knew Jews must soon be uprooted, which pointed against having a child. They were happy they took the chance.

By the time Sabina finished her story to Mrs. Ioanid and her cell-mates, the evening was spent and the women settled down for the night.

CHAPTER 11

Overcrowding in Jilava grew worse. Cell 4 had space for thirty people. By Christmas 1950 there were eighty. Because of the stench, inspectors ordered baths. Overjoyed, the women were taken to the showers. A disturbance was created and they were ordered back to their cells. The head guard had arranged with an informer to create the disturbance. The reason? The showers were nonfunctional.

Corporal Georgescu arrived next morning with a sheet of paper in her hand. "Everyone on this list must be ready to move at once." The list was read and the women departed.

On January 6, 1951, Mihai's birthday, Sabina's name was on the list. She was out of Cell 4 by eight a.m. and standing in line awaiting her fate. They waited in the bitter cold all day while women from other cells joined them. At long last they climbed into trucks which drove them to Ghencea, a transit camp near Bucharest.

On hearing the hopeful talk of new arrivals, a lanky girl said, "Release? This is the departure point for the Canal. You'll be packed off to there in a few days."

On the third day Sabina was brought before the commandant, Captain Zaharia Ion, who had been a Party member since the twenties. She looked so startled when she saw his emaciated body, he said, "Do you know why I look like this? Because I starved in jail under the bourgeoisie. People like you."

Sabina said, "I'm sorry you were unjustly imprisoned, but I don't belong to the bourgeoisie."

"I'll make you an offer," he said. "Instead of going to work on the Canal, you can stay here as a privileged detainee if you will report to me in confidence on the prisoners from time to time." Sabina declined the offer. "Then you won't see freedom again," snarled the commandant, who later died in prison under false charges.

Near Bucharest, Sabina boarded a train for the Canal. The long black prison car was crowded with politicals, thieves, prostitutes, and gypsies. They began to creak slowly south.

After many hours, the train stopped and they tumbled out, tired and aching. They were at a small town, Cernavoda, by the Danube. The camp was miles away. They marched through the black wintry night. They passed through gates strung with barbed-wire, under tall watchtowers. Searchlights played over rows of identical huts. It was late on Saturday evening and the prisoners were sprawled about after the day's work. Finding no empty bed, Sabina sat on the floor.

She was awake all night thinking of Mihai. Toward dawn she dozed off, then woke up with a pounding heart. Rats were jumping on the prisoners amid curses. One prisoner said cheerfully, "You should save some bread for them. It keeps them from biting."

On Sunday morning, Sabina hoped in vain for rest. The whole female section of the camp was ruled by Biddable Rina, a prisoner with a long criminal record and a hatred of politicals. While the criminal prisoners lounged about, the politicals were down on their knees scrubbing and scraping the floor.

"All new arrivals will gather outside for a visit to the bathhouse," Rina shouted. They were lined up and marched over the frozen mud under an escort of armed guards. As the prostitutes shrieked their obscenities, the guards laughed and stomped their boots. Under the strain of the journey, the hunger, and shame, Sabina fainted. She was carried back to the hut and placed on a bed.

Wearing a dirty gray and white striped jacket, a long pleated skirt given her by a nun at Jilava, and stockings full of holes, she made an outlandish appearance. The politicals decided she wasn't one of them and so the gypsies decided she was one of them. Sabina said, "I assure you I'm not a gypsy. I can't speak your language."

An old woman gypsy patted her arm and said, "We know, dear, we know." They had assumed that for some reason of her own, she was trying to hide her race. From that time on, in Cernavoda, she was an adopted gypsy.

Gypsies were strikingly beautiful people. Many of them stole anything they could put their hands on. Communists sent thousands of them to prisons and labor camps where they continued to steal. Sabina was the only political prisoner who lost nothing. Richard and Sabina had helped gypsies when they poured out of Nazi concentration camps at the end of the war. Now she had her reward.

The gypsies did a good business from fortune-telling. Since they had no cards, they threw grains of corn on the floor and read fortunes from the patterns formed. Sabina was to be re-united with Richard and Mihai and to travel many miles over sea and land to find happiness. They didn't tell her she would have to wait fifteen years.

Next day early in the morning, they left camp to march to work in an endless column. At the gate the leading guard shouted to the watchtowers, "Taking out 2000 (or whatever the count for the day was) criminals and counterrevolutionaries. "A bitter cold wind blew from off the Black Sea into Sabina's face.

Men and women worked together to build an embankment to contain the canal, which was to connect the Danube with the Black Sea. Sabina's job was filling wheelbarrows with earth, which would be taken by men to the top of the parapet and dumped. After several barrow loads, she staggered when she lifted the heavy shovel over the side of the barrow.

Each gang had a brigade-chief to check how much work one could do. The "norm" could be anything up to eight cubic meters a day. If the norm was fulfilled, it was raised by so many barrow-loads next day. A prisoner who failed to meet the norm was punished.

The "brigadiers" were trusted prisoners who had special rations and even some pay. They never did a stroke of work and ruled with the power of life and death. Rina wielded hers to the full.

Talking and all other forms of human contact were forbidden. Sabina took a risk and said a few cheerful words and quoted the Bible to the man waiting as she filled his barrow. The middle-aged man, who looked like a peasant, was startled. He quickly grabbed his wheelbarrow and trundled off.

Four barrows later, the man said, "Count Rakosi thanks you for your beautiful words and wants to know who you are." The "peasant" was a Hungarian aristocrat from Transylvania, a Romanian province thickly populated with Hungarians. Sabina was so surprised she left her spade in the earth for a moment.

"Come on. Wake up," said Rina. "Do you want a night in the carcer?" Sabina began to dig with frenzied strength. The carcer, a box six feet high and two and a half feet in width and depth, was a common punishment in canal camps. The prisoner had to stand in it all night and return to work the next day with a good chance of spending the next night in the carcer for not working fast enough.

The prisoners were given a pound of bread at midday, with some soup and oats. They toiled on for another four hours until dusk. The long column formed for the return to camp. On the way, several prisoners collapsed. One fell beside Sabina. Without a word, two of the stronger men picked him up, placed his arms around their shoulders and moved on. The icy wind never stopped blowing.

At the gates, the leading guard shouted, "Returning 2000 bandits."

"Bracing breeze," one of the guards called cheerfully, wrapped in his heavy overcoat. Sabina was chilled to the bone. Her hands and feet were blistered. Every muscle ached.

"Those of us who had faith," she recalls, "realized for the first time how rich we were. The youngest Christians and the weakest had more resources to call upon than the wealthiest old ladies and the most brilliant intellectuals. The latter, when deprived of their books and concerts, seemed to dry up like indoor plants exposed to the winds. 'Society' women were the most pitiful. In the material sense, they had lost the most, and they had few inner resources to fill the gap."

After work, women came to religious prisoners and asked, even begged, to be told something of what they remembered from the Bible. The prisoners had no Bible, and the religious ones hungered for it more than bread. Sabina wished she had learned more of it by heart. She repeated daily those passages she knew. Other Christians had deliberately committed long passages to memory, knowing that sooner or later they would be arrested.

Sabina believed deeply in, and practiced, meditation. She says she conversed often with Richard, especially during the years he spent in solitary confinement. He transmitted messages to her. She had a deep inner certainty that they were in contact, that he was present. She was quite sure that he received her thoughts too. These moments recurred through all the fourteen years of his imprisonment. She has a note in her Bible, dated 1953: *Richard came to see me today; he bent over me as I was reading.*

Sabina worried Mihai might be arrested and sent to the canal. He was twelve and there were twelve-year-old boys enslaved at the camps.

The Cernavoda prisoners were given postcards and told they might write their families and invite them to visit the camp on a certain Sunday. Sabina suspected a trick. She thought the recipients would be watched by the Secret Police. She spent days asking herself to whom she should write.

When the great day arrived, she woke long before reveille was sounded at 5 a.m. It was still dark. Ice was on the panes. She longed for daylight to come. When it did she ran out hoping to see the visitors waiting in the compounds by the gates. It was a long way off, separated from the camp itself by three fences of barbed wire and an outer no-man's-land zone.

Then she saw Mihai, taller, slimmer, and poorly clothed. She recognized the man at his side as the pastor of her church. She waved and waved, but they couldn't see her among all the other women lining the wire. She hurried back to tell the lady who had the bed next to hers. The lady looked at Sabina in her stained and ragged dress, her odd shoes, the remains of her summer coat, the piece of string she used for a belt.

"You'll frighten the poor child if he sees you like that. Borrow my blouse. It's in one piece."

Tania, the gypsy, offered a long bright skirt. Valia draped a white headscarf around her hair. Stockings and a grubby handkerchief were lent to her. While they were admiring her new elegance, a row broke out in the room.

Rina was in the middle of it, crowing triumphantly. Because so many had failed to fulfill their work norms, the visit was cancelled. They couldn't even receive the clothing and food the visitors brought with them.

The group of visitors waited all day at the gates in the hope the commandant would change her mind. The prisoners had no chance to look at the visitors or wave. Guards drove them away from the fence. The watchtower guns were trained on them. In the evening, the visitors were gone.

Postcards were distributed again. Several Sundays later, Mihai again made the journey to Cernavoda. This time there was no punishment. The visits proceeded alphabetically and Sabina's name was last. She feared she might not see him.

Again, borrowed clothes went from woman to woman. The prisoners were taken out to another barracks-hut near the gates. The visit was fifteen minutes, standing in the same room, ten yards apart, with the guards listening to every word.

When Sabina saw Mihai, she forgot she was a prisoner and what she looked like and where she was. She simply embraced him with her eyes. She gazed at him and he at her. In a flash the fifteen minutes had passed. They barely spoke. She called across the space that separated them, "Mihai, believe in Jesus with all your heart."

He looked very beautiful to her. She knew that every mother is convinced that her son is the most handsome. How he had received her words she learned only after her release.

She was pushed roughly on the shoulder and led out by the guards. Everyone crowded around asking about Mihai. Sabina just shook her head. For hours she couldn't speak. She was surrounded by weeping women who had waited for someone who never came.

At Cernavoda, the prisoners had to suffer indoctrination lectures every Sunday. In the afternoon the room-chief marched them to the assembly hall, where a woman speaker addressed them. She began by warning that anyone who spoke about God would be punished. "Outside, everyone is now Communist," she said. "Only you persist in this religious folly. We mean to educate you out of it. The Party knows best. You are not in prison. You are in a re-education institute. You are building your own future happiness. By exceeding the norms of work required, you may well hasten your own liberty as a rehabilitated citizen."

A propaganda concert followed. Among the prisoners were cabaret singers and actresses, some of whom were German. They had to sing Communist songs mocking Germany. The humiliation was intense. Sabina remembered Jesus speaking of being mocked, and she felt his pain.

A young woman read a poem dripping with gratitude to the Soviets for saving them from the Nazis:

> Mother Russia thank you
> for what you've done today.
> The glorious Red Army
> has shown us all the way.

This doggerel was loudly cheered by all present, the room-chiefs leading. Anyone showing a lack of enthusiasm was in for trouble. Informers were watching closely for socially-rotten reactions.

Sabina couldn't applaud at the meetings. When she heard God and fatherland slandered and saw beauty trampled in the dirt, she couldn't. She tried to bury herself among those standing at the back of the hall. But she didn't escape. Someone reported her.

In the evening she was marched into the commandant's office.

"I have information that you failed to clap during this afternoon's lecture and re-education class, Wurmbrand. All your behavior here has shown you to be a counterrevolutionary force, unamenable to proper re-education. We've tried to be good to you. Now other methods will be used."

Sabina was taken to the guard room and placed in a carcer. The iron door had a few holes to admit air. There was a slit through which food could be passed. After a few hours her feet were burning. The pulse in her temples beat with slow, painful thuds. She knew that people who had let thoughts of horror overcome them had been driven insane. To avoid this, she tried to count. Drops of water were falling on the roof of the box with a desolate sound. She counted these.

One: there is one God.

Two: there are two tablets of the Law.

Three: is for the Trinity.

Four: Christ will gather his elect from the four corners of the earth.

Five: for the five books of Moses.

Six: the number of the beast in Revelation is 666.

Seven: is the holy number.

The dripping went on but when she reached sixteen, the numbers meant nothing and she returned to one, two, three.

Sabina doesn't know how long she did this, but at a certain moment she simply cried aloud to avoid despair. One, two, three, four she cried over and over. After a time the words became inarticulate. Her mind had moved into rest. It blacked out. Yet her spirit continued to say something to God. This is one of the keys to survival in prison.

It is known there existed in the early church and also in the Greek mysteries a phenomenon known as *glossolalia*; speaking in unknown tongues. Religion couldn't find expression only in words because language is an imperfect tool. Therefore the use of music, the dance, and painting for expression. Between love and hatred there are as many nuances of feeling that cannot be put into words as there are fractions between one and two.

So there exists the phenomenon of *glossolalia*. Out of the depths of the heart, in moments of ecstasy or terrible suffering, come expressions of love towards God or fellow men, made up of words that exist in no dictionary. The mind blacks out. In the Bible it is written, "He that speaks in an unknown tongue speaks not unto men but unto God."

Sabina said that because of the above, the blacking out of her mind, her sanity was saved. After an hour or two her mind came back, rested.

One day soon after her experience in the carcer, there was an inspection by Colonel Albon. It was short and sharp. As he was about to leave, a gypsy girl ran up to him. She said she'd been secretly meeting a lieutenant in the Security Police and now she was pregnant.

Albon made a report to Bucharest. An inquiry was held and much of what had been happening came out. All the women were moved out of Cernavoda to a labor colony apart from the men a few miles further down the Canal. This was Camp Kilometer 4.

Early in the morning they left camp to work on the bank of the Danube. A bed of stones had to be laid in the water.

From morning to evening they loaded heavy rocks aboard a barge. Then the barge was ferried out into the river and the rocks were dropped over the side. The splashing drenched everyone within minutes of starting work. The icy wind blowing across the Baragan plain froze their clothes stiff. Sabina's fingers were cracked and swollen from the cold and crushed by the heavy stones.

In the evening when they returned to the hut, they went to bed in their wet clothes. There was nowhere to dry them and if hung to dry they would be stolen. Sabina slept with her wet dress under her head for a pillow and then put it on, still damp, in the morning. It dried out on the way to work just in time to get soaked again.

In the second week, Sabina was put to loading stones into barrows. At least she stayed dry. The stones were sharp and constantly tore her hands. Her knuckles were raw, her nails broken and bloody. She felt as though she were floating a few inches above ground as in a dream.

It snowed heavily during the night. More than the usual number of women tried to report sick. Ana Cretzeanu, camp doctor and a prisoner herself, wasn't interested. "Nothing wrong with you. Passed fit for work." Dr. Cretzeanu had sold herself for the right to stay indoors out of the snow and rain. She knew that in sending certain women out to work, she was condemning them to death. She had her orders from the medical board. The more women she allowed to go sick, the less was her own chance of survival or release.

Richard

Days later, the spring thaw came. The hard earth changed to mud. Sabina was working again on the ferry barges. As she threw the huge stones into the Danube, great chunks of ice floated past. Her hands and feet were numb and blue.

Male guards always accompanied the column to and from camp. They were the only men the women ever saw. On this day, especially among the prostitutes, ribald jokes flew thick and fast. Sabina was silent.

Annie Stanescu, a shrewish prostitute and leader of the pack, said, "Our little saint doesn't like nasty talk. Thinks we're horrid." The guards, loafing and smoking, looked at Sabina and grinned.

At the end of the day, they lined up, worn and sore. The muddy path ran along the riverbank. Sabina was aware that the eyes of Peter, the guard, were fixed on her. As he nudged his companion, he stuck out a boot and tripped her. She fell in the slushy mud. The women guards roared with laughter.

A hand reached out and dragged her up. Slippery with mud, she struggled in Peter's grasp. "What you need now, my lady," he said, "is a wash."

One guard caught her wrists and the other her ankles. She was swung once and flung through the air, landing in the rocky shallows. Knocked out of breath, she was stunned but was still conscious. The icy water was flowing so fast it dragged her over the rocks. The current swirled around her. Every time she tried to get up, the current knocked her down. She thrashed about, wounding herself on the stones.

Two hands seized her beneath the arms and pulled her through the shallows. Her rescuer tripped and fell backward into the water as Sabina sprawled on the bank. Someone forced her to sit up and slapped her on the back. For the first time she was aware of a sharp pain in her side. Dizziness made her lie down again.

"She's all right. Get up" A woman stood looking down at her. "Get moving or you'll freeze."

A young guard helped her sit up, then stand. Peter was nowhere in sight. She was shivering now, more with shock than with cold. The column was already a few hundred yards ahead. Sabina limped after it, helped along by pushes from a woman guard. She caught up with the column as they waited for the trucks.

Her clothes were cold and clammy and her shoes squished. The pain in her side was growing worse. Every bump of the truck sent a red-hot stab of agony through her. The swaying of the truck made her feel sick.

When they got back to the hut, Sabina wrung out her wet clothes. Her side was badly swollen and the skin was scraped from her hands and legs. She could find no comfortable position during the night.

In the morning she saw Dr. Cretzianu. A huge purple and yellow bruise spread down one side of her body. It was impossible to raise her arm above waist level.

"Fit for work," she pronounced.

Sabina fell in with the others.

"What's the matter with you?" The woman overseer was glaring. Sabina felt faint and was swaying.

"I can't go to work today. I'm in great pain. I think my ribs are broken."

Peter caught her by the wrist and pulled her out of line. "What's wrong with her is she didn't fulfill her norm yesterday. Get on with it." He spun her around and shoved her forward with a boot in her back.

Sabina went to work that day and every day after. On her release from prison, it was determined she had had two fractured ribs which had healed.

Spring arrived. New green patches of grass appeared. A little grass in the watery soup was a great treat. Eating grass was then forbidden as was everything else which might better the prisoners' condition. When the guards weren't looking, they pastured on it like cattle.

Frogs were also fair game. Their raw meat was considered a delicacy. They were hard to catch. When one ventured into the quarry, it was doomed.

Snakes were less popular. The fat, green grass snakes were devoured, however.

The longing for meat or any type of protein resulted from their watery potato, bean, or cabbage soup diet. Vitamin deficiency diseases were common. Diarrhea, scurvy, and skin diseases ravaged the prisoners. Abrasions and lacerations didn't heal and became infected, causing large ulcers.

Anything that moved was eaten. A priest told Sabina, "Dog is good, but I honestly cannot recommend rat."

The spring days began to lengthen. Gold and crimson sunsets filled the sky. Marching to work was less unpleasant. Nettles and pearly cow-parsley smelled moist and green. Trees put out shiny young leaves.

The balmy air affected them all. Everything in nature was changing. They couldn't help changing a little too. New friendships blossomed. Everyone became more willing to love, less ready to wound. One of the norm-checkers surprised Sabina with an accusation: "Wurmbrand keeps herself to herself. She doesn't make friends."

"Everyone here is my friend," Sabina said.

This angered the woman. "You and your clever talk."

Sabina wondered if it was true. Some accepted her as though she were a saint. Others suspected her of some dark motive. It was widely believed in Romania there was a Jewish plot to destroy Christianity by infiltrating it. Sabina was Jewish. Perhaps they thought she was part of the plot.

She had one friend who was truly close. It was silence that first linked them together. Sabina's eyes would sometimes rest on her as she tried to repair clothes by night. She would look up and meet Sabina's eyes calmly. Working in the quarries, Sabina would sense she was close.

Sabina asked, "Have you many years to serve?"

"No, only twelve."

"Only. Then it doesn't worry you?"

"God can release us if He wills. If He wishes me to stay here, I will stay."

Mrs. Djamil was the wife of a hajji. She and her husband were arrested because they had belonged to an organization called "Help Crimea," whose purpose was to help people who had suffered under Nazi occupation.

She seemed undismayed at finding herself among so many Christians, who explained the errors of the Muslim faith. She strictly followed the rules of her faith, which won for her respect.

With so many different sects and religions, the women had their share of religious argument, but the virulence of former days was gone. A new understanding arose. Outside, they couldn't share the world without quarreling. Here, they shared a hut and a bucket. They were sisters.

Officialdom decided an error had been made in planning the canal. The smaller irrigation projects would be flooded by the Danube's waters unless banks were built higher and root crops planted to prevent soil erosion. The prisoners moved from the quarries to the fields to spade and hoe with worn-out equipment on the Baragan plain.

Sabina worked beside Janetta, daughter of a former merchant. She was to become one of Sabina's closest friends and collaborators in the underground church. She would fulfill the norm for Sabina and others who couldn't work well. Sabina and Janetta discovered they had been born on the same day. On their birthday they exchanged raw potato for presents.

As they worked dizzily in the scorching sun on the treeless plain, Janetta said, "How we used to long for summer." They had been working eight hours in the dusty plain before the water truck appeared on the horizon. As it got closer, they saw that it was the food truck.

This was more than the women could take. Angrily they shouted, "Water. We want water" and surged toward the guards, who pulled their guns. They refused to return to work. A gun was jammed into Sabina's ribs.

The food truck arrived on the spot. The frightened driver, gaping at the rebellion, bounced the wagon over a rock, pulled the wrong rein and the horse veered. The wagon tottered on its side. The horse reared. Over went the canisters, spilling boiled macaroni in the dust.

The women charged the cordon, broke it, and fell on the macaroni. They snatched sticky handfuls and gobbled it, while they pushed and fought. Other women looked on in horror. The guards were content. Danger was past.

An hour later, whistles shrilled and they went back to work. Janetta and Sabina got no food or water that day.

Toward sunset, the prisoners marched back to camp. A mile short of camp, they passed some puddles of water in a swampy hollow. Some of the women fell on hands and knees to lap the muddy stagnant water.

The next day, an inquiry took place. The rebellion earned them some extra hours of work on Sunday. "This isn't a health resort," said the commandant.

One night, Sabina was awakened by Paula shaking her arm. "They've beaten up Diana. Come quickly. She's badly hurt."

The girl was unconscious, breathing heavily, lying on the bare floor. Blood ran from her nose, and her hair was matted and sticky. Her lips were swollen. They loosened her clothes and found her body badly bruised. Diana moaned and stirred. Her eyes opened. "It's all right. I didn't let them," she whispered.

They made her drink. When she recovered a little, she told how she was lured by two prostitutes to where some guards were waiting. She was nineteen, pretty, and her modesty provoked them. She wouldn't submit. After beating her, they threw her into the nearest hut and ran off.

Sabina and Paula spread their blankets over her, for even in that stuffy shed, she was shivering. They sat beside her until daybreak.

Sabina was brought before the deputy camp commandant. "You've been preaching about God to the prisoners. It must stop."

Sabina said, "Nothing can stop it."

Furious, the deputy raised her fist to strike Sabina. She stopped and stared. "What are you smiling about?" she demanded.

Sabina said, "If I am smiling, it is because of what I see in your eyes."

"And what is that?"

"Myself, Anyone who comes close to another person can see herself reflected. I was impulsive too. I used to rage and strike out, until I learned what it really means to love. That is to be one who can sacrifice self for truth. Since then, my hands do not clench into fists. If you look into my eyes, you'll see yourself as God could make you."

The deputy's hand dropped. She seemed turned to stone. She said quietly, "Go away."

Sabina continued to witness for Christ among the prisoners. The deputy commandant did not interfere.

As they hoed in the fields, Maria worked her way toward Sabina so she would be able to help her. The guards spotted them whispering and yelled, "Get to work."

They hoed vigorously. Sabina was feeling ill that morning. Dizzy spells made her halt often. Each time she dared straighten her back, the guards would shout, "You're for the carcer tonight."

Waves of darkness washed over her. Maria's voice seemed to come from a great distance as she chattered, trying to make Sabina forget how she felt.

Sabina managed to stay on her feet until noon. She drank the cup of watery soup and nibbled on the bread. In the afternoon she collapsed. The blazing sun spun round the sky. She saw Maria's face above her, her mouth moving, seeming to shout silently from a well of darkness.

Guards dragged Sabina to her feet. They poured water down her throat until she choked. "She's all right." They swore at Maria, "Don't stand there gaping. Get to work."

The experience had not only frightened Maria but Sabina as well. She explained that when you realize you have had a complete blackout, it makes you doubt the existence of the soul as a separate entity. In time, she convinced herself it meant no more than a dreamless sleep.

They went back to work, hacking at the weeds. The merciless sun sapped their strength. Sabina could barely hold the hoe.

Late in the afternoon storm clouds gathered on the horizon. Whistles blew for the end of work. They were working far from camp and battered trucks waited to take them back. As they crowded into the trucks, with no room to sit, lightning flashed and the first warm drops touched their upturned faces. In seconds they were drenched. Maria cried, "Lovely, lovely water."

The lovely water continued to descend as if poured from a

huge tub. A bolt of lightning made the women scream. The truck skidded and stopped. Its wheels were sunk deeply in mud. The women put their backs to the truck and heaved while the men watched. For an hour they worked in vain until the sergeant ordered them to march back to camp. Boots squishing, clothes clinging, they tramped through the rain.

Time stood still. Slavery was their whole life, the canal their world. They were worn down into a hopeless acceptance of their lot. The news from outside never changed. Hunger, queues, and oppression. The most often expressed hope was, "The Americans are coming. They won't let us remain slaves."

Despondency meant that work levels fell. Strange tricks were played in an effort to raise them. At a meeting, twenty women were picked out of the ranks and told, "You have been the hardest workers here. For this you will be released."

The commandant made a speech, "So it's farewell and thanks, Comrades. Together we have struggled to build Communism, and now the time has come to share the fruits of our labor. Now you are free. As a parting gift we give each of you an extra loaf of bread."

The twenty heroines leaned out the back of the truck, waving Red flags and singing the International.

Ten miles down the road at the next labor colony, the truck stopped and they were put back to work.

The effect on work norms at Camp K4 was electric. This trick was performed in other camps and soon the prisoners learned the truth.

CHAPTER 12

One morning after reveille, the guards ordered everyone to be ready to move in one hour. The whole camp was being alerted. Rumors spread: the Americans had broken through the Iron Curtain, the Russians had occupied East Berlin, they were being taken to be shot.

The women lined up and waited until almost dark before boarding the trucks. They were driven to the marshalling yards. The train was made up of freight cars and long black prison cars. The cars had small windows high up and covered by metal bars.

Train guards ordered them into the cars. K4 guards shoved them in. There was barely room to stand. "We can't take anymore here. We'll suffocate."

However, more and more women were pushed in until there were eighty-four in a car intended for forty. The big sliding door was slammed shut and the bar was secured. The train jolted into life, throwing them all together.

Sabina's car contained some benches, one of which was a toilet, waterless and paperless, but it had a lid. It was difficult to find a place to sit and impossible to stretch out. They dozed in snatches and were woken often by the grinding of brakes.

Slowly, dawn revealed the autumn landscape. In contrast to the barren plains of the Baragan, cows grazed in the fields, there were trees, peasants spread dung over the dark earth. Three little girls waved, not knowing they had caused eighty women to weep.

The train puffed and lurched across Romania. At a junction, guards handed in buckets of water while others stood by with machine guns.

Amateur politicians near Sabina were discussing the American elections. Eisenhower was going to save them all.

"Of course he'll be elected," said a "well-informed" lady from Ploesti. "He'll ask special powers as President to free the captive countries of Eastern Europe."

Sabina was tempted to say this same Eisenhower had handed hundreds of thousands of refugees from Communism at the end of the war to "Uncle Joe," as Roosevelt called Stalin. Some committed suicide, some were hanged, some perished in Siberian camps. She kept quiet. She thought, "Why dispel illusions, when people needed them as a thirsty man needs water?"

The car contained many literary women: writers, journalists, poets, novelists. An English and French literature professor from Cluj University astonished and amused the peasants by her ability to tell stories from the classics for hours. There was active discussion among the educated concerning the meaning of Dorian Gray and other characters.

The train stopped. The door was wrenched open and a bag of rations was thrown in. The newly-baked loaves of black bread smelled delicious. They were gobbled down at once. The rule of prison life was: food saved is food lost. They never knew what the next moment would bring.

On the third day, though the halts grew longer, neither water nor bread came. Late in the evening the doors were opened and a bag of bread was thrown in. The drunken sergeant said, "You women are lucky tonight. There's a spoonful of jam for each of you."

Maria asked boldly, "How much further to go, Sergeant-major?"

Flattered by the promotion, the sergeant said, "Another day."

"And where are we headed?"

"To be shot, of course." The sergeant roared with laughter.

The sliding doors crashed shut and argument ensued. There was weeping and wailing and questioning. The fact that he was drunk made him tell the truth. Sobbing Jewish women, having survived the Holocaust, began to clasp one another and exchange kisses of farewell. The train moved on, painfully slow. Stopped after an hour and moved on again.

It was a night of dread. At every halt the prisoners feared they would hear the crunching boots, the doors would open, and they would be dragged out to their death. Nothing happened that day or the next. As darkness fell again, they sank into a stupor of exhaustion and misery.

"Out. Everyone OUT."

The night was black as pitch. There was no station, not even siding. The women thought time for the massacre had arrived. Crying, screaming, swearing, they leaped or fell out. There were no steps and Sabina fell painfully on her knees. The guards waved machine guns and shouted like lunatics at the terrified prisoners. They were punched in the face, flung aside, slapped, struck with gun-butts. The women didn't have the slightest notion of what they were supposed to do.

"Line up. Line up. Keep near the sergeant." After an hour of utter confusion, several hundred prisoners were herded into a field beside the track.

"Everyone down. Lie down on your bellies. Get down." They were forced to lie face down in the mud. A ring of swearing guards encircled them. The women prayed and pled.

"On the road, bandits. Are you all deaf?"

They marched quickly through the darkness, spurred on by threats and blows. They struggled with their bundles, falling, skidding, gasping for breath. They were stunned with shock after four days of inactivity in the crowded train.

"Hold it. Get them into that field. Everyone down." Again they lay on their faces in the mud. Half the column was lost and they had to wait for it to catch up.

After hours of marching, they saw the walls of a new prison under the glare of electric lights. The heavy gates opened and they passed through in groups of five. Word went round: this was Tirgusor. A new name, new guards, same curses, same routine.

The checking of names and numbers began. It was long past midnight when they reached their cells.

Everyone questioned why they were in a famous maximum security prison, where murderers convicted of violent crimes were held. What did it mean? There were no answers.

Sabina was put to work in the sewing shop. They worked round the clock in twelve-hour shifts, sitting at benches in a large room with barred windows near the ceiling. The sewing machines appeared to date from the last century and broke down at least once a day. Sabina soon ceased to share Richard's pride about Singer, the Jew who invented sewing machines.

They stitched thick thread into prison mattresses. The heavy material had to be turned and twisted constantly as they pumped the foot pedals. If they fell asleep over their machines, they were slapped and punched awake.

The prisoners heard that Eisenhower had been elected president, then that several Communist leaders had been overthrown and purged from the Party. Was it the start of liberalization? "What do such puppets count?" said a woman journalist. "Nothing will change until Stalin goes."

A rumor, which became fact, spread throughout Romania: the canal was to be abandoned. The great labor camps were to be shut down. The basic plan was at fault. Officers were being arrested. Canal engineers were to be tried as criminals for "stealing State funds."

The thought was in every mind: with such an excess of laborers, would they be set free?

Mrs. Iliescu's contempt for the Communists was boundless. "We must show our superiority to these scum by working above their wretched norms. Under Communism or not, what we do will benefit the Fatherland."

She worked so hard in the sweatshop the norms were raised and everyone suffered. Sabina felt it was a stupid and revolting attitude. Yet it was difficult not to respect her. She had suffered so much and had such courage.

One of her often-repeated stories was of a woman interrogator who had a sadistic taste for torturing men prisoners. She landed in Jilava after the first Party purge. "Women whose husbands and sons had borne pain and indignity at her hands fell on her," said Mrs. Iliescu. "They threw a blanket over her head and beat her black and blue."

Sabina felt that even when such unspeakable hatred existed, reconciliation was still possible. Once, when asked, she refused to lead prayers in the cell so long as there were women present who would not make peace. She quoted Matthew: "Therefore if thou bring thy gift to the altar, and there remember that thy brother has ought against thee; leave there thy gift, and go thy way; first be reconciled to thy brother and then come and offer thy gift." She said men and women were persuaded to end long and bitter quarrels with these words. Their lives were changed.

An atmosphere of intense fear and suspicion reigned throughout Tirgusor. The Communists were using the wall-tapping grapevine for their own purposes. In every cell stool-pigeons spied and tapped out false messages. The answers obtained from unsuspecting new arrivals were used in the intense interrogations then in progress.

The Communists in prison were sure they would be shot. They had been ruthless, and ruthlessness would be returned.

In the meantime the loving and the lovable were executed.

"Gather all your things." Again they were on the move. Open trucks took them to the collective farm of Ferma Rosie. They started work at once in the fields. They had to cover vines with earth to save them from the cold. It was too late. The soil and the plants had long since frozen. The vineyard was ruined, and no one seemed to care.

This vineyard had been one of the most famous in Romania. Its owner was in prison. Big landlords, small farmers, and peasants had attempted to revolt against collectivization and were ruthlessly crushed. Sullen and indifferent, they worked as little as possible. For failing to discharge their obligation to the State, they were jailed by the thousands. The former "granary of Europe" faced famine.

While working in the fields one morning, Sabina collapsed. Guards put her on an improvised stretcher and placed her on a truck. She was taken to Vacaresti prison hospital which she knew well. She had done volunteer work there. She was put in an isolated cell that contained nothing but a dirty bucket. She slept on the bare concrete.

Next morning while the guard slept, she asked male prisoners if they knew anything about Richard. One said, "Wurmbrand? The pastor?"

"Yes," Sabina replied. "He is my husband."

He bowed to the earth. "I met him," he whispered. "My years in prison were worthwhile because the pastor brought me to Christ. And now I meet his wife." He had to move on without giving further information. Next time past the window, he said, "I met him in Tirgul-Ocna. He was in the cell for the dying. He always spoke about Christ."

Sabina remained another day in the cell, since no doctor called to examine her. She didn't believe that Richard was dead. A verse from the Bible came like music to her mind. It concerned Jacob's son, Reuben, which is Richard's Hebrew name: "Let Reuben live and not die." It was to Sabina a promise.

After forty-eight hours the hospital authorities remembered she had been admitted as an urgent case. She was put in a bed with sheets and blankets. A woman doctor attended. "You must eat everything you're given," she said. Her kind voice brought tears to Sabina's eyes.

Dr. Maria Cresin was fresh from medical school. With courage and patience she worked in understaffed, overcrowded Vacaresti and was adored by her patients.

Sabina had an ugly skin disease from malnutrition. In addition to a balanced diet she received vitamin injections. Sores and scabs on her body began to heal. The colitis and diarrhea ceased. Vitamin A improved her vision, especially at night.

In the bed next to Sabina was a once-wealthy woman whom the other patients called "The Millionairess." She was sure Eisenhower and Churchill wouldn't let Eastern Europe remain in slavery.

"When the Americans come they'll make the Russians pay war compensation. I shall ask for 5,000 lei a day for the six months I've been in prison. One million lei will make me secure for the rest of my life."

Sabina said, "You might as well ask for 10,000 lei a day. Then you'll have two million lei."

"What a good idea. You Jews are clever people."

Vacaresti was supervised by a political officer. One evening he came into the ward with some uniformed colleagues and made a pompous speech about the joys of Communism. When such fine hospitals as this were freely available, who needed God?

Sabina said, "Lieutenant, as long as there will be people on earth, we will need God and we will need Jesus, who gives life and health."

He was outraged. How did she dare interrupt, and how could she go on believing such stuff?

Sabina said, "Everyone who lives in a house knows it has been designed by an architect, just as everyone who attends a banquet knows it was prepared by a chef. We are all invited to the banquet of this world, which is so full of wonderful things, the sun, the moon, the stars, the rain, and fruits of all kinds. And we know the one who has prepared this is God."

The officer laughed and scoffed and walked out with his friends, banging the door.

Next morning, Sabina was told to pack. The same day she was sent back to labor. But this time it was a State pig farm. Fifty women tended several hundred swine. She found this the hardest assignment of all. Food was at starvation level. Each morning she dragged herself out of bed at 5 a.m., still wearing the filthy rags in which she had slept, and went out into the cold and darkness to feed the pigs.

The sties were ankle-deep in liquid manure, which never froze. The stench penetrated every angle of their huts. It clung to her body and hair. The soup she ate with her wooden spoon tasted of it.

The meaning fell away from things. Death stared her in the face. The whole world was made of tears and despair as never before, and a cry rose from her heart, "My God, my God, why hast Thou forsaken me?" She knew there was no hope for her, nor for the world, and expected only to die.

Happily it didn't last for many weeks. Sabina was convinced the Lord heard her prayers and took her out according to His plan. She had only to learn a very deep lesson, to drink the cup to its bitterest dregs. Now she was thankful she passed through this hard school, which teaches one the highest love, love for God, even when He gives nothing but suffering.

From the back of an open truck, she watched the pig farm recede. The wind was cold as steel. It tugged at her clothes and sent fine skeins of snow skittering across the land. No one knew or asked or cared where they were going. One collective was as bad as another.

To her surprise, Sabina arrived at Ghencea, the transit camp from which, over two years ago, she had been sent to the canal. It was after dark before they were checked and numbered and marched off to the huts. The hundreds of women were from all over Romania. Some of Sabina's gypsy friends from Cernavoda were there. Zenaida, who was queen of pre-war Bucharest, gave her a pair of men's trousers and a warm jacket which she had scrounged from somewhere. "It's Charlie Chaplin to the life. Even her boots have tabs on the back."

Then guards began to take them for questioning at the camp offices. Zenaida was one of the first and told Sabina of her experience. Like most prisoners, she did her best to give the impression she had seen the error of her ways and was now eager to work for a place in society.

Before the end of the month, small groups were trucked off to destinations unknown.

Eventually Sabina was taken to the office. Behind the desk was a chubby major. Special questions were reserved for religious prisoners. "In this place, Mrs. Wurmbrand (Mrs., no less), you must know I am more powerful than God. At least, He has not so far made any interventions in this office. Have you really accepted this? Have you seen through the sham of religion? Have you realized that in a Communist society God is superfluous? That you don't need him anymore? If you are ever released from here, you'll be astonished at the achievements of recent years, and we are only beginning."

Sabina said, "I see that you are powerful. Probably you have papers and documents there about me that I have never seen and that can decide my fate. God keeps records too, and neither you nor I would have life without him. So whether he keeps me here or sets me free, I'll accept that as best for me."

The major pounded the desk with both fists. "Ungrateful, Mrs. Wurmbrand, ungrateful. I'm sorry to see you've failed to learn your lesson, and I shall make a report to that effect." He shouted in rage for a few minutes.

Three days later Sabina's name was read out. She realized higher authorities than the major were deciding her fate. She stood waiting in the snow-covered yard holding her poor bundle. Even now she wasn't at all sure she would be freed. It was only when she'd been marched out through the gates of barbed-wire and stood shivering in the road that the guard began the long process of handing out slips of paper. "Wurmbrand, Sabina, born Cernauti, 1913 . . ." She accepted the document ordering her release, called "Certificate of Liberation"; it was growing too dark to read. They piled into a truck and drove off. They were dropped well outside the outskirts of Bucharest.

CHAPTER 13

Sabina walked with her greasy, smelly bundle through the suburbs. Home—that was where she was heading. If it existed. If anything existed, home, friends, family: she didn't know what had happened to any of them. Mihai would be fourteen now. She was almost frightened to find out what had happened to Mihai, yet longed to see him.

The lights dazzled Sabina's eyes, and the smell of food from restaurants shocked her senses. As the stream of people hurried by indifferently, a sense of dismay came over her. What if No. 7 tram stop no longer existed? But there it was. She suppressed her panic as she climbed aboard and then realized she had no money. She said loudly, "Would someone be so kind as to pay my fare?"

All heads turned to see who made this request. The sight of her was enough to tell anyone why it was made. A dozen people immediately offered to pay for her. They crowded around with sympathetic eyes. Everyone there, it seemed, had a relative or friend in prison. They mentioned names of their dear ones whom she might know.

They passed the police station on Victory Street where she had first been held. Gigantic portraits of mankind's four geniuses—Marx, Engels, Lenin, Stalin—still stared down on the crowds.

Sabina left the tram near a block of flats she knew and climbed the stairs. The door was opened by a friend who put her hands to her mouth and stepped back. "Sabina. Is it possible?" They embraced and her friend began to cry.

Someone ran to find Mihai. Sabina's heart stopped when she saw him come in. He was tall, pale, and thin, but a young man now. As they embraced, tears began to flow down her cheeks. "Don't cry too much, Mother," he said.

In her first few days of freedom, Sabina was like a woman back from the dead. She treasured the hours with Mihai, discovering him again. She found in him at once fine traits of character. She found him deeply religious and with wisdom beyond his years.

She was shocked to see the abject need and hunger all around. People were reduced to almost nothing. On many days they couldn't afford to buy black bread or use a little electricity to get warm.

A friend said to her, "Sabina, do be careful what you tell people. There are informers everywhere. The church is riddled with them."

A stream of friends and strangers came to see her, all begging for news of relatives in jail. Only rarely could she help them or answer their questions.

She soon learned about "applying" to officialdom. The queues at government offices were worse than those at food stores. She needed a ration card. Without one she couldn't even buy bread. She waited in line four hours one morning. When she reached the window, the girl snapped, "Where's your work card? Without that you can't get a ration card."

"But I'm an ex-prisoner."

"I can't help that. No work card and number, no ration book."

Sabina had to survive on the charity of others. For a time she and Mihai shared a room with a woman friend. But Mihai was a young man now. It wasn't wise for them to live jammed together. Sabina began a long search for another room.

The Wurmbrands' old home had been confiscated. So had all its contents, furniture, bedding, books. Friends lived in the house where their flat had once been. They said there was a small attic free. Small it was. The larger room was four yards by five, the other three by two.

After days of queuing and form-filling, Sabina was allowed to occupy this "accommodation space." The only furniture was a bed with broken springs and a sofa. No water, no toilet. Here they lived and cooked and slept. Janetta, when released, came to stay with them. She shared the sofa with Sabina.

One day Marietta came to their door. She stood there smiling girlishly and timidly and held out a little parcel tied with string. "It's nothing really," she said. "Two French pastries." She had queued two hours to buy them and they weren't very French.

Marietta was an old member of Sabina's congregation. She was a sweet girl but not too bright. People avoided her because she had epileptic fits.

"Come in and sit down, Marietta. We haven't lived here long and we're still not tidy." She squeezed in and sat down on a rickety chair they had just acquired. Mihai came to her assistance when the back fell off.

"How cozy you are here," she said, looking at the stove on which Sabina was frying potatoes. Marietta shared their fried potatoes. Later, when Mihai had gone to the other room to study, she told Sabina she had nobody in the world now and in a week she would be on the street. The family with whom she stayed had asked her to leave.

"Well, Marietta, as you can see, this isn't a flat. But if you like we can squeeze another bed in here. I expect we can find a mattress too."

Her face lit up with joy. "Really? Are you sure? I'd so much like to be with you."

So Marietta came to live with the Wurmbrands in the attic on Olteni Street.

On a mild, sunny spring day, church bells began to toll. Bucharest has many bells. Romania in the Middle Ages was a bastion of Christendom against the Turks. The country is filled with monasteries and churches. People stopped in the streets and asked each other what had happened. Despite the police ban on public gatherings, groups of people formed in the squares and whispered.

The loudspeakers on Victory Street crackled into life: "Dear Comrades and friends. Workers of the Romanian People's Republic. The Praesidium of the Supreme Soviet of the U.S.S.R. informs the Party and all Romanian workers with deep sorrow that on March 5th, 1953, the Chairman of the Council of Ministers of the Soviet Union and Secretary of the Central Committee of the Communist Party, Josef Vissarionovich Stalin, died after a grave illness. The life of the wise leader and teacher of the people, Lenin's comrade and faithful disciple, is over." Martial funeral music followed.

The sound of bells meant not death but the dawn of new hope to most of them. "Why are they doing it?" everyone asked when they heard religious services had been ordered to mark the demise of the President of the World Atheists' Organization, who had done so much to destroy Christianity.

Rumors spread that Stalin, in terror on his deathbed, had asked for the last rites, begged to be buried with a cross, and asked all Christians to pray for him.

Sabina says now we have the testimony of his daughter, Svetlana, who turned Christian and escaped to the West. She described "that incomprehensible and awesome gesture when he suddenly lifted his left hand as though pointing up to something...the next moment the spirit wrenched itself free of the flesh." Sabina asks, "Who knows what the dying Stalin meant?"

Slowly, Sabina regained her health and some of her old strength. The fractured ribs, which hadn't yet healed completely, caused pain. Her doctor advised some weeks in bed, but there was too much to be done.

She soon became a member of the underground church. Its title is not in directories or its buildings in the cities of Eastern Europe. Its priests are in worn working suits. They have no theological training. They know little of sectarian squabbles. The underground church had no name even behind the Iron Curtain. Only after Sabina reached the West did she come to know that they were referred to by this title among the few people abroad who knew what they were doing. If she had been asked earlier,

"Have you an underground church in Romania?" she wouldn't have understood the question. They simply did their Christian duty. They paid no heed to Communist laws. For the next twelve years this was to be Sabina's life.

She was distressed by the plight of churchgoers. They were persecuted by the police and harried by informers. Every means was used to stamp out belief. The old could worship, with difficulty, and under observation. The young weren't permitted to do so.

Many former friends, afraid of losing their jobs, didn't dare come near her house. Others wouldn't admit they had once worshipped beside her.

Passing the university, she saw a teacher she'd known well and went to greet him. He was with a colleague. "You're making a mistake, Madam. I don't know you." He turned away, unable to look her in the face.

A vital part of work in the underground church was to teach people to trust that God would not leave them. And Sabina, with a prison background, found it easier to win their trust.

She had to keep herself in her place. She was embarrassed by so many people asking her advice rather than that of the church's two young Lutheran pastors. Believers who had suffered for their faith were idolized by other Christians. Everything they said was "gospel." Sabina had to be firm and discourage people from treating her with exaggerated reverence.

Keeping her opinions to herself wasn't easy. The two young pastors did their best, but they preached what they had learned from Lutheran professors and out-of-date books. They had not gone through the fire that Sabina had. Communist methods of brainwashing and indoctrination were new. They needed new answers. These were found by the underground church as time went by.

Mihai came home early from school one day and told his mother he was finished with school. Sabina got the story by degrees. The Communist Youth Movement was being strengthened, and the best pupils were given the privilege of wearing a red tie. The children were asked to propose a candidate for the honor.

They selected Mihai. He refused. He said, "I won't wear the red tie. It's the symbol of the Party that keeps my father in prison."

The teacher, a Jewish girl, had to play the Communist. She scolded Mihai and sent him home. The fact was that the teachers hated what they had to do and the people who made them do it. Next day, Mihai's teacher smuggled him back into class and gave him a hug.

The propaganda in the schools was intense. Everyday Mihai came home with questions which Sabina had to answer.

Every Christian mother had this struggle. Life was a battlefield. Each evening they made up the ground gained by the Communists during the day. In this struggle for the youth, the Communists seemed to have all the weapons: the schools, the radio, the press. Mihai had always had before him the example of Christianity in action. When Sabina was at the canal in 1951, people from her church risked their liberty to help him. Old Mrs. Mihailovici, who'd been like an aunt to Mihai, came hundreds of miles from her village with a bag of potatoes, all she had to offer. Her visit was reported by informers, who always watch relatives of political prisoners. When she got home she was summoned by the militia and so badly beaten she never recovered her health. The people of the underground church never forgot their duty to the children of those in jails.

A woman came to Sabina in tears. "My child is working for the Secret Police. He's meeting a man regularly who asks him about everyone who comes to the house. I don't know what to do."

She couldn't turn her son out. She couldn't let him betray Christians who came to see them. Sabina advised her to break contact with the underground church for some time.

Some informers were trapped into cooperating. They didn't have the fortitude to lose their jobs or to go to jail. Some notified those they were informing on. Others left Bucharest and moved from town to town to avoid the weekly summonses to the Secret Police.

From this system arose the phenomenon of thousands and thousands of secret Christians who wore the red tie or Party badge.

Some even held high State posts while belonging to the underground church. They called a priest to baptize a child by night. They traveled to a remote town to be secretly married by a pastor. Many informers came to Sabina to tell of all they had to do and seek forgiveness for their betrayals.

Sabina would say to them, "Prove the sincerity of your repentance by telling us about how we're spied on. Let's have the names of the officers you took orders from. Tell us when and where you meet."

If they were in the habit of handing over their information at a certain street corner, one of the church members would sit in a cafe nearby to take a snapshot of the Secret Policeman. Then they'd follow him to see whom he met next. If their meetings took place in a "safe" house of the Secret Police, they'd watch the place and photograph those who came and went.

It was risky work, but they were able by these methods to list most of the informers, including Colonel Shircanu, who headed police spywork against the church. They watched him as closely as he watched them. They pinned down his chief informers. Some they succeeded in bringing to repentance. Others had to be dealt with by sterner means. In these ways they defended the underground church and enabled it to continue its work.

To compound Sabina's problems, Marietta fell in love with a crippled boy she had met at a hospital. From a factory accident, he had a left-sided paralysis and affected speech. Since his discharge from the hospital, he was sleeping in a cellar from which he was being evicted. Marietta married Peter and they moved in with Sabina. Now they numbered four, not counting the almost nightly guests: wives of arrested pastors, Christians who didn't dare make contact with an ex-prisoner by daylight.

Mihai graduated from school and could go no further since children of political prisoners weren't allowed higher education. After much red tape and saying his father wasn't a political prisoner, he landed a job looking after the instruments of the State Opera House. He received eight pounds a month, which to Sabina was a large sum of money. And he also got a ration card. Although he did an excellent job he was fired when it was discovered he had lied about his father's arrest. He had become so expert at repairing all kinds of instruments, he had a small clientele of his own among Bucharest's musicians. He earned enough money to buy books to study at home.

Sabina took on all sorts of strange jobs to keep the family going. The first was raising silkworms at home. She would get a box of one hundred from the Co-operative. Mihai picked mulberry leaves in the cemetery. After the worms spun their cocoon, they were taken back to the Silkworm Rearing Co-operative where she was paid enough to buy two days' food.

Silkworm larvae are fussy creatures that have been cultivated artificially for 4000 years. They like temperatures between 62 and 78, not too much light, and quiet when they are moulting. For several months Sabina's farm thrived. One day they developed a disease called grasserie, supposedly from being exposed to a draft. She threw them out and discontinued her farm.

She turned to other cottage industry ventures like sewing and knitting. And so with her small sums plus Mihai's earnings, they survived.

That was the year of the International Youth Festival. Young Communists and sympathizers from many parts of the world came to Bucharest. The previously empty shops were crammed with goods. For three wonderful weeks the inhabitants saw things that hadn't been seen in Romania since before the war. Then the festival ended. For months after, the shortages were worse than ever. They had squandered all the reserves on this display to deceive foreign visitors.

The young foreign Communists were as infected with informing as the Romanians. Many Romanians who made unwise remarks to youngsters from France and Italy were reported to the Secret Police. An acquaintance of Mihai was arrested.

The subterfuges and the way Sabina scraped a living were not the truly important things. It was to gather and keep in a life of prayer and trust her Christian brethren, and the wives and children of prisoners. This was Janetta's and Sabina's real work over the years Richard was in prison.

Since so many honest and good pastors were imprisoned, it fell more and more upon their wives to build up the underground church. Dozens of them became self-taught ministers. Women came from every part of the country to Bucharest to ask advice and to report how the church fared with them. Soon Sabina found that nearly all her time went to this work.

The underground church had innumerable secret meeting places in the city, often in cellars and attics such as Sabina's. On dark nights a light would show in a window, and people would flit up the stairs and give a coded knock.

The idea of using the tactics of the Communist cell against the Party arose in conversation with pastor Grecu, who sometimes joined them late at night. He was a minister of the approved church, and they allowed him some license because he was known to drink. Drunken priests made good Communist propaganda.

Pastor Grecu's heart was with Sabina's group. He was of enormous help. He carried on a secret ministry which went far beyond the limits imposed by the State. Many priests did this; there was no clear dividing line between the official church and the underground church. They were interwoven.

Under persecution, sectarian barriers fell more and more. Catholic, Orthodox, or Lutheran, they came down to the pure elements of faith, resembling the church of the first centuries.

Pastor Grecu and Sabina had many discussions on tactics. Janetta had become a pillar of the church. She and Sabina had both read Lenin's *What is to be Done?*, in which he set out his plan to conquer the world. It was written in 1903, when all the Bolsheviks in existence could be seated on one sofa; in fact, there's a picture of them doing so. One of Lenin's first principles is to infiltrate rival organizations. After the Communists took power in Romania, Sabina found they had long insinuated themselves into both "bourgeois" Ministries and the leadership of anti-Communist bodies. Seminaries and the priesthood itself were infiltrated.

Now the roles had to be reversed. Sabina and those working closely with her saw that the Underground Church couldn't survive unless they infiltrated the Communist organizations that were trying to destroy them.

The moral issue of Christians practicing deception was considered. There were enough examples of deception in the early church to justify their actions. People who came to the meetings were all eager to help. Sabina divided them into two groups: those who would shrink from playing a false role, and those who would think like St. Paul, who was a Jew to Jews and a Greek to Greeks. Even in the latter group, only a few were chosen. Only one in a hundred church members was aware of the infiltration policy.

Pastor Grecu pointed out that young people would find it easier to infiltrate but wondered if parents wouldn't object if they thought their children were taking on dangerous tasks. Sabina convinced him they would not if they were dedicated women.

Trudi, a pretty girl from a country town, often visited at Sabina's home. Sabina decided she was trustworthy and asked her to help. Colonel Shircanu, who worked with the Secret Police, was looking for a girl to help in his house. Sabina felt that if Trudi got this job, she would be a big asset. Trudi agreed, applied, and got the job.

After a month at the home of Shircanu, Trudi sent her first message. Pastor N., who attended the underground meetings, had agreed to spy. Challenged, he admitted he had been threatened with a long prison sentence unless he cooperated. Pastor N. left Bucharest for a provincial town.

Trudi's next message gave the name of a girl student. When challenged by Sabina, the girl denied everything. Sabina convinced her to tell the truth. The girl broke down and sobbed, "I was just walking in the street. A car drew up and two men said, 'We're police. Get in.' They drove me around for hours. They told me I had to report every week about everything that was said and done in your house and in the church. If I didn't, they said, awful things would happen to my family."

Trudi continued to turn up valuable information. Her most spectacular coup was to turn the colonel's home into a secret refuge for the very people he was trying to hunt down. The colonel began to enjoy the privileges of belonging to the Communist hierarchy. He took his family off on leisurely holidays to the mountains or to the sea. The trusted Trudi was left in charge as caretaker.

One day a message came through, "Why not have a meeting here, in the Shircanu's home? They're away for several days, and it's a big house with several exits. No one will suspect."

Sabina thought it was worth trying. Rather nervously, six members of the underground church arrived one by one at spaced intervals, received by a smiling Trudi. Everything went off perfectly. From then on, they met quite regularly at Shircanu's house when he and his family were away.

Trudi played her double role well. As time passed, more and more of the church members learned to do the same. They sang Red songs and the Party's praises. Several rose high in the ranks.

They had their failures, inevitably. For some workers, the strain of a double life proved too heavy. Others became too bold and paid the price. One of the members was manager of a State book store. To amuse the crowds, he put portraits of Marx, Engels, Lenin, and Stalin in the window. Under these, in large black letters, he advertised Hugo's masterpiece, LES MISERABLES. Colonel Shircanu investigated to see why the people were laughing and clapping. The manager was arrested and sent to a labor camp.

The Communist government encouraged divorce. A prisoner's will to resist, even to live, was often shattered when he learned he had been abandoned. It helped to get the wives involved in the Communist way of life. Once the State convinced a woman to accept divorce, she would be anxious to forget her husband by getting involved in Party activities.

An official from the Ministry of the Interior, carrying a briefcase, visited Sabina several months after her release. He ranted and raved about her stupidity in staying married to Richard. He accused her of being a poor mother; if she remarried, Mihai would have a chance to get a good education and an excellent position with the State.

Sabina remained mostly silent. Her only response was, "I didn't marry my husband only for happy times. We were united for ever, and whatever may come I will not divorce him."

Only one word was needed for her to make the break. If she had said "yes," the official would have done all the rest. A few days later, Richard would have been informed in the presence of his cellmates, "Your wife has decided to divorce you."

Sabina did everything she could to prevent divorce among her friends and church members. All too often she failed. The pressures were too severe.

More than once she was tempted during Richard's fourteen years in prison. The most serious was about a year after her release. A man who attended church meetings fell in love with her. She was forty-three, alone, with a son to help through the most difficult stage of adolescence, when boys need a father. The years were racing by with alarming speed, and she didn't know if Richard was alive or dead.

Mihai was fond of this Jewish Christian about the same age as his mother. He'd take Mihai to the movies or help him with his studies.

He was kind and gentle and knew how to make Sabina laugh. Sometimes he caught hold of her hand when he talked and looked into her eyes with longing. Sabina couldn't take her hand away, though in her heart she knew this was adultery in God's eyes.

Pastor Grecu saw what was happening and spoke to her. He spoke with rare emotion and sincerity. "Forgive me for asking; how is it with you and Paul? Don't imagine I haven't had such trials too."

"He's in love with me."

"Are you in love with him?"

"I don't know. Perhaps."

Pastor Grecu extracted a promise from Sabina not to see him again. With difficulty, she avoided Paul week after week. Then Paul stopped trying to see her. She learned later that Pastor Grecu had spoken to Paul as well. When she saw how close she had come to betraying years of waiting and trust, she knelt and prayed.

Sabina says there were other temptations. Fourteen years is a long time. Sometimes she came near to yielding.

Sometimes it was merely a passing weakness of the flesh. She felt that sexuality is a remorseless driving force, and one must, at times, not accuse oneself too harshly. One must have understanding for one's own weaknesses as well as for those of others.

While Sabina was in church scrubbing the floor, Marietta ran in breathlessly with a card from Richard, signed Vasile Georgescu. The message began: "Time and distance quench a small love, but make a great love grow stronger." He asked Sabina to visit him on a certain date at Tirgul-Ocna, the prison hospital.

Sabina wasn't permitted to go as she was restricted to Bucharest and had to report to the police station weekly. Mihai took her place. His visit has been previously described.

Richard's postcard message concerning love became known throughout Romania. It became a talisman of faith and was used by many. Richard helped prisoners write their cards because of his ability to say much in a few words.

Khrushchev was working his way toward supreme power in Russia, and there were signs of great changes to come. Throughout 1954, after Stalin's death, the Romanians hoped the West would do something for them. With 1955 came the Geneva Summit conference. The people were shocked when Romania was admitted to the United Nations in spite of its tens of thousands of political prisoners. The summit conference did bring some improvement in the prisons. Food was better and medicine became available. More visits were allowed. There were rumors of an amnesty.

The year 1956 began with the whole Communist bloc in a rebellious mood. "Five Year Plans" had gone nowhere. Food was scarce and wages were low. In February, at the Twentieth Congress of the Communist Party, Khrushchev denounced Stalin and his reign of terror. This was followed by a thaw from Moscow. Hundreds of political prisoners were freed each day.

Sabina didn't dare to hope that Richard would be among them. On a lovely morning in June of 1956, she went out to visit friends. On her return, Richard was home.

He had suffered beating and doping in prison. He had eighteen torture scars on his wasted body. Doctors found on his lungs many healed scars of tuberculosis. They had difficulty believing he had survived eight and a half years, three of them in solitary confinement underground, untreated. He was admitted to a hospital. All released prisoners were treated with kindness and generosity by the people wherever they went. They were the most privileged group in Romania, a fact that infuriated the Communists.

Richard had to move from hospital to hospital because brethren from all over the country came to see him. He did this to avoid attracting the Secret Police.

Soon after he got better, he and Sabina celebrated their twentieth wedding anniversary. Penniless, he wrote in a notebook love poems for Sabina.

Because of the political thaw, Richard was granted a license to preach. Persecution had brought the churches much closer. His first invitation to speak was in the Orthodox cathedral at Sibiu, where the priest was an old friend. He explained to Richard that it would be necessary for him to make the sign of the cross and so forth. Richard said he would make any prescribed sign as long as he could talk about Jesus.

Sabina went to Sibiu with him. Since he was still weak, something had to be found for him to sit on while he spoke. When the Metropolitan's throne was brought out, the rumor went round that the Metropolitan himself was going to speak. Instead, out came Richard, and the people whispered he was a Jew.

Richard crossed himself and spoke about the cross and its meaning. On the surface, the sermon was nonpolitical. Nevertheless, informers in the church reported every word to the Secret Police, who understood its hidden meaning.

When next he gave a series of talks to students at Cluj University, one of the top men from the Ministry of Cults was sent to listen. This man reported that Richard's lectures were a "torrent of sedition." The right to preach, which Richard had for six weeks, was cancelled.

Undaunted, he went on preaching secretly, speeding from place to place. He spoke briefly in small churches and at underground meetings and left at once before anyone could report to the local police. He often left the house without telling Sabina where he was going.

Mihai was studying theology at Sibiu when Richard was rearrested. He and Sabina knew it was coming. The new wave of terror began in 1958. They all saw now how they'd been tricked. Many people thought the Communists were interested in coming to terms with the West, that they would mellow.

In July 1958, new laws were enacted tougher than anything yet seen in the satellite countries. The death penalty was ordered for minor offenses, and was being liberally applied by autumn. Mass arrests began again. Thousands were sent to new slave labor projects. All juvenile delinquents (young people who criticized the government) became slave laborers.

A new purge began in official ranks. The fight against religion was renewed. Khrushchev ordered churches closed and priests arrested throughout Eastern Europe as part of a seven-year drive "to eradicate the vestiges of superstition."

The Wurmbrands' attic was a center for the underground church. Every evening Richard prayed, "God, if You know some prisoner to whom I could be of use, send me back to jail." To this, Sabina said a hesitant Amen.

One evening in January 1959, a woman from their church arrived in tears. The week before, she had borrowed some copies of Richard's sermons. Hundreds of these were circulating throughout Romania. It was strictly illegal. The police had raided the woman's flat and taken her remaining copies.

The Wurmbrands learned through an informant in the Party that Richard had been denounced by a young pastor who claimed to be his friend. He may have been forced to sign the denunciation under threat of prison. "Anyhow," Sabina said, "he did this and it's not for me to judge his motives. We were fond of him. It is better simply to continue to love."

On January 15 at 1 a.m., the police battered down the door and burst into their attic before they could get out of bed. "You're Richard Wurmbrand? Get into the other room and stay there."

The tiny flat was full of men opening cupboards, turning out drawers, throwing papers on the floor. On Richard's writing desk they found pages of notes, typewritten sermons, and worn Bibles, all of which they seized.

When they found Sabina's anniversary gift, in which Richard had written love verses, Sabina pleaded with them not to take it. They took it.

The captain brought Richard out of the other room in handcuffs. "Aren't you ashamed to treat innocent people like this?" Sabina asked.

Richard moved toward Sabina but was jerked back. "I shall not leave this house without a struggle unless you allow me to embrace my wife."

"Let him go," said the captain.

They knelt together in prayer, surrounded by police. Then they sang "The Church's one foundation is Jesus Christ, her Lord."

A hand fell on Richard's shoulder. "We've got to get going. It's nearly 5 a.m.," the captain said. He spoke quietly and his eyes glistened.

Sabina followed them down the staircase. Richard turned his head and said, "Give all my love to Mihai and the pastor who denounced me." The police pushed him into a van.

Sabina ran down the icy street, weeping and shouting, "Richard. Richard." The van disappeared around a corner. She stopped, breathless and confused.

Back at the attic, she fell on the floor weeping. She cried out, "Lord, I give my husband into your hands. I can do nothing, but you can pass through locked doors. You can put angels around him. You can bring him back." She sat in the darkness, praying, until the new day arrived.

CHAPTER 14

Sabina had many things to do. First, she must inform Mihai without letting informers at the university know, otherwise he would be expelled. She couldn't go to Sibiu herself, since she was known there. So her friend Alice took the news of Richard's arrest to Mihai.

Sabina saw Richard once more before he vanished for another six years. There was a trial which she was allowed to attend. Five judges sat on a raised platform under a red banner which read: JUSTICE FOR THE PEOPLE IN THE SERVICE OF THE PEOPLE. Above this were portraits of those in power.

Cases were heard and sentences given within minutes. As priests, peasants, gypsies, journalists came in one door and out another, it reminded Sabina of a conveyor belt. Richard followed a drunken sweeper. Sabina and Richard heard not one word of what followed. They simply looked at each other, perhaps for the last time.

Mihai told Sabina later that it was a rehash of his old secret trial in 1951. The amnesty was cancelled and he was sentenced to twenty-five years. As he went out, he gave Sabina and Mihai a last, cheerful smile. The procedure had taken two minutes.

Later, Sabina discovered the sentence included a heavy fine. Since she had no money, the few precious things she had collected since her release in 1953 were confiscated. This was a routine happening to the families of all political prisoners.

She was left with the beds, a table, and two chairs. Over the next six years, officials came again and again demanding money and confiscating what had been acquired.

Fear prevailed. Every day, friends were arrested. Nearly all of Sabina's close friends were back in jail. Churches were closed and men were kidnapped. While this was happening, Khrushchev made his "ice-breaking" visit to the U.S.A. and there was talk of a major summit in Paris in May 1960. Some felt that they would come to an agreement and prisoners would be freed.

While Sabina was visiting a friend, a neighbor called to inform her the police were in her attic. She was warned not to come home as Alice had already been arrested. The police searched for two hours. When Sabina returned she found a wrecked flat. Even the mattresses had been slashed.

When Sabina, years later, told people in the West about what happened to Pastor Armeanu, they thought she was joking. He was sentenced to twenty years for preaching on the text: "Cast your nets on the right side." This was declared to be imperialist propaganda because he didn't say "left side." An informer had reported his sermon.

The pastor left behind a wife and five young children, who were deported to the Baragan plain. One day, Mrs. Armeanu came to Sabina's door, exhausted and sick. Sabina took her in.

At an underground church meeting, Sabina challenged the man who had denounced Pastor Armeanu. She was bitter toward him and toward those partially responsible for Richard's arrest. She struggled with her hatred and prayed but could find no peace. Whenever her eyes fell on a picture pinned to the attic wall, a picture of the crucified Christ, she remembered His last words: "Father, forgive them, for they know not what they do" and "I thirst." She realized the betrayers thirsted for forgiveness, which she wouldn't give them because of her bitterness. Something changed in her. She resolved to give love and expect nothing in return.

When she wasn't busy with the underground church, she tramped the streets from government office to office trying to win a respite from Richard's fine. If she didn't pay it within a certain time, they would take all she had. It did no good.

Two tax department officials hammered on her door. They wanted more money. They made a list of all furnishings and household goods so that she could reclaim it when she found the cash. "You've got three days to pay. Otherwise you've had it."

Next morning when she finally got to see the correct functionary, he was furious. "You mean they haven't cleared you out yet? What business is it of mine what you do? The court instructions are clear. Either you pay immediately in full or your property's confiscated. You can't pay? That's it. They'll be round first thing tomorrow."

As Sabina walked down the stairs, she couldn't stop the tears from running down her cheeks. Shivering and coughing, she paused in the big hall before plunging into the icy street. Someone touched her arm.

A tall man in a dark suit had followed her down. She supposed he was another official with a new threat. He glanced quickly around. "I know your case," he said. "Here, take this." He vanished, hurrying back the way he had come.

Sabina looked at the folded money he had slipped into her hand. There was enough to stall them off for weeks. Walking home, Sabina didn't notice her sodden shoes, her frozen hands, or her exhaustion. Her heart was filled with glowing calm. The kind, generous man had shown her a sign of God's love. She wondered who he could be.

Mihai made discreet inquiries and learned he was from the tax office and was a friend of the underground church. Every month from then on, as long as Richard was in prison, he sent money out of his small salary.

Sabina was trying to earn a little extra by working at home. She had found an old knitting machine designed to make jerseys and pullovers. The trouble was that when she wanted to work, the machine didn't. She had a mechanic friend whom she called on almost daily for some repair. Finally the bearings wore out and she had to scrap the machine.

A week later, the mechanic arrived with a pair of simpler machines for making socks. Now, Sabina and Mrs. Armeanu were busy. The needles broke often and were not replaceable. As a result, sock production often stopped for months at a time. A socks blackmarket existed. It was not only illegal to make them privately but also illegal to sell without State permission. Finally Sabina gave sock manufacture up and limited her money-making ventures to language-teaching.

Richard

A young man in a dark raincoat came to her door after dark one evening. He gave her a summons to report to the Ministry of the Interior the next morning at nine. Early next day she packed a bag with toilet articles and warm clothes, not knowing if she would return.

The office was rather grand, with carpets, curtains, and pretty girl secretaries. Behind a grand-piano-size desk sat a plump man in civilian clothes.

"Sit down, Comrade Wurmbrand. We're taking an interest in your case. Tell me about yourself and your family. Nothing will go beyond these walls. You have a son, Mihai . . .how are his studies proceeding?"

Sabina had already caught the drift. It was another attempt to talk her into divorce. She answered, "I love my husband and whatever happens I shall stay married to him."

"Well now, let me make a little proposal. You want your child to complete his education. You want the right to work, to live your own life. You can have all this very simply. Just leave your I.D. card with me. In forty-eight hours we'll send it to you endorsed in your own name. Forget about big words like divorce. This is just a simple formality the State asks of you. Isn't it the intelligent thing to do? Of course, if you don't cooperate, there are other ways. When we want something, we get it."

Sabina looked him in the eye. "Suppose one day *you* are in prison, like so many other officials. Would you want your wife to divorce you?"

He sat up with a jerk and exploded, "Don't you know where you are, who I am? How dare you put questions to me?" He flung his pencil into the fireplace. "Now get out, get out. And don't forget what I've told you. Understand? Understand?"

Sabina walked out without answering. That was their last attempt to make her divorce Richard. Instead, on two occasions, they told her he was dead.

First, two haggard young men came to her door, saying they were ex-prisoners. They told a story of a depressed Richard and then his death, implying suicide. Sabina sent them on their way.

The second attempt to convince her of his death was contrived differently. It was officially stated that Richard was dead, but through a third person. A friend of hers was asked to inform her, but she continued to refuse to believe any reports of his death.

Richard's name was by now being whispered all over the country. He was becoming a legend. People prayed for his safety. To put an end to it, released prisoners were sent to Christian homes in several of the bigger towns to persuade people he had died in prison by his own hand. Very few believed them.

Sabina and Mihai knew they were in great danger. Although several underground church meetings had recently been broken up by the police, others had been left alone so informers could work in peace.

The meetings were increasing in size, up to fifty or sixty people at a time. They had to be especially careful if someone at a meeting had rank, a university professor or a Party member. Informers would be watching them. Sometimes meetings were limited to half a dozen trusted friends.

Informers were detected by planting false news. A suspect would be told that a meeting was to be held at a certain address. If an unusual number of plain-clothes snoopers were seen near the house, the suspect was considered guilty. Since a known informer was valuable, he was told that a change of address was necessary at the last minute.

So Sabina's life went on. On one hand she struggled to keep wind and snow, tax collectors, and secret police out of her attic; on the other hand she battled to hold together the underground church. She lived dangerously and was never bored.

In November 1960 she went to Cluj to witness a trial of leaders of the Army of the Lord, the forbidden religious organization Richard had done much to help. A close friend of the Wurmbrands, a teacher, was among them. The Army was made up mostly of country folk, and hundreds of them went to Cluj on the day of the trial. They stood in a silent mass outside the gates of the military tribunal in a heavy rain. They had come from all over Romania, in spite of the danger of being noted and denounced, to show their loyalty to those who were to be court-martialed for their faith.

When the prison vans arrived, the crowd surged forward to catch a glimpse of their loved ones. The accused men and women were hustled into the court as wives and families called out to them, clutching bundles of warm clothing and food.

"Get back. Get back." The militia brandished its rifles and some younger soldiers prepared to shoot, causing a panic.

An officer shouted, "Phone for reinforcements." Using their guns as staves, the guards pushed the crowd out of the yard into the street and then tried to close the gates. The cry went up: *Take us too. We are their brethren. We believe like them.*

In the end, the police, who were totally unprepared for such a demonstration, agreed to let in close relatives. A handful of wives and children were admitted. The rest stood all day outside the gates. The crowd was still large late at night.

At dusk, the prisoners were taken back to their cells. An officer announced sentences wouldn't be known until next day. Out-of-towners were taken in by local people who sympathized with them. Sabina was taken to the home of an underground church member along with six wives of prisoners. They decided to spend the night in prayer.

Next morning, Sabina returned to the courts. The sentences were posted. Her friend got eight years. She walked to the railway station in the rain and sat down to wait for the train to Bucharest.

In 1962, a warmer wind began to blow from Moscow. Sabina sniffed it cautiously. There was talk of a new thaw. More letters were coming in from abroad. Rumors spread that Romania was trying to break away from Comecon, the Soviet-controlled common market. There were rumors of an amnesty. People relaxed enough to tell jokes. One making the rounds was this:

Khrushchev: Mr. Kennedy, what can I do? I've tried brainwashing, I've tried prison, but these stupid Christians still go to church. How can I stop them?

Kennedy: Try replacing the ikons in the churches with your portrait.

On every Communist festival, Sabina listened intently to the radio, hoping for some announcement about a release of prisoners. May, August, and November holidays went by with release of only criminal convicts.

Yet, small signs continued to multiply. A trade deal was made with Yugoslavia. The "Institute for Russian Studies" became a lesser part of the "Institute for Foreign Languages." The "Russian Bookshop" became the "Universal Bookshop".

In August 1963, jamming of Romanian-language broadcasts from the West stopped. On August 23rd, Freedom Day, Sabina sat by the radio longing for news. There was none.

Early in 1964 a few politicals were released, some of whom were her friends. She asked them what it meant. They didn't know. On the day Alice was released, after four years in prison, Sabina couldn't sleep. She now had hope Richard would be home shortly. But months passed.

Every few weeks, Marcia, who became known as Sister Amnesty, announced the amnesty was imminent. The real amnesty, when it came, took them all by surprise. Sabina had risen early and gone out shopping for the family on a warm, blue June day. When she came home she found the daily paper, which had been brought by a friend, waiting for her. On page one was: AMNESTY. The announcement was hedged about in protective phrases. The State couldn't admit enslaving thousands of innocent people for years. And Moscow was watching.

Sabina joined a group of friends to discuss the amnesty, prayed with them, and then returned home. A neighbor ran in with a telephone message. An old friend had been released that morning from Gherla. He said Richard was on the list for today. He saw him waiting in the prison yard.

Another knock on the door. Sabina was summoned to the telephone in the apartment below. She went down and picked up the receiver. On the other end was Richard. When she heard his voice, she couldn't speak. She felt herself falling, falling; in her ears was a roar like the sea and darkness poured over her. When she regained consciousness, Mihai was talking to Richard, who was in the home of friends in Cluj. He would be home as soon as possible. But not today. His first underground meeting had already been arranged for that evening. He would take the overnight train and arrive in the morning.

There was no sleep that night. Every hour news came of fresh releases. Men and women Sabina hadn't seen in fifteen years crowded the attic. Large bunches of summer roses kept arriving from people who dare not show their face because of the danger.

Crowds of anxious, expectant people met every train. Then Richard's train arrived. Sabina saw him leaning from a window. He was thin and pale with a shaven head. In his shabby clothes, his oversized laceless boots, he shuffled toward Sabina and Mihai. He embraced them. "Don't speak," he said, "Let me just look at you."

CHAPTER 15

The story reverts to Richard's first prison release.

After his discharge from Jilava, he craved quietness and rest. He knew Communism was working everywhere to destroy the Church and that to seek the peace he so desired would be an escape from reality and dangerous to his soul.

Instruction in the public schools was both antitheistic and anticapitalistic. The students were told one thing in school and exactly the opposite by their parents. Because of their confusion, they often asked Richard for advice.

A young theology student from the university of Cluj wanted help in his thesis. "What is the subject?" Richard asked.

"The history of liturgical song in the Lutheran church."

Richard said, "You should begin by writing that we should not be filling young men's heads with historical trivialities, when tomorrow they may face death for their faith."

"What should I be studying, then?"

"How to be ready for sacrifice and martyrdom." Richard told him some of the things he had seen in prison. The student started bringing his friends, all of whom had trouble charting a course.

When Richard questioned them about their studies, one of them said, "Our theology teacher says God gave three revelations. The first was to Moses. The second was to Christ. The third was to Karl Marx."

"What does your pastor think of that?"

"The more he talks, the less he seems to say."

The upshot of these conversations was that Richard agreed to go to Cluj and preach in the cathedral there. The students also wanted Richard's books, but all his writings had been banned.

Before he left for Cluj, he had to pay a visit in fulfillment of a promise he had made in prison to members of the Army of the Lord. It was several years since he had met the Patriarch Justinian Marina, who Richard thought might help. The harm Marina had done to the church was great; it was also in his power to do some good.

When Richard found him walking in the grounds behind his palace, Richard said, "Everywhere you go you must preach and sing, and so I thought I should come and sing to you. It's a song of the Army of the Lord which I learned in prison." Richard sang the song and asked him to do something for the people of the "Army." Marina said he would try, and they had a long talk. Richard tried to bring the Patriarch back to God, but he remained submissive to the Party's demands. If he went too far, he would be replaced by the Metropolitan of Iasi.

Later, Richard heard he had raised the matter of the "Army" in the Holy Synod, where he was opposed by the Metropolitan, who, by the way, had become the Orthodox representative for the World Council of Churches. Next, he was reproved by the Ministry of Cults for receiving Richard. His secretary had reported the visit, just as Marina always informed on his secretary. Marina had agreed to meet representatives from the "Army", but when they arrived he sent them away, saying, "So Wurmbrand told you to come, did he? It's time he was back in jail."

The news that Richard had promised to deliver a series of talks at Cluj was at once reported to the authorities. The informer was a Baptist minister who told him what he had done.

His action didn't surprise Richard, who had met many of his colleagues since his release. Priests, pastors, and bishops reported to the Ministry of Cults. Those who refused to answer questions about their congregations were dismissed and either replaced or the church was closed. Richard divided the clergy into four categories: those in prison, those who informed under pressure, those who shrugged it off and did as they were told, and those who had acquired a taste for informing.

An official spy called Rugojanu was a fanatic who went from church to church sniffing out counterrevolutionaries. He attended Richard's lectures.

On the first evening there was a group of fifty students and a few theology teachers. Richard, who was strictly anti-evolution, declared it was strange the Communists accepted the teachings of the English bourgeois, Sir Charles Darwin. He continued, "If you believe you were created by God, you will try to become Godlike. If you believe you sprang from apes, you're in danger of turning into a beast."

He started his lectures on a Monday. On Tuesday the audience had doubled. By the end of the week, more than a thousand faces looked up at him. He knew that many of them were eager to hear the truth but feared the consequences of embracing it. He told them of the advice given him by a pastor who died for his faith at the hands of the Fascists. He said, "You give your body as a sacrifice to God when you give it to all who wish to beat and mock you. Jesus, knowing His crucifixion was near, said, 'My time is at hand.' His time was the time of suffering, and it was His joy to suffer for the salvation of mankind. We, too, should regard suffering as a charge given us by God. St. Paul wrote in the epistle to the Romans, 'My brothers, I implore you by God's mercy to offer your very selves to Him, a living sacrifice dedicated and fit for His acceptance.'"

Richard looked out at the silent congregation. It took him back to the time he was preaching in his church during the war when the Iron Guard bullies filed in with their guns. Again, he was surrounded by menace. Rugojanu was taking notes.

Richard continued, "Don't let suffering take you by surprise. Meditate on it often. Take the virtues of Christ and His saints to yourself, by thought. The pastor I spoke of, my teacher who died for his faith, gave me a recipe for a tea against suffering, and I will give it to you. It contains seven herbs:

1. contentedness
2. common sense
3. remembrance of past sins
4. thought of the sorrows which Christ bore gladly for us
5. knowledge that suffering has been given to us by God as from a father, not to harm us, but to cleanse and sanctify us
6. knowledge that no suffering can harm a Christian life
7. hope."

Richard paused for a moment. The crowded church was silent. "I have drunk barrels of this tea since then. I can recommend it to you all. It has proved good."

As Richard finished speaking, Rugojanu stomped out of the cathedral. Richard came down from the pulpit and the audience broke into a hubbub of talk. Outside, students applauded and cheered. He telephoned Sabina. She approved of what he had done but knew there would be reprisals.

Next day, he was summoned by his bishop, who informed him Rugojanu was making trouble. As he was telling about protests from the Ministry of Cults, Rugojanu walked in. "Ah, you. What excuses are you trying to make. I heard your torrent of sedition."

Richard asked him what in particular had displeased him. He said everything had but especially his cure for suffering.

"What was wrong with my poor tea?" Richard asked. "Which herb did you not like?"

He said violently, "You told them the wheel always turns. In this counterrevolutionary outburst, you are mistaken. The wheel will not turn. Communism is here forever." His face was distorted with hatred.

"I didn't mention Communism. I said simply that the wheel of life keeps turning."

"You meant that Communism would fall, and they all knew what you meant. Don't imagine you've heard the last of this."

Rugojanu called a meeting of the church leaders at the bishop's palace in Cluj. Richard was denounced for trying to poison youth with concealed attacks on the government. "You may be sure he will never preach again," shouted Rugojanu in an ugly rage. "Wurmbrand is finished, Wurmbrand is finished, Wurmbrand is finished." He grabbed his coat and hat and stormed out of the building.

A hundred yards from the door, a car, swerving to avoid a dog, mounted the pavement and crushed Rugojanu against the wall. He died on the spot.

The revocation of Richard's license as a pastor didn't stop him from preaching. Now he had to work as secretly as he did among Soviet soldiers after the war. A new danger arose by visits from old prison friends asking for advice and help. Some of these had turned informer and were trying to provoke him. These unhappy men had expected too much after release. Their domestic world was turned upside down, and they had turned to the pursuit of sexual pleasure to win back their lost youth. To pay for this they needed the quick profits from providing the Party with information.

Sometimes the Underground Church met in open country. Richard beautifully described this: "The sky was our cathedral, the birds supplied our music, the flowers our incense, the stars our candles, the angels were the acolytes who lit them, and the shabby suit of a martyr just freed from prison meant far more to us than the most precious priestly robes."

After the revolution in Hungary the situation grew gradually more difficult. Khrushchev announced a new Seven-Year Plan, "to eradicate the vestiges of superstition." Churches were closed or converted for other uses.

Richard prayed, "God, if You know men in prison whom I can help, souls that I can save, send me back and I will bear it willingly." Sabina would hesitate and then say Amen. There was an inner joy about her from knowing they would serve Christ more fully soon. Richard wondered if the image of the mother of the Lord, standing grief-stricken by the Cross, is not mistaken. Was she not also filled with joy that her Son would be Savior of the world?

They came for Richard at 1 a.m. on January 15, 1959.

It was still dark and the streets were covered with icy slush when they reached Police Headquarters in Bucharest. After putting him through the familiar reception process, the guards led him to a cell in which was a man of about thirty, called Draghici, who jumped each time the door was opened. He was jittery, he explained, because he never knew whether they had come to take him for a bath or to be shot. He had been under sentence of death for four years.

Draghici told Richard the story of his life: how as a boy he had left the church because of a dishonest priest whom he had revered, his drunken father had disappeared with the family savings, and at fourteen he had joined the Iron Guard for the sake of the green shirt, the marching songs, and the admiration of girls. When the Guard was overthrown he was sent to prison, and when the Communists took power, he was sentenced to eleven years as a Fascist. Promised freedom if he would beat the other prisoners, he accepted. "And now I must die for it."

Richard sensed that the young man was dying already of tuberculosis. As he lay awake listening to Draghici cough, he thought, "Man is a sinner, but the guilt is not his. Satan and his fallen angels are at work to make us as wretched as they are themselves."

For ten days and nights he reasoned with Draghici. "It is not of your free choice that you became a criminal. Your sense of guilt demands atonement. Jesus has taken on Himself the punishment you feel you deserve."

On the tenth evening Draghici broke down in tears. They prayed together, and his remorse and fear were lifted. Richard was happy that his request to be allowed to help other prisoners was answered in his first days back in prison.

When he was taken for interrogation at Bucharest's Uranus jail, a Secret Police major asked him to name counterrevolutionaries he had met. "I will be glad to name counterrevolutionaries, in Russia as well as at home," he replied. "Several thousand of them were killed in the Soviet Union during the thirties by Yagoda, then Minister of Interior, but in the end the real counterrevolutionary was revealed as Yagoda himself. Then, under his successor, Beria, the Soviet secret police drove hundreds of thousands to their death until Beria, too, was shot. The supreme enemy of the revolution, the killer of millions, was Josef Stalin, who has since been turned out of his tomb in Red Square. It would be best to look elsewhere than in my poor church for counterrevolutionaries."

The officer ordered him to be beaten and kept in solitary confinement. He stayed there until his trial. Sabina and Mihai were present this time to hear him denounced after a ten-minute trial and sentenced to twenty-five years.

There were other newly-sentenced clergy with Richard in the Secret Police truck. After a short journey it descended a steep ramp and halted. His heart sank. He knew he was back in the underground prison of Jilava.

A party of baton-swinging guards drove them with blows along a passage. At the sight of priests there was a whoop of joy. Gray grubby uniforms were thrown at them. Those who were slow in stripping had the clothes torn off their backs. Beards were cut off amid roars of laughter. Heads were roughly shaved. Bleeding and half-naked, they were driven into a large cell.

They sat on the stone floor, huddling together in the February cold. A guard lurched in, bawling, "All priests outside." Amid suppressed giggles and snorts, they filed out into another gauntlet of baton-blows. Those who fell were kicked with heavy boots and spat on.

Half an hour later all priests were again called out. No one moved. Guards rushed into the cell, lashing out indiscriminately.

Richard tried to comfort those near him. One man had lost some teeth and his lip was badly split. As he cleaned the blood from the priest's face, the man said, "I'm Miron Cristescu." They had met years before, but now, shaven and with a bloody, dirty face, he was unrecognizable.

A few days later, Richard and Miron joined a convoy that headed into the mountains. After many hours the Transylvanian town of Gherla and its prison came into view. Gherla brought back memories. Sabina had visited him here in 1956. From the high walls he had seen life going on in the town. When the children came from school, shouting and laughing as they chased each other, he and the other prisoners had to turn away. It made them think of their own families.

Ten thousand prisoners were packed into primitive accommodations intended for 2,000, and the régime was as harsh as in the worst days of the re-education campaign. The previous summer there had been serious rioting at Gherla. As a punishment food was reduced to starvation level and hundreds of convicts were dispersed to other jails.

Richard and the other priests and pastors took their place along with thousands of other political prisoners caught in the new wave of arrest—landowners, army officers, doctors, shopkeepers, artisans, farmers.

The cells were long, dark, echoing barracks rooms, each containing up to one hundred men but only fifty to sixty bunks. Many shared a bed. Sleep was difficult with night-long processions to the overflowing buckets and a dozen snorers. No one could rest by day when discipline was enforced by whips and studded boots. The guards made surprise "security visits" to the cells, banging the iron bars across the windows with their batons to make sure they had not been filed. The prisoners lay face down on the floor in rows, to be counted. The guards walked on each man in turn as his name was called.

The slightest breach of the rules brought a minimum of twenty-five lashes, with a doctor standing by, because men had died under such castigation. There was scarcely a man in prison who hadn't been flogged, and some several times. The blows burned like fire. The floggings had a brutalizing effect on the guards. Blood and power seemed to affect even the best among them.

Richard and Miron carried the lavatory buckets each day to the one flush-toilet on the landing. Though fastidious and cultured men, they forced themselves to do these demeaning chores.

In the cell were some tough characters, including murderers and thieves. Others were war criminals serving life sentences. They were bitter, angry men, and all his attempts to offer religious consolation were shouted down. When he began speaking quietly to a single man in a corner, others formed a menacing circle around them.

"We told you to shut up," snarled the leader. Richard stood up and someone pushed him. Another put a leg out and he fell on his face. He felt a violent kick in the ribs. As the pack fell on him there was a shout of warning.

A guard called for help. The crowd scattered. When the cell door opened everyone was in his bunk. The commandant was told the story. He demanded, "Wurmbrand, who did it?"

"I cannot answer."

"Why not?"

"As a Christian I love and forgive my enemies. I don't denounce them."

"Then you're an idiot."

"There you are right. Anyone who isn't a Christian with all his heart is an idiot."

"Are you calling me an idiot?" thundered the commandant.

"I didn't say that. I meant I wasn't as good a Christian as I should be."

The commandant smote himself on the forehead with the palm of his hand. "Take him away and give him thirty strokes." He waddled off, growling, "Crazy monks."

When Richard returned from his beating, the guards were still questioning prisoners, who gave no information. No one was punished. After this there were few interruptions when he preached.

In spite of the grim conditions, humor wasn't lacking in prison. Richard found that some quarrels were comical. Each cell of 60 to 80 occupants had two parties: those who slept near the two narrow windows were for keeping them closed; those who slept in the fetid air far from the windows were for keeping them open. The topic was debated, literally for hours, day after day, as though they were in Parliament.

Laughter was often heard. Gladness, in the Acts of the Apostles, is called a witness to the existence of God. Without such a belief the presence of joy in prison is inexplicable. Some could even laugh at their sufferings.

Stories and riddles were told by the hour. Everyone had to contribute. There was a certain kind of nonsense that made them laugh better than anything. "What has three colors, hangs on trees, and sings tara-boom-cha-cha?" asked Florescu, a half-gypsy thief. No one had an answer. "A herring," said Florescu.

"A herring hasn't three colors."

"If I paint it, it has."

"They don't hang on trees, either."

"They do if I tie them on."

"They don't sing tara-boom-cha-cha."

"I only said that so you wouldn't guess the answer."

In a batch of new prisoners Richard was shocked to see Professor Popp. He looked ill and moved like an old man. Richard hadn't seen or heard from him since the amnesty of 1956. That evening Popp explained why. Like many other released prisoners he had plunged into a hunt for pleasure. "I felt starved," he said. "I was afraid life had passed me by. I had to prove I could enjoy myself again. I spent lavishly. I drank too much. I left my wife for a younger woman.

"Then I was sorry. I hadn't forgotten my Christian vows. I wanted to see you, but you were far away. I told everything to another pastor and blamed Communism for destroying the country. He listened and then denounced me."

Popp had been given another twelve-year sentence. His will was weak. Richard tried to bring him back to God, but life seemed empty of meaning to him.

On the second day he was put to work with Richard. They had to clean the floor of the large cell, scrubbing it from end to end. A prisoner, elected as room leader, kicked over the bucket of dirty water when they were almost finished and said, "Now do it again." A guard came in with muddy boots to inspect the floor. They scrubbed for another hour to the accompaniment of kicks from the room leader. Richard remarked, "There is no oppressor worse than the oppressed."

This experience left Popp shaking with exhaustion. As the days passed he withdrew further into himself. Richard had to urge him to eat and help him get ready each morning. He neither laughed nor wept nor joined in the life of the cell. One morning, stung by a jeering remark from the room leader, he seized the man's throat, clinging to it like a madman until two guards clubbed him down. He was carried unconscious to the hospital wing. Next day they heard he was dead.

The tragedy filled the cell with sorrow. There was talk in the cell that evening of life after death. Florescu, who had pulled up a stool, said, "I believe in what I can see, taste, and feel. We're all matter, like this bit of wood I'm sitting on, and when you're dead, that's it."

Richard went over and kicked the stool from under him. It shot across the floor and Florescu went down with a bump. He scrambled up furiously and made for Richard, but the others held him. "What's the idea?" he snarled.

Richard replied, "But you said you were matter like the stool. I didn't hear the stool complain." There was laughter. "I'm sorry, Florescu," he said. "I just wanted to prove that since matter doesn't react with love or hate, it is, after all, different from us."

Florescu sulked for a while, then said, "I might believe if the dead ever came back to talk to us."

"I am sure that men have been in touch with the dead. Great scientists from Newton to Sir Oliver Lodge have believed in spiritualism. The Bible describes the evocation of dead King Saul. Scripture forbids it but says it is possible."

The row over the stool had brought others to listen, and he began to preach earnestly about life after death. It was for them no academic matter but rather a topic of burning and immediate interest. Men died every day in Gherla.

He forgot the guards and raised his voice to preach to prisoners lying in bunks that rose in tiers to the ceiling. Eyes watched him in the dim light which the weak bulb hanging above them seemed to make still more dismal.

While he spoke of life after death, there was a silence such as there never is in church. No one yawned or fidgeted. The prisoners, in soiled clothes, their cheeks hollow, and their eyes big with hunger, received the thought of survival after death as thirsty soil receives rain.

At sunrise, before reveille, Richard got up to join another prisoner looking out the barred window. The light was ashen. Mist hung in the yard, but they could see a row of black coffins lying by the main gate. They contained men who had died in the last twenty-four hours. One would be Popp. This was a daily scene at Gherla. A guard crossed the yard and raised the lids of the coffins. Behind him came a hulking figure with a steel stake in his hand. He plunged the steel into each corpse in turn. They were making sure that no life remained and that no would-be escapees had replaced the dead. The coffins were closed and loaded onto the truck that would take them to the cemetery.

The prisoner with whom Richard watched the sordid coffin scene was Gaston, a Unitarian pastor, who, since Popp's death, had been morose to the point of considering suicide. With all the shifting in cells, Richard had lost sight of him. Many months went by. After a beating for preaching, Richard was thrown into an isolation cell. There he found Gaston, who had also been beaten for preaching.

Gaston's back was a mass of bloody wounds. Richard tried to ease the pain with applications of a shirt soaked in water. His body shook and he couldn't speak at first. Finally, he said, "I want to tell you something."

"You mustn't talk."

"Now or never. About Professor Popp . . .and the pastor who betrayed him . . ." He stopped, his lips trembling.

"You needn't tell me."

"I couldn't stand the pressure. I've suffered. When he died . . ." He began to sob.

They prayed together. He said he could never forgive himself. "The professor didn't. How could anyone else?"

"Of course they can. So would Popp if he had known everything. Let me tell you about a man who was far worse than you. It

RICHARD AND SABINA

will help us to pass the night. He was the murderer of my wife's family. She forgave him, and he became one of our closest friends.

"When Romania entered the war on Germany's side, a pogrom began in which many thousands of Jews were killed or deported. At Iasi alone 11,000 were massacred in a day. My wife, who shares my Protestant faith, is also of Jewish origin. We lived in Bucharest, from which the Jews were not deported, but her parents, one of her brothers, three sisters, and other relatives who lived in Bucovine were taken to Transmistria, a wild border province. Jews who were not murdered at the end of this journey were left to starve, and there Sabina's family died.

"I had to break this news. She recovered herself and said, 'I will not weep. You are entitled to a happy wife, and Mihai to a happy mother, and our church to a servant with courage.' From that day I never saw Sabina weep again.

"Some time later our landlord, a good Christian, told me of a man who was staying in the house while on leave from the front. 'I knew him before the war,' he said, 'but he's changed completely. He has become a brute who likes to boast of how he volunteered to exterminate Jews in Transmistria and killed hundreds with his own hands.'

"I was deeply distressed and decided to pass the night in prayer. To avoid disturbing Sabina, who was unwell and who would have wished to join in my vigil, I went upstairs after supper to the landlord's flat to pray with him.

"Lounging in an armchair was a giant of a man whom the landlord introduced as Borila, the killer of Jews from Transmistria. When he rose he was even taller than I, and there seemed to be about him an aura of horror that was like a smell of blood. Soon he was telling us of his adventures in the war and of the Jews he had slaughtered.

"I said it was a frightening story but that I didn't fear for the Jews, that God would compensate them for what they had suffered. I said I ask myself with anguish what will happen to the murderers when they stand before God's judgment.

"An ugly scene was prevented by the landlord, who said we

were both guests in his house and turned the talk to more neutral channels. The murderer proved to be not only a murderer. He was a pleasant talker, and eventually it came out that he had a great love of music.

"He mentioned that while serving in the Ukraine he had been captivated by the songs there. 'I wish I could hear them again,' he said.

"I knew some of these old songs. I thought to myself, **The fish has entered my net**. I told him if he'd like to hear some of them, he should come to my flat, that I was not a pianist but could play a few Ukrainian melodies.

"The landlord, his wife, and daughter accompanied us. Sabina was in bed. She was used to my playing softly at night and didn't awaken. I played the folk-songs, which are alive with feeling, and I could see that Borila was deeply moved. I remembered how, when King Saul was afflicted by an evil spirit, the boy David had played the harp before him.

"I stopped and turned to Borila and told him I had something very important to say to him. 'Please speak,' he said.

"I told him if he'd look through the curtain, he'd see my wife Sabina asleep. Her parents, her sisters, and her six-year-old brother were killed with the rest of the family. I reminded him he had killed hundreds of Jews near Golta, and that was where they had been taken. I told him we could assume he was the murderer of her family.

"He jumped up, his eyes blazing, looking as if he were about to strangle me. I held up my hand and told him we would try an experiment. I said I would wake Sabina and tell her what Borila had done. I predicted what would happen. I said Sabina wouldn't speak one word of reproach but would embrace him as if he were her brother and bring him some supper. I said if Sabina, who is a sinner like us all, could forgive and love like that, imagine how Jesus, who is perfect love, could forgive and love him. I asked him to return to Jesus and assured him that everything he had done would be forgiven.

"Borila was not heartless. Within he was consumed by guilt

and misery at what he had done. One tap at his weak spot, and his defenses crumbled. The music had already moved his heart, and now came, instead of the attack he expected, words of forgiveness. His reaction was amazing. He jumped up and tore at his collar with both hands, so that his shirt was rent apart. 'Oh God, what shall I do, what shall I do?' he cried. He put his head in his hands and sobbed loudly as he rocked himself back and forth. 'I'm a murderer, I'm soaked in blood! What shall I do?' Tears ran down his cheeks.

"In the name of the Lord Jesus Christ I commanded the devil of hatred to go out of his soul.

"Borila fell on his knees trembling, and we began to pray aloud. He knew no prayers; he simply asked again and again for forgiveness and said that he hoped and he knew it would be granted. We were on our knees together for some time. Then we stood up and embraced each other. I reminded him that I had promised to make an experiment, and now I would keep my word.

"I went into the other room and found Sabina still sleeping calmly. She was weak and exhausted at that time. I woke her gently and told her there was a man in the house whom she must meet; that we believe he murdered her family and that he had repented and was now their brother.

"She came out in her dressing-gown and put out her arms to embrace him. Both began to weep and kiss each other. As I foretold, she went to the kitchen to bring him food.

"While she was in the kitchen, the thought came to me that Borila's crime had been so terrible, some further lesson was needed. I went to the next room and returned with my son Mihai, who was then two, asleep in my arms. It was only a few hours since Borila had boasted to us how he had killed Jewish children in their parents' arms. He was horrified. The sight was an unbearable reproach. He expected me to accuse him. But I asked him if he saw how quietly he slept. I told him that he was also like a newborn child who could rest in the Father's arms, that the blood Jesus shed had cleansed him.

"Borila's happiness was very moving. He stayed with us that

night. The next morning he said, 'It's a long time since I slept like that.'

"He wanted to meet our Jewish friends. I took him to many Hebrew Christian homes. He told his story everywhere and was received as the returning prodigal son. With a New Testament which I gave him, he went to join his regiment in another town.

"Borila later came to say his unit had been ordered to the front. 'What shall I do?' he asked. 'I'll have to start killing again.' I told him he had killed more than a soldier needs to. I explained I didn't mean a Christian shouldn't defend his country if attacked. I told him that he shouldn't kill any more, that it would be better to allow others to kill him."

As Richard told the story, Gaston grew quieter. At the end, he reached to clasp his hand and fell into an untroubled sleep.

In the morning they were moved together into another cell. Among the prisoners, Richard found Grigore, who was also a war criminal responsible for massacring Jews. He knew Borila. Richard told Gaston, "There's an epilogue to the story of the man who killed my wife's family. This man can tell it to you."

Grigore told how he had served with Borila in Transmistria, where they had massacred the Jews. "When we went to Russia again, he was a changed man. We couldn't understand it. He put aside his weapons, and instead of taking lives, he saved them. He volunteered to rescue the wounded under fire, and in the end he saved his officer."

The months turned into years. Two had gone by and the only thing that changed were the faces. Prison made of some men saints, and of others brutes, and it was difficult to tell who would become which. One thing was certain—the majority of prisoners would go on living in a vacuum. They sprawled on their bunks, hour after hour, with nothing to do. Talk became their whole life. Richard wondered what would happen if science made work unnecessary.

As his third year in Gherla progressed, things eased a little.

They gained a little more freedom of speech, a few more mouthfuls of food. They believed conditions outside were changing again. They didn't know in what way, nor that the greatest trials lay ahead.

CHAPTER 16

On a March morning, 1962, guards burst into the cells shouting, "All priests outside." The priests gathered their few belongings and dutifully filed into the corridors, but Richard didn't stir.

Gherla had a new commandant, a martinet called Alexandrescu. Richard stayed where he was to avoid interference with his preaching, not knowing what mischief the new move would engender. It turned out the whole jail was being divided into class groups: intellectuals in one cell, peasants in another, and so on.

A guard asked Richard what he was. "A pastor," he replied in a country accent. He was placed in a cell with shepherds and farm hands. "Pastor" is the usual word for shepherd in Romania.

He remained in this cell for a few weeks until an informer betrayed him. After a beating, he was taken to the priests' cell, which was his home for the remainder of his stay in Gherla. It was a cavernous room with dirty, gray cement walls. The only light was from two narrow windows. Bunks were closely packed in tiers four-high. He saw some low benches and a table. The prisoners, mostly clergy but with other Christians, numbered about a hundred.

As Richard entered his new cell, a deep voice cried, "Welcome, welcome." It was old Bishop Mirza, an exemplar of the Orthodox faith and a man of great goodness. Heads were raised as he greeted men he knew, including Miron, who had a bunk above the bishop and Gaston.

That evening, in the hour which the priests' room had set aside for prayer, Catholics collected in one corner, the Orthodox occupied another, and Unitarians a third. The Jehovah's Witnesses had a nest on the upper bunks; the Calvinists assembled down below. Twice a day the various services were held. Far from fostering understanding, their common plight made for conflict.

When mass was celebrated a few feet from his bunk day after day, the evangelical pastor Haupt evoked some words of Martin Luther. "What's that?" one of the Catholics demanded.

Haupt raised his voice obligingly, "I repeated the words of Luther. 'All the brothels which God condemns, all murders, thefts, adulteries do not make so much harm as the abomination of the Papal mass.'"

After the services had finished, one of the Catholics, Father Fazekas, said, "Dear brother, have you not heard the saying, 'Mankind has suffered three great catastrophes—the fall of Lucifer, and of Adam, and the revolt of Martin Luther.'"

Father Andricu, an Orthodox priest, joined in the counterattack, "Luther and Lucifer are one and the same." So Catholic and Orthodox followers became temporary allies.

Before nightfall they were squabbling over the supremacy of Rome.

Fazekas was of Hungarian origin and this was held against him even by his fellow-Catholics. When he prayed aloud to the Virgin Mary as "patron of Hungary," general displeasure was shown. "Isn't the Blessed Virgin Romania's patron too?" asked a patriotic Orthodox priest.

"Certainly not. She is Hungary's patron."

Gaston ironically wondered if the Virgin was not patron of Palestine, since it seemed treacherous to leave the country of her birth to become patron of another. "Perhaps you haven't heard the Jews murdered her son." said Fazekas.

Bishop Mirza, smiling gently, tried to calm everyone down. "The Virgin is not bound to any one country," he said. "She leads the church, is queen of heaven, she moves the planets, and she heads the choirs of angels."

Richard said, "That doesn't leave God much to do." Other Protestants supported him but in a manner he disliked.

"Why should I venerate God's mother like this?" asked one. "She cannot save."

Fazekas replied, "Poor man. Do you venerate only those who will save you? The mother of the Lord sings in the Magnificat, 'All generations will call me blessed.' They do so because she was Jesus' mother, not because she distributes favors."

Richard thought it was a good answer, but he felt that as much as he honored the Virgin Mary, her role had been exaggerated by her following and that this distortion began in ancient times. When Christians first thought about heaven, they had visions of an Oriental court: a place of music, luxury, and sweet scents. There developed the idea of a spiritual hierarchy in which simple men put their requests to priests, priests to the saints, and saints to the Virgin.

He further stated that the bedrock of his faith is that a man may speak directly to God, but there are times when difference of opinion only encourages anger. He told the others of the two martyrs of different confessions who were sent together to the stake. They were asked if they had a last wish before the fire was lit. Both said, "Yes. Tie us back to back so I don't have to see that damned heretic as I die."

Sometimes Richard couldn't hide his feelings. For hours he listened to Father Ranghet, a Dominican in the bunk below, telling his beads. At last he said, "Why do you have to appeal a thousand times a day to the Virgin? Is she deaf, or indifferent, or reluctant to hear?"

Ranghet was cross. "Since you Lutherans have no belief in the infallibility of the Holy Father, you have still less cause to believe in your own. What's wrong in your impaired sight is right in mine." He went back to repeating "Hail Mary" louder than before.

"You speak often of the Holy Father. Do you mean God?"

"I mean his Holiness the Pope."

"To me it seems blasphemy to use divine titles for a human being. You call him Christ's Vicar on earth, which means his substitute. I can't accept such a substitute, any more than I could allow my wife to have a substitute for me."

"You go too far," he said.

And Richard had thought it was he who had gone too far. Only that day Father Ranghet had said that all the sacrifices of life and liberty offered by all men were as nothing compared with the offering he made at the altar when he sacrificed the son of God. He couldn't accept the idea that a priest made God from a piece of bread or that there was any need for such a thing. He couldn't believe his eternal destiny depended on absolution from a man who might not be too sure of heaven himself.

He looked for topics on which they could agree. When Pastor Weingartner, a modernist Protestant, took issue with Catholics on the Virgin Birth, he felt bound to take their side.

Weingartner said he couldn't accept such a scientific improbability. He believed it to be a myth.

Richard replied, "It is too late to make an historical inquiry into the Virgin Birth, but it is also too early to dismiss it as scientifically impossible. An American biologist called Loeb has already produced a birth without male seed in lower organisms. What a biologist can do for a small being, surely God can do for man."

Next morning a pleasing thing happened. Bishop Mirza came to Richard and said, "I thought in the night of the Lord's Prayer, which tells us to say, 'Our Father which art in heaven . . .forgive our trespasses.' Jesus didn't tell us to confess to a priest or receive absolution from him—he told us to pray for it to the Father. Of course the question is not a simple one, but if I were a Protestant, I should use this argument. So I thought that in friendship I would make you a present of it in exchange for your defense of the Virgin Mary."

The bishop had set them an example. If they failed to live in peace together, they fell into the trap the Communists had laid: by locking the clergy together, they deprived the other prisoners of spiritual guidance while the clergy vitiated their own cause with quarrels.

CHAPTER 17

Richard wondered what else the Communists had in mind. Electricians had been working in the prison for some time, and in many cells loudspeakers had been installed, one to each wall. It appeared they were to have broadcasts. Gaston said, "It won't be light music."

When the entire prison had been divided into classes, a series of lectures began. To Richard and others they seemed absurd. A brash young political officer explained that an eclipse of the sun was about to occur, but there was no cause for alarm—socialist science had freed them from superstition. He proceeded to explain the workings of a solar eclipse to a yawning audience of dons and doctors. The event was to take place on February 15, and since it was the duty of the People's Republic to broaden their views, they could watch from the courtyard.

Weingartner's hand went up. "Please, if it rains can we have the eclipse in the hall instead?"

"No," said the lecturer seriously and began his explanation again from the start. The indoctrination lectures lasted for hours. The same points were driven home over and over again. At the end of the day, exhausted and ill-tempered, they were left to their own disputes.

As the prison lectures continued, Richard saw that although in themselves they were ridiculous, there lay behind them a clever plan. The speakers turned from politics to appeals directed at the pleasure-seeking, irresponsible side in everyone. They told the prisoners how much they were missing in the world. They talked of food, drink, and sex. They told of the conflict between Christianity and science in America, where millions were starving as a consequence.

At first, they were encouraged to argue. When a lecturer said only a handful of chemicals remained of the body after death, Richard asked why, if that were so, some Communists had given their lives for their beliefs. "For a Christian to sacrifice himself," he said, "may be considered wise. To give up the transitory things of life to win eternity is like laying down ten dollars to win a million. But why should a Communist give his life, unless he too has something to gain for himself?"

The political officer could find no reply. Richard said, "Atheism is a mask for your feelings. In the depths of your heart, which is never reached unless a man practices meditation or prayer, you too believe there is a reward for living up to ideals. Deep in your heart you also believe in God."

"Let's see what Lenin has to say about that," the lecturer retorted. He read from a booklet: "Even flirting with the idea of God is unutterable vileness, contagion of the most abominable kind. Filthy deeds, acts of violence, and physical contagions are far less dangerous." He grinned victoriously. "Any more questions?"

"Have you a child?"

"I have a daughter in the Young Pioneers."

"Would you prefer that she be stricken with a horrible disease rather than come to believe in her Creator? That is what Lenin says, that cancer is better than religion."

The political officer called Richard up and slapped his face. He considered the blow a modest price to pay for upholding his beliefs.

Clearly, there was more indoctrination to come. They puzzled over the silent loudspeakers. Until recently they had been starved, beaten, abused, but no one seemed to care what they thought. Commandant Dorabantu, removed for falsifying accounts, used to say, "Invent all the new cabinets you like in your cells, you bandits. We have the government in Bucharest."

The lectures showed how this attitude had changed, following the new policy of Gheorghiu-Dej, Romania's dictator, who was trying to ease the Kremlin's grip in order to do business with the West. For this Dej had to show a more democratic façade. The army of political prisoners was an embarrassment to him, yet he couldn't simply set them free to spread counterrevolutionary beliefs. Their ways of thought were to be altered by mass brainwashing.

To prisoners in Gherla in 1962, this was one theory among many, and few believed it. There was uncertainty about what actually happened in brainwashing. Feelings were summed up by Radu Ghinda, a well-known author and Christian writer, who recently had joined them: "If they haven't changed me in fifteen years, how will they do so now?"

When theories about brainwashing were being discussed one evening, Ghinda scoffed: "Rubbish. Pavlov played tricks with the behavior-patterns of dogs, and the Communists in Korea adapted some of his ideas to make American prisoners change sides. These methods won't work on people of education and intelligence. We're not G.I.s."

"Nor dogs," said another.

No one disagreed.

The loudspeaker on the wall at last crackled into life. "One-two-three-four-testing," said a voice repeatedly. Then came the words, "Communism is good." A pause. More crackling. The voice returned with increased volume, resonance, and authority:

Communism is good
Communism is good
Communism is good
Communism is good

It continued all night and into the next day. Soon Richard was only intermittently conscious of the tape-recorded words, but still they penetrated his mind, and when finally the voice stopped, the words rang in his head: "Communism is good, Communism is good, Communism is good."

Weingartner said this was the first stage in a long process. "Our rulers have learned it from the Russians and the Russians from Peking. Next it will be public confession. Under Mao-Tse-Tung, the Chinese must attend lectures in their factories, offices, and streets. Then they are made to denounce themselves, to say how they plotted against the proletariat, five, ten, or twenty years ago. If you don't confess you're imprisoned as a stubborn counter-revolutionary. If you do confess, you go to jail for what you have said. So people try to confess and yet not to confess, to admit to treacherous thoughts, while denying they have acted on them. They denounce each other. Trust between friends and in families is destroyed. The same procedure has begun with us."

"How long will it last?" asked Gaston.

"Until you believe Communism is good; perhaps for years," said Weingartner.

The next lecturer was plump and jolly. He told of the wonderful new Romania that was developing under Gheorghiu-Dej's Sixteen-year Plan and of the paradise those whom the Party considered worthy were already enjoying. He described the privileges granted to loyal workers, the good food, the flowing wine, the glorious holidays at Black Sea resorts with girls in bikinis everywhere.

"But I forget," he laughed. "Most of you fellows have never seen a bikini. You don't even know what it is, poor chaps. Let me explain. The best things in life aren't left to the decadent West."

His eyes gleamed and his voice became thick as he began a gloating description of breast and belly and thigh, and mixed the pleasures of wine and travel into his gross talk. Richard had never seen on human faces such hungry lust as he then saw on most of those around him in the big hall. He felt they were ugly and frightening, suggesting animals in heat. Their human decency was stripped away by the man's unbridled talk, and only sensual greed remained.

The lecturer concluded, "So much pleasure waits for you outside. There's the door. You can open it, if you choose. Throw off the reactionary garbage of ideas that have made criminals of you. Come to our side. Learn to be free."

Little was said after these talks. No one thought of the wives and hard work that awaited them outside. The raw desire that is part of one's will to live had been skillfully revived.

The prisoners had been kept for months on low rations and were weighed regularly to ensure they remained forty pounds below normal. The food improved, but Richard thought it had a strange flavor and he suspected the presence of aphrodisiacs. Imprisoned doctors later agreed with him that sexually-stimulating drugs had been added to their meals. The doctors and the clerks who came to read out an announcement or a court verdict were nearly always young women who wore tight, teasing dresses and used perfume and make-up. They seemed to linger deliberately in the cells.

"You've only one life," the lecturer said each day. "It passes quickly. How much time have you left? Throw in your lot with us. We want to help you make the most of it."

This appeal to the ego, the self-enhancing, self-protective side of one's nature, came when primitive emotions were in ferment. Finally, as the veneer cracked, came the appeal to the super-ego, their conscience, social values, and ethical standards. The lecturers told them their patriotism had been false, their ideals a fraud, and in their place they tried to plant Communist ideology.

These mass-suggestion sessions were called "struggle meetings." The struggle never stopped. "What are your wives doing now?" asked the jolly lecturer. "What you'd like to be doing yourselves." They were exhausted and hysteria was close. Every hour that lectures weren't in progress, the tape-recorders ground out the message that Communism was good. Prisoners quarreled among themselves.

Daianu, poet and Professor of Mystical Theology, was the first to break. At the end of a lecture, he jumped to his feet and began to babble about his crimes against the State. "I see it now, I see it all. I have thrown away my life for a false cause." He blamed his landowning parents for putting him on the wrong road. He repudiated his faith, the saints, and the sacraments. He ranted against superstition and blasphemed against God. On and on he went.

Radu Ghinda stood up and continued in the same vein. "I have been a fool," he shouted. "I have been misled by capitalist and Christian lies. Never again will I set foot in a church except to spit in it."

With greater enthusiasm than the lecturers themselves, Daianu and Ghinda called on the prisoners to give up their old beliefs. Both were gifted speakers, and many who heard their eloquent praise of the joy and liberty Communism brings were deeply shaken, convinced they spoke from genuine faith.

When Ghinda sat down, a gaunt, trembling old man shouted, "You all know me—General Silvianu of the Royal Army. I disown my rank and loyalty. I am ashamed at the role I played in making criminal war on our ally, Russia. I served the exploiting classes. I disgraced my country."

The general was followed by an ex-police chief, who confessed that Communism would have come to power sooner had the police not hindered it.

One after another, men stood and parroted their confessions. Richard realized this was the first fruit of months of planned starvation, degradation, and exposure to mass suggestion. The first to give way were those, like Daianu and Ghinda, whose lives were already eaten by private guilt. Daianu had preached asceticism but practiced gluttony and womanizing. After telling students to give up the world for God, he became a propagandist for Hitler. His poems, fine as they were, expressed aspirations, not fulfillment. Ghinda, too, was torn ideologically by anti-Semitism on the one hand and his faith on the other. Both men were growing old. They had served more than fifteen years in prison and faced many more.

Others in the priests' room didn't yield so quickly. For them further suffering lay in store. Quarrels, at least, came to a halt. They learned that all their denominations could be reduced to two factors: hatred, which makes ritual and dogma a pretext for attacking others; love, in which men of all kinds realize their oneness and brotherhood before God. Now it was as if the cell were ablaze with the spirit of self-sacrifice and renewed faith. To Richard it seemed the angels were all around them.

Many were ready to sacrifice their ration of bread for communion. The Orthodox ritual required that the bread be consecrated over an altar containing a relic from the body of a martyr. There was no relic.

"We have living martyrs with us," said Father Andricu. They consecrated the bread and a little wine in a chipped cup, which had been smuggled from the hospital over the body of Bishop Mirza as he lay ill in bed.

Soon the prisoners who had been "converted" to Communism, were asked to lecture to the others. They did so with passion, believing their release depended on their efforts. Word went around of a terrible sequel to the defection of Daianu and Ghinda. Two members of the Iron Guard stole a chisel from the carpenter's shop, opened their veins, and bled to death in protest.

Richard found Daianu and Ghinda in a corner of the cell. "What do you think of yourselves now that your betrayal has cost the lives of two men who believed in you?" he asked.

Ghinda said, "They died so that the people may live."

"A week ago you were counted among the enemies of the people yourselves."

Daianu burst out, "I mean to get out of here, whoever suffers."

Feeling against them became so strong they were moved to another cell. Miron said, "Strange that men who wrote with what seemed deep Christian faith should turn traitor so easily."

Richard felt perhaps the answer was that in their writings they praised Christ for His gifts—peace, love, and salvation. He thought a real disciple doesn't seek gifts, but Christ himself, and so is ready for self-sacrifice to the end. They weren't followers of Jesus, but customers.

When the Communists opened a shop next door with goods at lower prices, they took their business there.

During 1963 Richard became very ill again and was moved to the prison hospital. He had been there one week when every man was ordered up. Some could hardly walk. They helped each other out into a big yard where the whole prison had been assembled. They stood while an hour-long play was acted by chosen prisoners. The play mocked Christianity. When the officers surrounding the commandant clapped or laughed, the audience did the same.

When it was over, Alexandrescu asked for positive comments. It wasn't enough to show approval; reasons had to be given. Daianu and Ghinda led the way. One after another, men went up to repeat slogans against religion. As they rejoined the ranks, some embraced Richard tearfully, and said, "We *must* say these things until it's over."

When the commandant called Richard up, he remembered what Sabina had said to him many years before at the Congress of Cults: "Go and wash this shame from the face of Christ."

He was well known at Gherla; he had been in so many cells. Hundreds of eyes were on him, and they all seemed to ask one question: "Will he praise Communism too?"

Major Alexandrescu called, "Go on. Speak."

Richard began cautiously, "It is Sunday morning, and our wives and mothers and children are praying for us, in church or at home. We should have liked to pray for them too. Instead, we have watched this play."

As he spoke of their families, tears came into the eyes of prisoners. He continued, "Many here have spoken against Jesus. What is it you have against Him? You speak of the proletariat; wasn't Jesus a carpenter? You say that he who doesn't work shall not eat. This was said long ago in St. Paul's Epistle to the Thessalonians. You speak against the wealthy. Jesus drove the moneylenders from the temple with whips. You want Communism. Don't forget the first Christians lived in a community, sharing all they had. You wish to raise up the poor. The Magnificat, the virgin Mary's song at Jesus' birth, says God will exalt the poor above the rich. All that is good in Communism comes from the Christians.

"Marx said that all proletarians must unite, but some are Communists, some are Socialists, and some are Christian. If we mock each other, we cannot unite. I would never mock an atheist. Even from the Marxist point of view this is wrong, for if you mock, you split the proletariat.

"In his introduction to *Das Kapital*, Marx says Christianity is the ideal religion for remaking a life destroyed by sin. Is there anybody, even a Communist, who is without sin? If you haven't sinned against God, then you have against the Party." He gave them many quotations from their own authors. Major Alexandrescu shifted in his chair and kicked the ground with his toe, but he didn't interrupt.

The prisoners, too, were quiet, and seeing they were moved, Richard forgot where he was and began to preach openly about Christ, and what He had done for them, and what He meant to them. He said, "Just as no one has heard of a school without examinations, or a factory where work isn't scrutinized to see that it is good, so all of us will be judged, by ourselves, by our fellows, by God. You too will be judged, Major Alexandrescu."

The major let it pass again. Richard concluded, "Jesus teaches love and gives eternal life." As he returned to his place, the prisoners burst into cheers.

Miron said, "You have undone all their work."

Gaston whispered, "Did you hear the cheers?"

Richard answered, "They were cheering what they had found in their own hearts, not me."

Until now only a noisy minority of priests had fallen under the influence of brainwashing. Those who opposed it openly were also few, but their sympathizers were many, even if they lacked the courage or the wit to fight back. As a result of his speech, Richard lost his sanctuary in the prison hospital and was sent back to the priests' room.

Daianu and Rada Ghinda, in their private cells, volunteered to write about the wonders of the People's Republic, which neither of them had seen for fifteen years. For this task they were given pen and paper, Party literature, and tourist propaganda. The two men made full use of this chance to prove their new convictions. Some weeks later they were freed. It was a powerful blow against the open resistance.

Lieutenant Konya, the political officer, brought a newspaper into the priests' room and told Father Andricu to read it aloud. He read the headline: "A COUNTRY THAT LAUGHS AND HEARTS THAT SING." It was an article by Ghinda with a smiling photograph of himself. Daianu also lent his name to glorification of freedom in Socialist Romania.

Konya said, "We want you to know everyone of you has the same chance of freedom and work, as soon as you give up your nonsensical, out-of-date beliefs and join the people of the new Romania." He didn't tell them that Daianu's and Ghinda's articles were published only in the West and couldn't be obtained in Romania.

Everyone was excited at the two men's release. Many who had suffered cruelty and humiliation for years, without giving way, began to waver. But those who did yield, instead of being freed, had to prove their conversion by volunteering to work sixteen hours a day. On returning to their cells they had to attend more lectures, or else give them. They had to keep a "temperature chart of political health," which meant everyone had to write about his neighbors' attitude to Communism, whether it was lukewarm, cold, or hostile.

The reports on Richard evidently weren't good. Konya brought him two pieces of news: that Sabina had been in prison for a long time and that he was to be flogged at ten that evening because of his repeated defiance and insolence.

The news about Sabina was a terrible shock, and his pain at the thought of it added to his fear of the beating to come. They all dreaded this period of waiting. Time dragged until he heard footsteps coming down the passage. The tramping boots went by. Someone had been taken from the adjacent cell. Presently he heard blows and screams from the room at the end of the corridor. Nobody came for him that night.

Each morning he was again warned. For six days the suspense was maintained. Then he was led up the passage. The blows burned like fire. When it was over, Konya, who supervised, shouted, "Give him some more." He was slow in getting to his feet. "Ten more," ordered Konya. He was half carried back to the cell, where the loudspeakers were blaring:

> *Christianity is stupid*
> *Christianity is stupid*
> *Christianity is stupid*
> *Why not give it up?*
> *Why not give it up?*
> *Why not give it up?*
> *Christianity is stupid*
> *Christianity is stupid*
> *Christianity is stupid*
> *Why not give it up?*

Sometimes beatings were administered by guards in the cells for "minor irregularities."

"Drop your trousers for a beating." They dropped them. "Lie on your bellies." They did. "Turn over on your backs. Hold your feet up." They rolled over.

They kept trying to pray. Sometimes a priest would lament, "I call on 'Our Father' but what kind of father, what kind of God abandons me to my enemies like this?"

The others urged him, "Don't give way. Go on saying 'Our Father.' Be obstinate. By persisting you will renew your faith." He could listen to them because they shared his suffering.

One evening, Konya told Richard to gather his things. "Since you haven't responded to treatment," he said, "a spell in the special block might help." There were many rumors about this section of the prison. Those who returned from it were few. They either died or succumbed to brainwashing and were moved out. Some joined the indoctrination staff and learned to brainwash others.

They crossed the yard, turned several corners, and stopped before a row of doors. One was opened and double-locked behind him.

He found himself alone in a white-tiled cell. The ceiling reflected blinding white light from concealed lamps. Although it was summer, the steam heating, which functioned nowhere else in Gherla, was full on. Konya had left him in handcuffs so that he could lie only on his side or back. He was soon soaked in sweat. The spy-hole clicked open and the guard giggled, "Something wrong with the heating?" His stomach ached. There had been a peculiar taste in the food, and he thought it was drugged again. The loudspeakers here had a new message:

> *Nobody believes in Christ now*
> *Nobody believes in Christ now*
> *Nobody believes in Christ now*
> *No one goes to church*
> *No one goes to church*
> *Give it up*
> *Give it up*
> *Give it up*
> *Nobody believes in Christ now*

In the morning Konya unlocked his handcuffs and ordered him to follow him down the corridor.

A new cell and fresh clothes awaited him. He saw a bed with sheets, a table with a cloth, flowers in a vase. It was too much. He sat down and wept. When Konya left, Richard regained his composure. He looked at a newspaper on the table, the first he had seen in all his years of imprisonment. He searched for news to confirm a rumor going around Gherla, that the U.S. Sixth Fleet had entered the Black Sea to demand free elections in the captive countries. Instead, he found an item about a Communist dictator who had taken power in Cuba and was defying America on her own doorstep.

His first visitor was Commandant Alexandrescu, who told him his new surroundings were a sample of the good life which was open to him. He began to attack religion. Christ, he said, was a fantasy invented by the Apostles to delude slaves into hopes of freedom in paradise.

Richard picked up the newspaper and handed it to him. "This is printed on the Party presses. It is dated July, 1963. That means 1,963 years since the birth of someone who, according to you, never existed. You don't believe in Christ, but you accept him as the founder of our civilization."

"It means nothing; it's customary to count that way."

"But if Christ never came on earth, how did the custom arise?"

"Some liars started it."

"Suppose you tell me the Russians have landed on Mars. I need not believe you, but if I hear on the radio the Americans congratulate them, I know it must be true. In the same way, we must accept Christ's existence as a historical fact when it is recognized in the Talmud by his worst enemies, the Pharisees, who also name his mother and some of the Apostles. Only Communists deny this plain fact of history, because it doesn't suit their theory."

Alexandrescu didn't pursue the argument. Instead, he sent him a book. It pleased him to have a book in his hands after all these years, even if it was only *The Atheist's Guide*. This manual, unknown in the West, was essential reading for all those who wished to make themselves careers behind the Iron Curtain.

During the next few weeks Richard alternated between promises and threats, between his flowery private room and the blinding cell with loudspeakers, between good meals and starvation, between argument and punishment.

While undergoing the heat treatment one morning, he was joined by Father Andricu, the former "Red priest" who had repented. Andricu sat panting until he could bear no more. He jumped up and pounded on the door, begging to be let out. Alexandrescu came and said, "It can be hotter yet, or you could be free men if you chose. If you were released, how would you act and what kind of sermons would you preach? I want you to write a draft." He gave them pen and paper and left.

They sat down and wrote. When they had finished they exchanged papers. Defensively, Andricu said, "You can hear sermons like that every Sunday, progressive, in a scientific Marxist way."

"Don't deceive yourself, Father Andricu. You know this is a recantation of all you believe. Even if a priest loses his faith he should be silent. I don't speak of judgment before God. What would your parishioners, your friends, your family think if they heard you preach this stuff? Don't let the Communists cheat you again. They buy you with promises they never keep."

Richard argued for a long time with Andricu, telling him that in his heart he knew the truth of Christianity. At last he said, "Give me back the sermons." He tore them into pieces.

A new series of "struggle meetings" attended by hundreds of prisoners began in the main hall. The special block prisoners were sent to hear them. Most lectures were now being delivered by men recently "converted." After instruction, they came back to sing praises of the Communism that had given them years of suffering. Attacks on religion were often based on modern theologians who deny the scriptures: propagandists like those of the "God is dead" school. "Study your own thinkers. They have proved there is no objective truth in Christianity."

For twelve hours a day they listened to lectures, joined discussions, absorbed the tape-recorded slogans.

In each cell a few men reported daily on the political health of the others. Those who knuckled under to them were fairly safe. Those who didn't usually ended in the special block. Informing touched everyone like a fever.

On August 23, the anniversary of the armistice with Russia, most prisoners were ready to believe whatever they were told. A large meeting in the hall was addressed by Alexandrescu. "We have good news." He announced that the peasants' seized farms were flourishing in the collectives. Former merchants and bankers applauded when told that trade was booming.

"Some of you," said the commandant, "are seeing reason at last. Others are being very foolish. You idiots! You have sat in prison for fifteen years waiting for the Americans to come and free you. I have news for you. The Americans are coming, but not to release you. They are coming to do business with us."

Alexandrescu said the Party had taken steps to win commercial favor in the West. Loans were being raised, factories built, nuclear plants operated, all with Western aid. "You fools. You've all been living in illusion. We know the Americans better than you. If you beg, they give you nothing. If you insult and mock them, you get all you want. We've been cleverer than you."

Somebody laughed. Others joined in. Soon the whole hall was rocking with laughter. The commandant raised his hand and announced they would be allowed to watch the Freedom Day celebrations on the newly installed television. When it was over, Alexandrescu said, "We shall now discuss the celebrations."

One after another the prisoners testified, ending with the cry, "August 23 has brought us freedom."

Richard started in the mood of the day. "If there's anyone to whom August 23 has brought liberty, it is I. The Fascists hated me, and if Hitler had won his war I should be a piece of soap by now. But I'm alive." There were approving murmurs.

"But in another way, I was free before August 23. Let me tell you how. In ancient times the Tyrant of Syracuse read the book of Epictetus, the philosopher-slave, and admired it so greatly he offered to set him free. 'Free yourself,' said Epictetus. The Tyrant protested, 'But I'm the king.' The slave answered, 'A tyrant ruled by his lusts is in bondage; a slave who rules his passions is free. King, free yourself.'"

The hall was quiet now. "Although I'm in prison, I'm free. I have been freed by Jesus from my guilt and from darkness in my mind. I can thank the events of August 23 for freeing me from Fascism. For the other freedom, the freedom from all that is transitory, from death, I thank Jesus."

The commandant jumped to his feet. "Tell that nonsense to Gargarin. He's been up in space, but he saw no sign of God." He laughed and the prisoners laughed with him.

"If an ant walked around the sole of my shoe, it could say it saw no sign of Wurmbrand."

He was punished by another term in the special block. It was there that Alexandrescu made a special visit to inform him of President Kennedy's assassination. "What do you think about that?"

"I can't believe it." He showed him a newspaper in which it was reported in a single paragraph.

"Well?" he insisted.

"If Kennedy was a Christian he is now happy in heaven." Alexandrescu walked out.

At a later time guards came for him, blindfolded him, and led him to a distant part of the prison, he thought perhaps for execution. He remained outside a door with a guard who, in the past, had listened when he spoke of Christ. The guard whispered, "My poor friend. You're having a hard time, but in God's name, go on." He moved some paces away. Richard said his words warmed him.

Richard addressing VOM

He was led into the presence of General Negrea, the Deputy-Minister of the Interior, who was flanked by a political officer and some officials from Bucharest.

Negrea said, "I've been studying your case, Mr. Wurmbrand. I don't care for your views, but I like a man who sticks to his guns. We Communists are obstinate too. I've often been in prison myself and plenty was done to make me change my mind, but I stood firm.

"I believe it's time we met half-way. If you're prepared to forget what you've suffered, we'd forget what you've done against us. We could become friends instead of enemies. You could enter a period of fruitful cooperation. I've even read your sermons. The explanations of the Bible are beautifully put, but you must realize we live in a scientific age." He went into the Party's science lecture. At last, his discourse came to an end.

"We need men like you. We don't want people to join us out of opportunism, but because they see the fallacies of their past thinking. If you are prepared to help us in the struggle against superstition, you can start a new life at once. You will have a post with a high salary and your family around you again in comfort and in safety. What do you say?"

He replied that he found joy in the life he was already leading; but as for helping the Party, he had thought of a way of doing so if released.

"You mean you'll work for us?"

"I suggest you send me from town to town and village to village along with the best Marxist teacher you have. First I shall expose my ignorance and the stupidities of my retrograde Christian religion; then your Marxist can explain his theories, and the people will be able to make up their own minds."

Negrea gave him a hard stare. "You're provoking us, Mr. Wurmbrand. That's what I like about you. It's just the way we Communists used to answer the bosses in the old days. So let's not argue. I'll make you a better proposal still. Nobody wants you to become an atheist propagandist. If you're really so attached to an outworn faith, though I can't understand how a cultured man can accept such nonsense, then keep to it. But also keep in mind that we have the power. Communism has conquered a third of the world; the Church must come to terms with us.

"Let's put our cards on the table for once. Frankly we're tired of church leaders who do everything in the eyes of the people; they're no longer in touch with what's going on." One by one, Negrea named the remaining bishops. All were powerless or Party men, and everybody knew it, he said. "Now if a man like you became a bishop, you could have your faith and still be loyal to the régime. Your Bible says you should submit to authority because it comes from God. So why not to ours?"

Richard made no response. Negrea asked the other officials to leave. He was convinced that Richard would accept the offer, and gave him his confidence on something he didn't want the others to hear.

"The Party made a mistake in attacking your World Council of Churches. It began as a spy-ring; but the pastors concerned are often of proletarian origin. They aren't shareholders, so to speak, but superior servants. Instead of opposing such men we should win them over to our side so that the council itself becomes our instrument.

"Mr. Wurmbrand, this is where you can help. You've worked for the World Council of Churches. You're known widely abroad; we still get many enquiries about you. If you became a bishop, you could help our other WCC allies to build a bulwark for us, not of atheism, but of Socialism and peace. Surely you recognize the universal idealism behind our campaigns to ban the bomb and outlaw war. And you'll be able to worship to your heart's content. There we won't interfere."

Richard thought for a moment. "How far must this cooperation go? Bishops who worked with you in the past have had to inform on their own priests. Will I be expected to do that too?"

Negrea laughed. "You'd be under no special obligation by virtue of your office. Everyone who knows of any act which may harm the State is obliged to denounce the man who does. As a bishop you'll certainly hear such things."

He asked for time to reflect and Negrea agreed. "We'll meet before I leave for Bucharest to put your release papers through."

He was taken back to an isolation cell and lay thinking for many hours. On one hand he felt that "no" was the only answer and that he should have replied at once. On the other hand, he knew the official church in a Communist country can survive only through some compromise. It was easy to say the church could go underground, but an underground church needs cover for its work. Lacking this cover, millions of people would be left with nowhere to meet for worship, no pastor to preach, no one to baptize them, marry them, bury their dead; an unthinkable alternative, when he could help to avoid it by saying a few words in favor of collectivization or the so-called peace campaigns.

And then, he hadn't seen Sabina or Mihai for many years. He didn't know if they were alive. The political officer had said Sabina was in prison. What would become of her and Mihai if he refused this proposal?

He needed strength from above to say no, when doing so meant eleven more years of prison, with the sacrifice of his family and almost certain death under horrible conditions. At that moment faith failed him. His imagination was overcome by the danger of dying, being beaten again and again, and the hunger and privations to which he was condemning his wife and son. His soul was like a ship driven from side to side, rocked by a violent tempest. In those hours he drank the cup of Christ; it was for him the Garden of Gethsemane. Like Jesus, he threw himself facedown upon the earth and prayed with broken cries, asking God to help him overcome this horrible temptation.

After prayer he felt a little quieter. He began to think carefully of all the times he had argued the truth of Christianity. He asked himself: is the way of love better than hatred? Has Christ lifted the burden of sin and doubt from his shoulders? Is He the Savior? There was no difficulty eventually in answering "yes." When he had done so, it was as if a great weight had been lifted from his mind.

For an hour he lay on his bed saying to himself, "I shall try now not to think of Christ." The effort failed. He could think of nothing else. In his heart was a void without Christianity. For one last time he thought of Negrea's proposal. His visiting card would read: "Richard Wurmbrand, Lutheran Bishop of Romania, by appointment of the Secret Police." He would not be a bishop of Christ in a holy place, but a police spy in a state institution. He prayed again and afterwards felt tranquillity of soul.

Next day he was called again before Negrea.

Alexandrescu and others were present. When he said he could not accept, the whole question was argued again. When they reached the subject of the World Council of Churches, Negrea again asked the others to leave and asked him to reconsider his refusal.

Richard replied that he didn't feel worthy to be a bishop, or a pastor, or even a simple Christian because he had considered Negrea's shameful offer. Again he refused to accept it.

"We'll find another one who will."

"If you believe you can prove I'm wrong, bring me your atheist arguments. I have the arguments for my faith, and I seek only the truth."

"You know what this will mean for your future?"

"I have considered well and weighed the dangers, and I rejoice to suffer for what I'm sure is the ultimate truth."

Polite to the last, Negrea nodded to him, closed his briefcase, walked to the window, and stood looking out while the guards handcuffed and led him away.

For a long time he remained in the special block, for how long he isn't sure. Time telescoped all the days of certain periods in his prison life into one enormous day. Brainwashing increased in intensity. The loudspeakers now said:

Christianity is dead
Christianity is dead
Christianity is dead

He recalls one day. Prisoners had been given postcards to invite families to come and bring parcels. On visiting day, he was shaved and washed and given a clean shirt. Hours passed. He sat in the cell staring at the glittering white tiles, but no one came. Evening brought only a change of guards. He was not to know then that his postcard had never been sent. The same trick was played on other stubborn prisoners. The loudspeakers were saying:

> *Nobody loves you now*
> *Nobody loves you now*
> *Nobody loves you now*

He began to weep. The loudspeaker said:

> *They don't want to know you anymore*
> *They don't want to know you anymore*
> *They don't want to know you anymore*

He could not bear to hear these words, nor could he shut them out.

Next day brought a brutal "struggle meeting," confined to the disappointed men. Plenty of other wives had come, the lecturer told them. They were the fools. They had been abandoned. Their womenfolk were in bed with other men, at that very moment. He went into obscene detail. "And where are your children? Out in the streets, all atheists." They had no wish to see their fathers. How stupid they were.

In the special block, he listened to the speaker day after day.

> *Christianity is dead*
> *Christianity is dead*
> *Christianity is dead*

In time he came to believe what they had told them for all those months. Christianity was dead. The Bible foretells a time of great apostasy, and he believed it had arrived.

Then he thought of Mary Magdalene. Perhaps this thought, more than any other, helped to save him from the soul-killing poison of the last and worst stage of brainwashing. He remembered how she was faithful to Christ even when he cried on the Cross, "My God, why have You forsaken Me?" And when He was a corpse in the tomb, she wept nearby and waited until He arose. So when at last he believed Christianity was dead, he said, "Even so, I will believe in it, and I will weep at its tomb until it arises again, as it surely will."

In June 1964, all prisoners were gathered in the main hall. Major Alexandrescu announced that under the terms of a general amnesty granted by the government, political prisoners of every category were to be freed. Richard had trouble believing it. At first, he thought it must be another trick.

But it wasn't. The summer of that year saw the release of innumerable thousands of prisoners. For this they had to thank another so-called thaw between East and West. Also Richard learned later that Prime Minister Gheorghiu-Dej had had a true change of heart. After many years of doubting Communist dogma, he had returned to the faith in which his mother had raised him. Dej had been converted through a maidservant in his home, and her uncle, a good old man who often spoke to him of the Bible. Christianity, although he didn't confess it openly, gave him the strength to defy his Soviet masters. Ignoring their threats, he opened new relations with the West and in doing so set an example for other captive countries. He died a few months later, his end being hastened, it is said, by Soviet agents.

Richard's turn for release finally came. He was one of the last group of a hundred or so men gathered in the big hall. They were almost the last prisoners left in Gherla. The corridors were strangely silent. His hair was cut and he was given worn but clean clothes.

While waiting, he heard a man call, "Brother Wurmbrand." The man came up and said he was from Sibiu. Richard assumed he was a member of their church there. "I've heard so much about you from your son. We shared a cell."

"My son? In prison? No, no, you're mistaken."

"You mean you didn't know? He's been in jail six years now."

He turned away and the man left. The blow was almost more than he could bear. His mind was still frozen with pain and shock when Alexandrescu came up. "Well, Wurmbrand, where will you go now that you are free?"

"I don't know. I've been told officially my wife is in prison, and now I hear my only son is too. I have nobody else."

"The boy too? How do you feel having a jailbird for a son?"

"I am sure he isn't in jail for theft or any other crime. If he is there for Christ's sake, then I am proud of him."

"What! We spend all this money keeping you for years, and you think it's something to be proud of to have a family in prison for such things?"

"I didn't want you to spend anything on me." They parted. Richard walked out of prison. The streets of Gherla dazzled him. He startled when cars whizzed past. Colors shocked his eyes. Radio music coming through an open window had a rich texture. The air smelled clean and fresh. But everything was saddened by the thought of Sabina and Mihai in prison.

He went by bus to the nearby town of Cluj, where he had friends. They had moved. He tramped from house to house until he found them. His overjoyed friends brought out cake and fruit and all kinds of good things. A beautiful brown onion was on the table and that was what he wanted. Often he had hankered for an onion to take away the taste of prison food.

He made a telephone call to a neighbor in Bucharest. Sabina answered. "It's Richard," he said. "I thought you were in prison."

Noisy confusion took over. Mihai came on the phone. "Mother's fainted. Hold on." After another noisy interval, Mihai said, "She's all right. We thought you were dead."

Richard learned that Mihai had never been in prison and the news had been given as a last turn of the screw to test his reactions to brainwashing.

He took the train to Bucharest. As it drew into the station, he saw a crowd of men, women, and children with arms full of flowers. He wondered what lucky person was receiving such a welcome. Then he recognized faces and leaned from a window to wave. As he climbed down, it seemed as if the entire congregation of his church was running to meet him. Then his arms were around Sabina and Mihai.

That night Sabina told him she had been given news of his death years before. She said she refused to believe it even when strangers called on her who claimed to be ex-prisoners and said they had attended his burial. "I will wait for him," she had said. The years passed and no word came until his call from Cluj.

For Sabina it was as if he had been resurrected from the dead.

CHAPTER 18

While in the depths of despair in prison, Richard composed and memorized a poem which he later recorded in Romanian and translated into English. It is presented here as:

Richard's Lament

From childhood I frequented temples and churches.
In them God was glorified.
Priests sang and censed with zeal.
They claimed it right to love You.
But as I grew
I saw such deep sorrow in this God's world that I said to myself,
"He has a heart of stone.
Otherwise He would ease the difficulties of the way for us."
Sick children struggle in hospital.
Sad parents pray for them.
Heaven is deaf.
The ones we love go to the valley of death even when our prayers are long.
Innocent men are burned alive in furnaces.
And heaven is silent.
It lets things be.
Can God wonder if in undertones even the believers begin to doubt?

Hungry, tortured, persecuted in their own land, they have
    no answers.
The Almighty is disgraced
by the horrors that befall us.
How can I love the creator
of microbes and tigers
that tear men?
How can I love Him
who tortures all His servants
because one ate from a tree?
Sadder than Job, I have neither
wife, child, nor comforters,
and in this prison there
is neither sun nor air
and the regime is hard
to endure.
From my bed of planks
they will make my coffin.
Stretched upon it, I try
to find why my thoughts
run to You, why my
writings all turn
towards You.
Why is this passionate love
in my soul, why does my song
go only to You?
I know I am rejected; soon
I will putrefy in a tomb.
The bride of the Song of Songs
did not love when she asked
if You are "rightly loved."
Love is its own justification.
Love is not for the wise.
Through a thousand ordeals
she will not cease to love.

Though fire burns
and the waves drown her
she will kiss the hand that hurts.
If she finds no answer
to her questions
she is confident and waits.
One day the sun will shine
in hidden places
and all will be made plain.
Forgiveness of many sins
only increased Magdalene's
burning love.
But she gave perfume
and shed tears before You
said Your forgiving word.
And had You not said it,
still she would have sat
and wept for the love
she has towards You,
even being in sin.
She loved You before Your
blood was shed.
She loved You before You forgave.
Neither do I ask if it is right
to give You love.
I do not love in hope
of salvation. I would love
You in everlasting
misfortune.
I would love You even
in consuming fire.
If You had refused
to descend to men, You would have been
my distant dream.
If You had refused to sow

Your word, I would love You
without hearing it.
If You had hesitated and fled
from the Crucifixion,
and I were not saved,
still I would love You.
And even if I found sin in You,
I would cover it with my love.
Now I will dare to say mad words,
so that all may know how
much I love.
Now I will touch untouched strings
and magnify You with
a new music.
If the prophets had predicted
another, I would leave
them, not You.
Let them produce
a thousand proofs,
I will keep my love for You.
If I divined that You were
a deceiver, I would pray
for You weeping and, though
I could not follow you in falsehood,
it would not lessen my love.
For Saul, Samuel passed a life
in weeping and severe fasting.
So my love would resist
even if I knew You lost.
If You, not Satan, had risen
wrongly in revolt against
Heaven and lost the loveliness
of wings and fallen like
an archangel from high, hopeless,
I would hope that the Father

would forgive You and that
one day You would walk with Him
again in the gold streets of Heaven.

If You were a myth, I would leave
reality and live with You
in a dream.

If they proved
You did not exist, You would receive life
from my love.
My love is mad, without motive,
as Your love is, too.
Lord Jesus, find some happiness
here. For more I cannot
give You.

Richard said that when he completed this poem, he no longer felt the nearness of Satan. In the silence he felt the kiss of Christ. Quiet and joy returned to him.

CHAPTER 19

Richard Wurmbrand was born March 24, 1909 in Bucharest, Romania to Henry and Emilia (Eckstein) Wurmbrand. The Wurmbrands, of German extraction, had moved to Bucharest from the German-speaking province of Bukovina, then under Russian control. German was the dominant language in the Wurmbrand home, but Richard heard enough Russian to be able to speak it fluently.

Richard had a sister and three older brothers, one of whom, Max, is still (1996) living at the age of 92. A sister, Mary, died before Richard was born. When he was one year of age, his father, a dentist, moved the family to Istanbul, seeking better living conditions, it is believed, although the move has been vaguely described as war-related.

Richard received little formal education, but Henry had a well-stocked library that he availed himself of avidly. By the time he was ten he had read every available book including Voltaire, who no doubt influenced his thinking so that by the age of 14 he was an avowed atheist and considered religion harmful to the human mind.

Nevertheless, while living in Istanbul he was fascinated by places of worship. He had no religious training at home and wondered what it was all about. He never had a bar mitzvah, the Jewish rite of passage.

One day while walking with a friend in Istanbul, he was asked to wait outside while his friend delivered a message to the priest.

Curiosity made Richard follow. The priest put his hand on Richard's head and asked what he could do for him. When he had no request, the priest said, "As a Christian I must do something for you. Please let me get you a glass of cold water." This little episode made a lasting impression on him.

Richard describes his father as taciturn and feels he never really knew him. He cannot recall his father ever speaking to him, even in the hospital on the day of his death from pandemic influenza in 1918. He was aware that his father had been in touch with the Gospel but was apparently unable to communicate what he knew.

Henry was buried with a simple ceremony, as was the custom with the poor. The coffin was made of unpainted planks. An elderly Jew said the prayer, "*El mole rahamim*," meaning "God full of mercy." When they returned to their home his mother fainted.

In 1922, when Richard was 13, Emilia took her family back to Bucharest. She provided them with what little food and clothing she could secure. But times were difficult and Richard's early years were lived in poverty. A brief review of history sheds light on Romania in the twenties. In 1878, the Congress of Berlin gave Romania its independence and a German prince for its king, influencing Romania to be on Germany's side at the beginning of World War I. When King Carol died in 1916 he was succeeded by Ferdinand, whose wife was Queen Marie, granddaughter of Queen Victoria. She caused Romania to switch its allegiance to the Allies. An army of Germans, Bulgarians, and Turks immediately occupied Romania, and a period of starvation and epidemics ensued.

In contrast to his relationship with his father, Richard has better memories of his mother. He remembers turning the handle of her sewing machine as she sewed. Sometimes she would sing to him—but always the same two songs, both of which were Christian hymns. Her favorite was "Silent Night." He doesn't know where his mother, a Jewess, learned them. When he became a Christian, he read to her the story of the Passion. She wept over it but never spoke about it afterwards. He says that when he became a Christian it was a deadly blow to her.

He is probably oversensitive about his sinful life as a child. He admits to throwing a knife at his mother when he was about six. He considered himself a disobedient son.

As he grew older, he wasn't happy as an atheist. He kept searching for a god who he believed didn't exist. Not believing in a higher power left a void in his life. He found it difficult to pass churches. He was fascinated by statuary in Catholic churches but was disenchanted because he couldn't understand the Latin services. He was displeased with the synagogue because he didn't understand Hebrew and the rabbis ignored him. He disliked the Greek Orthodox church because of its anti-Semitism. He remembers that a priest sicced his dogs on him because he was a Jew.

In the early 1930s Richard entered the race for material wealth. He admits to shady deals but at the time dismissed dishonesty as clever dealing. By the age of 25 he was financially comfortable as a stockbroker.

In 1935 he was introduced to Sabina Osten, who had accompanied her uncle to the Wurmbrands' home. Richard, who was in a fit of anger, watched from the balcony as they approached. After introductions he explained his angry countenance to them. His mother was nagging him to get married to a wealthy heiress to whom he wasn't attracted. He said that if she were like Sabina he would be interested. An immediate courtship ensued.

Sabina Osten was born in Czernowitz on July 10, 1913 to Elias Osten, a merchant, and Rebecca (Geisler) Osten. Sabina says her family was divided into two parts. She and two older brothers were born before her father went off to war for four years. On his return, he had four more children, a boy and three girls. These four and her parents, still living in Czernowitz, perished in the Holocaust, either by starvation or by execution. Sabina and her brothers, Maurice and Dagoder, living elsewhere, survived.

When Sabina met Richard she was on vacation from the Sorbonne in Paris, where she had been studying law and chemistry and working to supplement her allowance. She didn't return to

Paris but got work in Bucharest so that she and Richard could further their relationship.

It was a whirlwind courtship consisting of nightly parties, bars, theatres, casinos, night clubs, and whatever else gave them pleasure. On October 23, 1935 Richard and Sabina, although both were atheists, were married in a rabbi's home to please their parents.

Their love of gaiety continued into their marriage. Having children was out of the question as it would interfere with their fun. Their revelry lasted less than one year.

In late summer, 1936, Richard developed a productive cough, sometimes with blood. When he returned from a doctor's appointment with a diagnosis of tuberculosis of the lungs, Sabina was devastated by the sudden turn in their carefree life. Richard, however, was terrified at the thought that there might be such a thing as judgment after death.

He prayed, "God, I know You do not exist. But if perchance You do exist, which I deny, it is for You to reveal Yourself to me. It is not my duty to seek You."

He was admitted to a sanatorium in the Carpathian mountains, where he continued to think about his sins and his relationship to a "nonexistent" God. With prayer, he gained some relief from his turmoil.

Sabina visited him every second weekend, and found him gradually becoming more quiet and less resentful. When she asked him what was the source of his new-found peace, he told her about a book he was reading entitled *The Brothers Ratisbonne*. The brothers had founded an order to convert Jews.

Richard felt the order must be praying for him without knowing him. He thought, *If strangers consider my life so important, do I have the right to waste it?* Sabina was impatient with his thoughts. She wanted to resume the lively life they enjoyed before his illness.

He was released from the sanatorium in the spring of 1937 and elected to convalesce in the Carpathian mountains. Having 12,000 villages from which to choose, he chose a small village called Noua in which lived an old carpenter, Christian Wolfkes, who for many years had been praying for a Jew whom he might convert to Christianity. No Jews lived in his small village.

Wolfkes was delighted when he met Richard and learned that he was a Jew. He told him about Jesus and presented him with a Bible over which he and his wife had prayed.

He read the New Testament over and over. Jesus fascinated him, but he rebelled against following the Cross. He hesitates to tell what followed lest he be accused of exaggerating. He said he was vividly aware of His presence and it seemed a voice spoke clearly: "Do not fear the Cross. You will find it the greatest of joys."

Richard now knew that Jesus was God. He remembered the Wurmbrand family legend. Around the 14th century, one of his ancestors, a rabbi, was requested to pray for a member of another family who was considering becoming a Christian. The rabbi said, "Don't worry about him. He will be true to his faith. The worry is in my family. In the future a Wurmbrand will become a Christian."

As far as Richard has been able to ascertain, he is the first in this rabbi's line of descendents to convert to Christianity. To this day the thought astonishes him. It has helped shape his vision of God's overruling provenance. Add to this the strange facts that his Jewish mother sang Christian hymns to him, and his father seemed to be aware of the Gospels.

After Richard acknowledged that Jesus was God, he went through a period of intense struggling. He told several rabbis of his new faith only to be urged to return to his old faith, a faith he never had. He visited Rabbi H. who had officiated at his marriage. The rabbi knew at the time that Richard and Sabina were atheists, but he said nothing about it. But now that he believed in Jesus, the rabbi was displeased and asked, "What makes you believe in Christ?"

He told the rabbi that the prophesy of Isaiah in the 53rd chapter had particularly impressed him. The rabbi stroked his beard and said to Richard and Sabina, "You should not have read that. That chapter is forbidden to you." Then the rabbi urged them, "My children, leave these things alone."

Richard answered, "I should like to do so, but the prophesies will not leave me in peace. What other interpretation of this part of the Bible can you give me?" The rabbi shook his head sadly and dismissed them without giving an explanation.

In 1940, during a pogrom, Fascists killed two of the rabbi's sons before his very eyes. They also shot at the rabbi but missed. The rabbi conducted his sons' funeral. Richard attended but was ostracized by the others.

After the ceremony, the rabbi saw Richard and called out to him, embracing him in sight of all. Among thousands of Jews, the rabbi had chosen him to whom to pour out his sorrow. Later Richard observed, "It is difficult to bring a Jew to Christianity."

Another rabbi with whom Richard spoke about Jesus at the beginning of his belief, while he was still doubting and suffering intellectual scruples, was Rabbi R. from Satu-Mare.

They met one evening in a synagogue. When Richard mentioned the Savior to him, he answered, "If you are prepared to listen to me quietly for half an hour, I will free you from this delusion."

He answered, "I am prepared to listen to you, not for half an hour, but for many days."

The rabbi went home with him and they agreed to read the New Testament together, so that the rabbi would have the opportunity of interrupting from time to time to point out anything that was incorrect. They read from eight in the evening until one o'clock next morning.

He listened attentively, interrupting from time to time with: "*Oi, vi shein, oi vi shein! Dus hob ich nicht gewist.*" (Ah, how beautiful! How beautiful! I never knew that.) Not once did he contradict. That night he slept at Richard's house. Next day, he pleaded, "Please don't tell anyone in the synagogue what has taken place."

Richard agreed but added, "I think it should be a point of honor for you to tell the Jews that you consider the New Testament a wonderfully beautiful book."

Rabbi R. moved to Cernauti and a year later Richard visited him, finding him sitting among his pupils. When he mentioned

Jesus, the rabbi reviled Him with ugly jokes. During the war, Rabbi R. was killed by the Nazis.

When Rabbi G. heard that Richard was a lost sheep, he asked that he visit him. Again Richard was asked what it was that attracted him to Christianity. Briefly he told the story of his life of sin and of the peace he had achieved in his conscience through the certainty that Jesus had forgiven his sins.

"Jesus gives me peace in my soul, and joy. I know that He has given peace to millions of people. I know of no evil that He has done. Tell me, Rabbi, why should I abandon Him?"

The rabbi answered, "Jesus did no evil. On the contrary, through Him many people have been saved from the worship of idols and made to know the true God. But you are a Jew. It is your duty to remain in the Jewish religion."

"No," he said vehemently. "The Jewish religion is false because it is Jewish. Religion must provide men with an exact knowledge of God and of how man can achieve unity with Him. There can never be a Jewish religion. There is only religion or nonreligion. Religion is either true for everyone or else wrong for everyone.

"In religion we must apply the same principle as in justice. No form of justice to which we give a prefix such as race, caste, class, military, or emergency, can be true justice. Justice stands by itself, without any prefix. And for the same reason I accept no prefixes in my belief. I am seeking for contact with God and union with Him. Any religion which has a prefix may prove an obstacle in this search for a union. The Jewish religion binds me to Judaism, the Orthodox and Roman Catholic religions to certain traditions, the Protestant religions to the ideas of their reformers. All these are horizontal unions, not vertical unions with God. It is this vertical union that I seek."

The rabbi said, "I must say with great regret and profound sympathy—not with scorn and malice—that in you I see a person uprooted from his people. Do you not hear within you the voices of your forefathers, calling you back?"

Richard replied, "Yes, every Jew with sidecurls, the music of a synagogue, the mere sight of the letters in the Hebrew Bible—all these remind me of my forefathers. It is almost like the sight of Abraham with his family, coming to Canaan on his camel. I see before me the scenes from the Bible. I feel myself experiencing the departure of the Jews from Egypt, all their difficulties in the desert, the miraculous event when the Jews received the tablets of the law through Moses. I experience the whole shattering history of my people. But personal biographies and history are one thing, objective truth another.

"The most profound philosophers, politicians, and religious thinkers have always offered as objective thinking a system which was nothing but the result of the tragedy of their own personal lives, and they themselves sometimes admit this. Marx wrote in a letter to Engels: 'If Titus had not destroyed my fatherland, I would not have been the enemy of all fatherlands.' One must not allow oneself to be guided by a criterion of this kind in deciding whether to be a patriot or an antipatriot. And so, even in the religious sphere we must not allow ourselves to be guided by feelings, but we must seek the true religion. That is what I want."

The rabbi shook his head skeptically. "Which *is* the true religion?"

Richard said, "I don't know, not yet. But I think I have made a long step toward discovering it, insofar as I have discovered the religion that is certainly incomplete. That is the religion to which I belong by birth. In my opinion it is absurd that religious convictions should depend on the results of a sexual association. A man of the Mosaic faith enters into a union with a woman of the same faith. The child born of this union is regarded as an apostate if he does not believe in Moses. One of his neighbors is a man who is the child of a marriage between a Catholic man and a Catholic woman. He believes that he is compelled to abide by all Catholic dogma. The same applies to a Protestant, or a Mohammedan, or a Buddhist. The result of this is incomparable confusion. This kind of religion is obviously not the true one, and I do not intend to abide by it."

The rabbi said, "Jesus did not do what you are doing. He followed in the paths of His forefathers. He kept the sabbath, the laws pertaining to food, and the other laws. He worshipped God in the synagogue. Why don't you do the same?"

Richard replied, "Jesus was a unique person with a unique vocation. The revelation He made was new. He presented a new and eternally valid truth. In order to win the goodwill of those who heard Him, He did what every sensible creature does; He clothed His teaching in a form that was acceptable and attractive to His listeners. This is how we can understand His conformism. But through Him the prophesy of Jeremiah, in chapter 31, is fulfilled: 'Behold, the day will come, saith the Lord, that I will make a new covenant with the House of Israel, and with the House of Judah; not according to the covenant that I made with their fathers in the day that I took them by the hand to bring them out of the land of Egypt; which my covenant they brake, although I was an husband unto them, saith the Lord: but this shall be the covenant that I will make with the House of Israel; after those days, saith the Lord, I will put my law in their inward parts, and write it in their hearts; and I will be their God, and they shall be my people.'

"We are no longer governed by an old covenant, but by a new revelation, which I can characterize in a few words: freedom in our daily life, and love. One of the renowned Christian teachers, Augustine, declared that the Christian norm in the conduct of life is: 'Love, and do what you will!' I no longer find Jewish customs imperative or necessary."

To Richard's amazement, the rabbi answered, "I cannot recall such a passage in Jeremiah."

Richard showed him the reference in the Bible. The rabbi tried to put an end to their discussion. "I realize that there is no point in arguing. I shall never be able to convince you that you should return to Judaism."

"You do not possess the truth, and therefore you have no confidence either," Richard replied. "You have given up all hope of bringing me back to the Mosaic faith, to which I never subscribed. But I shall never give up the hope that one day you will become a disciple of Jesus." The rabbi shook hands with him and dismissed him.

As a result of what Christians had told him about Jesus, Richard was still in doubt as to whether He really was the Savior. The rabbis removed the last shred of doubt on this score, thanks to the complete inability they showed in contradicting the Christian arguments.

Richard's inner struggle became more acute each day. He said his understanding was one thing, his feelings something quite different. With his understanding he knew that Jesus was the Savior; but his life, instead of conforming more and more to His teaching, became, if anything, worse. To his horror, he discovered that he possessed the will to do good, but not the power to carry it out.

There were two aspects to his inner conflict. On the one hand he knew, or rather felt, instinctively that conversion would mean that he would have to live a life of suffering and conflict. He would have to take his stand against some of his own people, against their customs and ideas which had survived for thousands of years. He knew that, while it was his duty to remain patient and mild, he would have to suffer abuse and condemnation, and yet remain unbowed in every storm. He would have to be prepared to oppose his people in which he was rooted with all his soul.

Richard heard a voice inside him saying, "Are you, you alone, wiser than all your people? The Jewish nation has fostered so many geniuses, so many mystics, so many men of action, and countless martyrs for the faith of their forefathers. Are all these people wrong, and only you, a small group of Jesus' disciples among the Jewish people, right?" It was not until later that he realized that the multitude and the famous men who support a cause are no argument against God's unequivocal word.

It was in this period of conflict that he experienced the presence of Jesus. "I cannot say that I saw Him," he testifies. "He had no outward appearance, but He was present. This phenomenon was repeated for several days running. It was at midday. I had cast myself down on a sofa. Tears ran down my cheeks. It was as though I heard a voice calling me, not with words, but if I were to describe what I felt, it would be something like this: 'Come! I will give you happiness. All your sins will be forgiven. Unspeakable joys await you.' My wife was at my side, saddened by the conflict within me, which she shared with all her heart. But I answered, 'No, no, I shall not come. You are calling me to tread a heavy path. Too much renunciation, too many sufferings await me. I do not want them. Depart from me!'"

Richard admits, "I didn't accept, because I was evil. Nevertheless, I believe that some sermons and Christian books on which I fed my soul at that time were in part responsible for the answer I gave. In those sermons and books the picture of Jesus was falsified. He was shown as a police officer, demanding rigid obedience to hundreds of laws. These laws started by insisting that one should renounce smoking and the wearing of jewelry, and ended by insisting that one should sacrifice one's life for Him. The emphasis was on all these 'don'ts,' and on our duty to give to God, instead of depicting Him as the giver of gifts of immeasurable worth—forgiveness of sins, peace of heart, communion with God, truth, life in the Light, the Spirit which gives power and holiness, the joy in fighting the good fight—with the angels fighting on your side—an eternal life of glory, and so much more—and all these gifts bestowed without any conditions.

"The salvation bestowed by Jesus is free, unconditional; it does not depend on what is in us, or on what we do. It springs from His loving character, and for this reason is eternal.

"Christian preaching is often bound up with 'don'ts' and demands, and this gave me a false sense of Jesus. But what restrained me more than anything else was the fact that I was in bondage to sin: love of money, love of illicit pleasures, hatred, evil, dishonesty, and much besides. I continued to commit grave and gross sins, even after I was intellectually convinced that Jesus is the Savior.

"The seed God planted in my heart wasn't corrupted by visible sins. The inner man continued to grow; and the Holy Ghost triumphed by transplanting my belief from my reason to my heart."

The man who was to play a very special role in Richard's life was Isac Feinstein. For this reason, a short summary of his life is given.

At the time of Isac's conversion he was a minor business executive. One evening, in a Christian gathering, he heard the message of Jesus. Immediately he believed. At home, he told his parents, "I have found the Messiah." From that evening he never wavered in his faith, although he encountered great resistance from his family.

His father, a pious Jew, tried to persuade him to deny Jesus. When this proved unsuccessful, he arranged for the ceremony to be carried out which is prescribed by rabbis in cases of this kind. He declared that his son was dead, carried out a symbolic burial with a coffin in which the branch of a tree was placed, tore his clothes, and wept for his son together with his family, sitting on the floor for seven whole days.

All this time the "dead man" rejoiced in a life which was richer than ever, and, according to Richard, he grew in grace and the knowledge of God.

After he had been a Christian for some time, he prepared to work heart and soul to spread the Gospel among the Jews of Romania. He took missionary training in Poland. On his return to Romania he entered the service of the Norwegian Israel Mission in Galatz.

Isac had an unlimited capacity for work. He published a periodical for adults and one for children, as well as countless Christian pamphlets. He preached all over the country and wrote numerous letters. He became an outstanding personality among the disciples of Jesus in Romania, a pillar of God's temple.

Feinstein was still a young man when war broke out. At that time he was thirty-seven years old, a pastor in a Jewish-Christian congregation he had formed in Jassy (Iasi). From there his benevolent activity spread throughout the whole country.

Anti-Semitism was rampant in Jassy, with the threat of a pogrom. Once when Feinstein was on a short visit in Bucharest, Richard, in whose apartment he stayed, suggested that he shouldn't return to Jassy, where death lay in wait for him. He also offered to send a Romanian brother to Jassy to bring Isac's wife and six small children to Bucharest.

He answered, "The shepherd's duty is to die with his flock. I know they will kill me, but I cannot abandon my brethren. I am returning to Jassy."

A few days after his return, on 28 June 1941, the pogrom started. Eleven thousand Jews were killed, along with Romanians who looked like Jews. Christian Jews were also killed by the Fascists and by the incensed populace who maintained the country was waging a holy crusade.

Feinstein was among those arrested and jailed. Criminal prisoners have recounted that Feinstein told the Jews not to have any illusions. He knew that they would be killed, and he exhorted them to be converted in order that they might prepare to meet their God.

Thousands of Jews were crammed together in sealed cattle trucks and sent off in intense heat and without water, with the result that most of them were suffocated. Among these was Isac. The few survivors were interned in a concentration camp. Some of these related how Isac, realizing death was near, turned to a rabbi and said, "It is time for us to sing the psalms."

He died while the rabbi was reciting the psalms aloud, and Isac was explaining what they foretold about Jesus. When death came, his head was resting on the rabbi's shoulder. The rabbi died a few minutes later.

Richard concluded: "A mosaic Jew and a Christian Jew were the victims of the same hatred, the hatred which in Romania was doubly vile because it masqueraded behind the name of 'Christian.'"

Not a single man from the Jewish-Christian congregation in Jassy survived. Only a few girls escaped with their lives.

"I have described Feinstein's death; he was a martyr of the Christian faith who was of the Jewish race. This outstanding man, who had a shepherd's heart such as I have seldom come across since, played an important role in the spiritual crisis through which I passed."

Isac used to visit the Wurmbrand home, and Richard would talk to him about his sin and how impossible it was for him to rid himself of it. He told Richard that Jesus' words, "Judge not," referred not only to other people but also to him.

"Don't judge yourself," was the advice Isac always gave him. "Don't distress yourself. Don't worry yourself about your sin. It is written, 'Take no thought for your soul' (Matt. 6.25, in the original Greek version). The care of the soul is Jesus' concern. Just tell Him quite simply about your sin, and from that moment it will be His concern to deal with . . .Be zealous in thinking what is right and Christian, and you will not need to run away from sin, for sin will run away from you."

Richard gives Isac, who had a beautiful singing voice, credit for introducing him to Bach's hymn "O Sacred Head." The song went straight to his heart.

One afternoon in 1937, the day before Yom-Kippur, the great Jewish day of repentance and fasting, Richard was in Isac's office. As usual, his soul was greatly troubled. To Isac he said, "The demands of Christianity are too extreme; they are impossible to fulfill. It is written in the Bible that he who says he is Christ's must also live as Jesus lived. But is that possible? It's like asking a wolf to live like a lamb, and then condemning it for not succeeding. Since I have not been Christ through all eternity, since I was not born of a virgin, since I have not had Jesus' especially chosen and holy upbringing, since I have no clear perception of spiritual realities nor do I have His mind, since God's angels are not continually ascending and descending upon me, since I do not live in celibacy, nor am I a carpenter—how, then, should I be able to live as He did? Must the snail run like the hare? From the little I have seen of Christians so far, conversion for some means merely making Jesus an interesting subject of conversion. It does not mean that they are converted to be a Jesus in miniature. At any rate, I have not seen people of Jesus' type."

Smiling, Isac answered, "Don't allow yourself to be guided by what you see, because it is possible that you do not see very well. The Jews who lived two thousand years ago didn't see in Jesus anything that made Him worthy of honor, despite the fact that He was the incarnation of God. Unless a man is born anew he cannot see God's kingdom, even though it is perfectly incarnate in the man who is standing face to face with him.

"But is it not expected of us that we should be like Jesus, that we should live like Him? The verse in St. John's Epistle to which you referred—'He that saith he abideth in Him ought himself also to walk' (1 John 2:6)—does not make our belief absurd; it is merely a warning to those who go around proudly declaring, 'I am in Christ.'

"Only a very proud person could imagine himself capable of living like Jesus. The commandment to live like Jesus, like all the other commandments in the Bible, was not given to us so that we should fulfill it, but merely so that we should understand, as a result of our constantly unsuccessful attempts, that it is impossible for us to accomplish it, and so that it should reveal to us the depth of our sinfulness. We should not attempt to live like Jesus, but we should daily polish our hearts by concentrated meditation and by faith, and then the beauty of Jesus will be reflected in us; it will give a still more beautiful picture than the picture of His own life, because the living Christ, incarnate in a human being who had been broken and had gone astray, is more beautiful than the Christ incarnate born of a virgin."

"No, no!" Richard cried with tears in his eyes. "I do not want a Jesus who has been calculated, explained, and believed in, but a real Jesus. And the hope of ever having this Jesus seems to me to be an impossible ideal." So saying, he ran out of Isac's office without taking leave of him.

Isac ran after him; Richard couldn't escape from him. He went into a shop. Isac followed him inside. He was so insistent that he persuaded Richard to accompany him that very evening to a prayer meeting which was being held by a small group of Christians in Bucharest at the Anglican Mission to the Jews.

There, after most of the congregation had offered up prayers, Richard said he was involuntarily lifted up by the Spirit. He was astonished to hear himself, for the first time, praying aloud in a public gathering. He heard his own words, but they did not seem to be words that he had formulated. They sprang from the depths of his soul. He said, "Proof that my depths had been stirred was the fact that I prayed in Yiddish, a language which in other circumstances I had never spoken."

He continued, "I consider the eve of Yom-Kippur 1937 as the day of my rebirth, because the teaching of Jesus cannot be written clearly on a page which already bears some other writing. What is required is a complete break with the past, and a completely new beginning, the starting point of which is a constant and uncompromising siege of one's thinking.

"The person who was most astonished at this change, a man who had once been a militant atheist and an active participant in the worst anarchic disturbances, was myself. My will was not free when this change occurred. My hand was forced. Everything is of the grace of God.

"I believe that just as there is in nature a biological timetable which governs the time when a bird has to emerge from its egg and when it has to migrate to another country, and to return at another date, and just as there is a biological timetable in man's physical life, so there is a spiritual timetable which is also determined in the same way. For every person who is chosen by God, there is a particular foreordained hour when he discovers the Son of God, who has always been in him but who has waited patiently for the moment when He is to reveal Himself. In that particular hour, internal and external factors, which have been prepared a long time ago, come together in order to produce this rebirth."

Richard was determined to be faithful to Jesus. He said, "The man who has made this decision must discover the true face of Jesus among the countless forgeries that have accumulated in the course of time. He must decide for himself on one version of this face, in order to be able to serve Him wholly and entirely, and without doubting that he has chosen the right confession. I was very interested in the difference between the confessions. I was anxious to be well informed before I commenced my life as a Christian. It wasn't easy to make a choice."

"The convert seeks in vain for 'the House of the Father,'" Richard said, "the Church that was founded by Jesus. In its place he finds many other churches with barbarian names, which the one-time carpenter, Jesus, would not even have understood: Catholic, Orthodox, Lutheran, Baptist, and many others. It was in this labyrinth that I had to find my way."

In his search, Richard describes several encounters, some of which were horrendous. But he said, "I find a great deal of good, too, in the various confessions and their leaders, just as my experience with rabbis wasn't always unfavorable."

He tells of visiting an Orthodox monastery in Sinaia. The old monk was drunk. He told Richard, "The rich man is easily saved. He gives money to the church and to the needy, and he goes to Heaven. But it is difficult for a poor man to be saved, since he has nothing to give." Richard pointed out that this is the very opposite of what Jesus had taught. After more discussion, the monk said, "Do you know, young man, you are very enlightened?" Richard departed, knowing he had helped the monk take the first steps in the right direction.

He visited the office of Catholic Bishop X with two priests by his side. When the bishop learned that Richard was a Jew, he burst out laughing. "Dumb Jew! Have you ever heard a more presumptuous dirty Jew, wanting to be a Christian?" The two priests joined in his laughter. Richard wasn't surprised. He had been warned by Isac, and he also knew that bishops and priests had been nourished on the so-called holy tradition, on the writings of the church fathers. But many of the "holy church fathers" were rabid anti-Semites.

Richard said, "Until recently (1937), every Good Friday, worshippers in the Catholic Church prayed for the 'perfidious Jews.' This formula has now been omitted from Roman Catholic services, but in the anti-Semitic writings of their church fathers future priests continue to imbibe this doctrine. It was normal for the disciples of the 'holy' fathers to laugh at me. They were following in the footsteps of their teachers."

Richard rose from the chair in which he was sitting, strode over to the bishop's desk, and struck it with his clenched fist. "Aren't you ashamed of yourself?" he asked. "You are a Christian bishop, and yet you laugh at a Jew because he believes in Jesus. What nationality was Jesus? And His mother? And the Apostles? You fill your churches with pictures of 'dirty' Jews, yet you laugh at Jews. Do you not fear God?"

The priests moved as if to protect the bishop. "Stop! Let him be!" said the bishop. "There is good in this young man. I wish to speak with him."

A calm conversation ensued. The bishop congratulated him on the new path on which he had set his feet. He also expressed a desire that Richard should win over other Jews to Christ. He felt it was useless to ask the bishop for details on how to do this.

The Orthodox priest in the parish to which Richard belonged was sitting in the yard in front of his house. When he told him he was a Jew who believed in Jesus, the priest set his dogs on him. He had numerous encounters of this kind with Orthodox priests and had no desire to join the Orthodox church. Richard said, "In fairness, I must say that I have since met Orthodox priests who were saints, but my early experiences were bad."

In spite of the fact that Luther was anti-Semitic, Richard finally decided to become a Lutheran. "The Lutheran Church is a remarkable one," he said, "a church which exists against the wishes of the man who founded it."

He explained that Luther didn't want a church named after him. Luther felt that all those who believed in Jesus should be called Christians. He felt that having many sects divided God into many gods.

Richard considered Luther a split personality because, although anti-Semitic, he wrote some beautiful things about Jews. "We shouldn't treat the Jews so badly," he said, "because among them are future Christians . . . . If the apostles, who also were Jews, had treated us, the Gentiles, as we treat the Jews, no Gentile would have ever become a Christian."

"So far I haven't discovered a single Christian organization which is qualified to tackle the task of preparing the world for the Kingdom of God and making disciples of all nations. Not a single one of them takes this task seriously, striving toward it according to a definite strategic plan. Many of their efforts are wasted in trivial everyday affairs.

"For my own part," Richard said, "after seeking long, to right and left, I have found what I am seeking: my confession is love. My brothers and sisters are all those who love one another, no matter to what denomination they belong. My Lord is Jesus, because He is the incarnation of love.

"Most of the Christian Jews who have subsequently comprised our congregation have adopted the same interdenominational attitude, despite the fact that our church was formally Lutheran. It was known as 'The Church of Love.' Pastor Solheim's greeting was 'Love.' We were the only church in Romania which, long before the modern ecumenical trend, had people of all denominations kneeling together at the communion rail."

Richard states that in his wife he has truly found what the Bible describes as "a helper who is his like."

"There is a certain value in celibacy," he said, "but I have also noticed that the competence of many laborers in God's vineyard has been to a large extent due to the fact that they had found an excellent helpmeet in their wives."

He had had much difficulty with Sabina when he went off to be baptized. She wanted to commit suicide. His mother fainted when she heard of his decision. Later, Sabina had a change of heart and requested baptism, as described in another chapter. Richard's mother maintained her faith in Judaism.

He said that if he could do it over again, he would use a different approach. "Complexes of this kind must be carefully dealt with," he said. "The duty of love is greater than the duty to be baptized. A person should never be in a hurry to be baptized, before his family is familiar with the idea, and realizes what it involves and means . . . .But at that time I was of a different mind. I went to my baptism leaving behind a weeping wife and a sorrowing mother.

"I cannot say into what confession I was baptized. My baptism took place in the chapel of the Lutheran Norwegian Israel Mission, the head of which was a Free Church Christian, Isac Feinstein. The act of baptism was carried out by Brother Ellison, who had been an Anglican priest, but who had left that church after being baptized a second time as an adult. He continued nevertheless to conduct services in the Anglican Mission. It sufficed for me to know that Ellison was a true-hearted disciple of Jesus, as were the others who assisted at the baptism of myself and two others.

"Our baptism took place in a cordial atmosphere. Ellison, who was of a high spirituality, warned us: 'You have now received robes of white, and it is your duty to keep them pure.' Feinstein, who was more down-to-earth in his approach, also preached: 'You are human beings, and you will still sin like all human beings. You will not keep your robes white, but when you do sin, go immediately to Jesus so that He can cleanse you of your stains.'"

When Sabina expressed a desire to be baptized, the ceremony was also performed by Ellison.

One night while returning home from a party, Sabina said, "I should like to wake the pastor so that he can baptize me, and cleanse me of all my impurity." Richard persuaded her to wait til morning.

Clarutza, a girl of sixteen, put the finishing touches to Richard's conversion. She was the first Jew converted by him. "Clarutza was young in the faith," he said, "but I, her spiritual father, was also young in the faith. I, who had not yet been cured, began to cure others. It was bound to have consequences."

One day, Clarutza, while having dinner at the Wurmbrands' home, suddenly asked, "Brother, do you buy lottery tickets?"

He had a ticket in his pocket, Richard said. For a long time he had been engaged in a spiritual struggle, because an inner voice had told him that God's children are not allowed to indulge in a game of chance, while at the same time the prospect of winning a large sum tempted him considerably. His conscience hadn't been appeased. Before he had time to consider, the answer came from his lips: "No," when he should have said "Yes." This wasn't the only lie he told at this time. Lying had become second nature to him, and he confessed that even after he had become converted it played many tricks on him.

Richard wished he could unsay the lie that had escaped his lips, but it was no longer possible. Pride, and maybe fear too, fear of undermining the confidence which this young girl had in him, prevented him from putting things right immediately. For a week afterwards he found it impossible to pray. When he knelt down to recite "Our Father," he seemed to hear a voice answering: "Liar."

In the anguish of his soul, he went to Tudor Popescu, who at that time was the "senior" believer among them in Romania. He had once been an Orthodox priest, but like Luther he had had the courage to oppose his church's hierarchy and to preach the true gospel. For this reason he had been expelled from the church. Thousands of believers followed him, and he was now a leading personality in Christian circles in Romania. He was a sincere friend of Christian Jews, and he preached to them with great blessing.

Richard told this old brother of his affliction and asked him what he should do. He told him of his fear that if he confessed to the girl that he had lied to her, she who had planted the seed of the love of Christ in her, perhaps she would lose her faith.

Tudor answered, "You are right to be afraid. The least sin a man commits may prove a stumbling-block to another soul and condemn that soul to perdition. For this reason you must be more vigilant another time. Nevertheless, my advice is that you should simply confess to her that you have lied. If, as a consequence of this, the girl loses her faith, this will show that she was not one of the chosen of the Lord. You, on the other hand, will continue in the way of the Lord, fulfilling His commandments."

This experience, Richard said, revealed to him how profitable it is for believers to confess their sins not only to God, but also to a wise brother, who can give them advice. "It is not wise for us to wallow in our own sin, and allow it to remain within us until it chokes our spiritual life," he said.

He called Clarutza to him and placed her in a comfortable chair facing him and told her what had happened. He asked her humbly to forgive him.

Clarutza listened earnestly and said, "This time I shall forgive you, but you must not do it again."

He was full of joy that the burden had fallen from him. He related this to all who were present at the meeting the following Sunday. Immediately, one after the other, Christian Jews, stood up and confessed various lies, dishonesties, and thefts. These confessions proved a great blessing to them all, he said.

Clarutza had completed Richard's conversion.

CHAPTER 20

After Richard and Sabina converted to Christianity they changed their minds about not having children. As a result, on 6 January 1939, a son, Mihai, was born. In spite of the fact his parents were in jail and slave-labor camps much of his young life, he developed into an intelligent Christian, wise beyond his years and devoted to his parents.

Now an American citizen, with an Anglicized name of Michael, he manages a correspondence school in California. He has a daughter, Amy, and a son, Alex. Michael and his ex-wife Judy are divorced.

At first, Richard tried to convert rabbis. Finding this practically impossible, he shifted to lay Jews. The Wurmbrands' first mission trip was to Sabina's family in Czernowitz. As a result, her brother and three sisters attended Messianic meetings and soon accepted the faith.

As noted previously, Clarutza was Richard's first convert. He told of a trip they took to the summer resort, Sinaia, to spread the Gospel. They got permission from the abbot of the Orthodox monastery to sell Gospels and Christian literature outside the church on Sunday morning. This was a bold move because lay members of the Orthodox Church weren't permitted to read the Bible themselves, and the literature was Protestant.

They set up a stall in front of the church entrance. A crowd gathered, and copies of St. John's Gospel and other books sold like hot cakes.

A police constable patrolling the fringe of the crowd observed that the two salespeople looked decidedly Jewish and thus came under suspicion. He walked over and asked Richard for his name. On hearing "Richard Wurmbrand," he was jolted by the German name and left with a salute. A little further off, he paused and looked back. He evidently decided they weren't Aryan and approached again, asking them to produce identity cards. That was their undoing. Their cards identified them as Jews.

An uproar followed. At the top of his voice, the constable shouted, "These dirty Jews have desecrated our church and our gospel."

People wanted their money back because they refused to read anything written by a Jew. Richard and Clarutza were arrested and taken to the police station. When he asked her if she was frightened, she replied, "Far from it; I'm enjoying myself. It is lovely to have an experience of this kind with Jesus."

Because it was Sunday and the station was manned by only one person, through a series of misunderstandings, the "culprits" were released. They stopped the first taxi and left Sinaia.

Shortly after Richard became a Christian, he accepted the position of secretary to the Anglican Mission to Jews in Bucharest. The mission was sponsored by the Church of England, and the Reverend George Stevens was pastor.

Richard clung to his old ways of foxy dealings. For example, he tried to bribe an insurance agent to drop a just claim against the Mission. He was scolded severely by Stevens. In time, Richard learned that a Christian cannot have double standards.

The Sinaia experience was in the summer of 1939. On September 1, 1939, World War II began with Germany's invasion of Poland. King Carol sided with the Allies, but political pressures forced him to make an economic treaty with Germany, placing oil and other war-necessary items at Hitler's disposal.

During the spring and summer of 1940, Romania vacillated between Germany and the Allies. When Romania realized that Russia had plans to take Bessarabia, the government looked to Germany for support against Russia.

When Corneliu Codreanu, founder of the Iron Guard, a militant Fascist organization, was executed on November 30, 1938, the Iron Guard disbanded and fled to Germany. There they received further training and returned to Romania in the summer of 1940.

Thus, the Jews were in jeopardy because of two anti-Semitic powers—the Russian Communists and the Green Shirts, as Romania's Iron Guard was called. Jews who could afford it fled the country. With Romania openly allied with Germany, English people, including Reverend Stevens, left Bucharest.

Meanwhile, Richard, who for three years off and on had studied theology at Cluj University, was ordained a pastor. When Stevens left, he took over the Mission.

In her book *A Ransom for Wurmbrand* Anutza Moise said that in the beginning Richard's sermons weren't very biblical; that he took his illustrations from science, history, geography—anything but the Bible. She once took him to task about this. "The Bible is full of stories and events which you could use as illustrations. Why don't you?"

To her astonishment he calmly replied, "Because it isn't necessary." He continued as before, she noted, but as time went on he learned to love and use the Bible. Another thing that irked her was the length of his sermons, which never lasted less than three-quarters of an hour, except on one occasion when she landed in the police station.

Anutza recounts her first impression of the Wurmbrands on their initial encounter. Sabina, called Bintzea by her close friends, was a small, vivacious young woman who looked even more diminutive beside her handsome giant of a husband. She at once embraced Anutza and gave her a warm smile that went straight to her heart.

Richard also impressed her deeply. She found him very different from Bintzea in that he was serious and rarely smiled. She remarked that he only learned to smile and laugh many years later during his long period of suffering in prison.

In their early years as Christians she was often in the Wurmbrands' home. On one occasion, during dinner, a guest told a joke. Richard scolded him and said, "This is a Christian home. At the table we speak only of Christ." In later years he developed a rich sense of humor and had an appropriate story for every occasion.

One of his stories was about a congregant we will call Vasile. This gentleman had difficulty controlling his exuberance. During Richard's sermons he often jumped up and shouted "Hallelujah!" which was a disturbing practice to most of the congregation.

One of the affluent members took him aside and said, "Vasile, if you will stay quiet during the service, you may come to my home every Sunday and eat roast beef and other goodies." Vasile agreed to this and for several Sundays controlled his excitement.

It was Easter morning. When Richard read the Easter message, "Christ is risen," Vasile jumped to his feet and shouted, "Roast or no roast, Hallelujah!"

Over time the Wurmbrand home became a sanctuary. First they shielded Jews against the Green Shirts, then escaped Russian prisoners of war against German soldiers, and finally German soldiers against the Red Army. Somehow, they managed to keep them separated.

One Sunday, a group of Green Shirts came to the Anglican Mission for the purpose of heckling. Richard preached directly to them about their hateful mode of living. Finally, realizing he was in great danger, Richard cut his sermon short and slipped out a secret door and through a corridor to a side street while the Green Shirts shouted, "Where's Wurmbrand? Where's Wurmbrand?"

Richard arrived home without detection, but Anutza and Mr. Ellison and some other members of the congregation were arrested and taken to the police station.

Evidently convinced that they didn't know where Richard was, the police were obliged to release them.

When the Green Shirts gained power, they invalidated the permit for the Anglican Mission. Although the Orthodox Church supported their persecution of the Jews, Richard visited the Inspector of Cults, who was both an Orthodox priest and a Green

Shirt, to get a new permit. The priest mocked him for being a Christian Jew, but he was really testing Richard. Finally he conceded, "You are worthier of bearing the name of Christian than I am." Richard got his permit.

The Wurmbrands lived in an anti-Semitic community but were tolerated because they were Christian. In time they won the friendship of their neighbors. Sabina said, "His blue eyes could look into your soul." His acquaintances called him a great actor because of his ability to win converts.

Richard took this as a compliment. "I can't see how it is possible to be a good missionary," he said, "unless one has a certain artistic flair and a knack of playing different roles."

The Wurmbrand home was always crowded with refugees from oppression. Mihai wrote in his diary: "If mother has to slice the bread thinner or add more water to the soup, there is always a place for a hungry stranger." Sabina gave a powerful witness in her gentle acts of love. As a result, many people came to her for advice.

In September 1940, King Carol was forced to abdicate. He had tried to placate both Germany and the Allies and pleased no one. Young Michael succeeded to the throne for the second time. Because of his youth, the real power was in the hands of Prime Minister Ion Antonescu. In fact, he established a Fascist dictatorship that briefly brought the Green Shirts to power. After a period of Iron Guard revolutionary and criminal excesses, with fighting in the streets of Bucharest, he was forced to suppress them.

When Richard and Sabina aided the families of the Iron Guard, they were much criticized. Richard's response was simply, "Jesus taught us to love our enemies."

Antonescu had requested Hitler's help in breaking the power of the Green Shirts and then led Romania into the war on Germany's side. German troops immediately occupied Romania and persecution of Jews increased. It was the winter of 1941, and soon Sabina's parents, little brother, and three sisters along with many others, were herded out of Czernowitz to a forest where they were frozen, starved, or shot. Sabina never had news of them again.

Richard preached against this reign of terror in any church that invited him, as well as in bars, in brothels, and in prisons. When the Nazis forbade him to do so, he preached at secret meetings in homes. Somehow he always managed to escape when an arrest was attempted.

On 28 June 1941, in Jassy, 11,000 Jews were butchered. Only seven Jewish Christian girls and a Norwegian missionary, Sister Olga, survived. Through a Christian police officer Richard arranged for them to be arrested and brought by train to Bucharest. On arrival they were released to Richard and Sabina who sheltered them in their home until they could escape to safety.

Under the Antonescu-Hitler regime, worship permits for Christian Jews were again invalidated. When diplomatic relations with Britain were discontinued, the Anglican Mission to Jews was dissolved. The assembly hall was closed, and the Wurmbrands, who had taken an apartment in the same building, were evicted.

The Romanian branch of the Swedish Mission to Israel, a Lutheran mission, embraced Richard and his flock of about one hundred members. Typically, Richard applied for a permit to preach, but was refused.

He wrote in his journal: "At that moment, God had taken from me all my powers of reasoning, so that I completely forgot that I was a Jew, without any rights, in an anti-Semitic atmosphere, the office of a minister of State. All he had to do was ring his bell, and I should have been arrested and should have vanished without a trace."

When the minister refused the permit, Richard told him they would all stand in judgment before God. Instead of reacting with rage, the minister asked, "What can I do to be saved, wretched sinner that I am?" He received his answer and Richard got his permit.

But not for long. The Wurmbrands and several others were arrested for holding illegal religious meetings. When they were released after serving a short term in prison, they found that the permit had been canceled and that the minister who issued it had been dismissed. Secret worship meetings were resumed.

Again Richard was arrested and served fourteen days in prison before being released through the intervention of the Swedish ambassador. This was a faux pas on the part of the ambassador, who was responsible for the Swedish Mission but not for Romanian citizens. As a result he was retired by the Swedish government.

Richard and Sabina resumed their works of mercy. They did what they could to help Gypsies who were also being exterminated by the Fascists. They rescued Jewish children from ghettoes and planned escape routes across the border to Hungary. They distributed Gospels to German soldiers and to Russian prisoners of war, to whom he also preached in his fluent Russian. The young Russian soldiers, raised under Communism, had never heard of Jesus Christ.

Richard told of an incident that happened while Bucharest was under constant attacks by the Russian air force. He and six other members of his church were in the midst of a trial when the air-raid alert sounded. Prisoners, judges, lawyers, and court officials, all terrified, rushed to the shelter. There they all knelt while Richard prayed. When the all-clear sounded, the guards grasped the prisoners by the collar and led them back to court, where they were freed by the judge. According to Richard, they were the first Jews released by a Fascist court.

Between 1941 and 1944 Richard was jailed several times by the Nazis, but never more than three or four weeks at a time. When he raised enough money for a bribe, he would be released.

On 23 August 1944, the anti-Fascist Communist People's Party toppled Antonescu from power. King Michael then declared war on Germany. Bucharest was now bombed by Germans instead of Russians.

On 31 August 1944, as described in another chapter, Richard and Sabina went out to meet the Russian army. Ivan, the driver of the first tank, was converted to Christianity in their home. A Russian couple they met in the shopping district, fascinated by the story of Jesus of whom they had never heard, also converted in their home.

Soon Richard left the Swedish Mission and became pastor of the Norwegian Mission to Jews along with the Norwegian pastor, Reverend Solheim. They were both asked to represent the World Council of Churches, an appointment they accepted. Their sole duty was to administer funds sent for Romanian relief.

They distributed food, clothing, and money. The mission was turned into a canteen, which fed about 200 daily. Needing additional space, they rented an enormous home. The Wurmbrands took some rooms for their own use, the ballroom became a church, and the remaining rooms were used for other mission activities.

During 1945, Richard and Sabina took as their own, six Jewish children, three boys and three girls, who had been released from a concentration camp. On 30 December 1947, King Michael was deposed by Groza. Richard and Sabina then decided their six foster children (adoption was not possible) would be safer in the new State of Israel. The Turkish steamer *Bulbul*, on which the children embarked, never reached its destination and was never heard of again.

By now, Richard felt that he had two missions: to give aid to the Romanians and to bring the Good News to the Russian soldiers, a million of whom were occupying Romania. It was about this time that Sabina discovered she had a talent for preaching, a gift which she exercised diligently.

Then followed the Congress of Cults, Richard's defiance, and finally the beginning of his years of persecution when he was kidnapped by the Communist government on 29 February 1948.

CHAPTER 21

When released from prison because of the amnesty of June 1, 1964, Richard weighed 98 pounds in spite of his 6'3" stature. He spent several weeks in hospital in Bucharest, during which time he partially regained his weight and health. After fourteen years of imprisonment and torture, he was exhausted and had thoughts of retirement, but his religious zeal negated this contemplation. Soon he and Sabina became active again in the underground church.

The Western world, whose delegations had been cleverly duped by the Communists, believed, at least seemingly, that Romania enjoyed religious freedom. Realizing this, the leaders of the underground church felt that Richard would be more effective in the West, where he could dispel this false impression. Richard and Sabina accepted this idea, but the problem was how they would make their escape.

In the meantime, their close friend Anutza Moise, who had escaped to Norway, was working diligently to raise $10,000, which the Communists were demanding for Richard's ransom, instead of the usual $2,500. Under the aegis of the Norwegian Mission, she finally succeeded.

Richard was notified that his ransom had been paid and that he was free to leave the country. He was warned by the Romanian government that he could preach Jesus all he desired but that he was not to disparage Communism or the Romanian government. He was reminded that other Romanians had been captured and returned to Romania for imprisonment or execution. "We can easily hire thugs in the West to kill or capture you," he was told.

This wasn't the end of his hassle. When he applied for visas he was told that only he was being released. Sabina and Mihai were to stay. After much negotiation (it isn't clear whether money was involved), all three were issued visas for the new state of Israel.

On December 6, 1965, the Wurmbrands flew to Rome, landing at the Cimpino airport. Here they met another roadblock. Because they were Christian Jews, the Jewish Welfare Agency refused to accept the validity of their Israel visas. Subsequently, the Norwegian Mission to Israel secured visas for them to visit their headquarters in Norway.

Their plane was scheduled to arrive at Oslo's Fornebu airport on December 23 at 7:30 in the evening. Because it had been snowing all day, landing was impossible and their plane was diverted to another airport some distance from Oslo. When the bus arrived at 11:30 at Fornebu, Richard was the first one off and was greeted by Anutza with hugs and kisses. When "Bintzea" alighted, Anutza sobbed uncontrollably. Sabina's eyes just sparkled because she knew that if she started sobbing she would never stop.

At the headquarters of the *Israelsmisjonen* a reception was waiting. Food was abundant but appetites were not. The excitement was overwhelming.

Anutza remarks in her book that Richard's scars were deep and numerous, his legs and feet were swollen, his face was haggard, and there were deep shadows under his eyes.

A few days after their arrival in Norway, Richard and Sabina were sent to a rest home in the mountains. At their request, Anutza accompanied them, although she didn't consider the mountains a good place for a vacation in the winter.

Richard was in a terrible state of nerves. If a car passed them while they were walking, he was convinced it was the secret police. A group of two or three people talking on the street had the same effect on him.

Often, during a meal or when they sat together in conversation, a veil of unutterable sadness or despair came over his face, Anutza observed. Telling a joke would bring him back and he would roar with laughter, which surprised her because she remembered him as puritanical. In the old days in Romania he would frown disapprovingly at a frivolous remark. When Anutza asked him about this change in him, he told her about telling himself a daily joke while in solitary confinement so that he could keep his sanity.

The Wurmbrands' rest soon ended. When news got around of their arrival, people who had been praying for years about starting a project behind the iron curtain came to see Richard. Invitations to preach poured in and several times he left the rest home to oblige. He returned to Oslo after only ten days of so-called rest.

On Christmas Day, the Wurmbrands attended the American Church since they wouldn't understand the Norwegian at Anutza's church. Richard introduced himself to the pastor, the Rev. Myrus Knudson, who greeted him warmly and asked him to come again. After checking with the American authorities and the Mission to make sure Richard wasn't a fake, he invited Richard to preach.

During Richard's sermon, he noticed two ladies who spent the whole service quietly weeping. After the service he learned that they were tears of joy. One, an invalid who had been praying for him for many years, was totally unaware that he was to preach that morning. The other had also upheld them in prayer over the years.

The NATO personnel in Oslo, whose pastor at that time was Colonel Sturdy, were impressed with Richard's background and decided that he had a most important message for the world, particularly for America. They collected money to pay his fare to the States.

The *Israelsmisjonen* wanted Richard to work for them in Paris, but he felt that he needed to work for the Communist world. He agreed provisionally to go to Paris and leave Sabina and Mihai there while he went on a preaching tour of America. There wasn't enough money for all three to go to the States.

This arrangement wasn't agreeable to Sabina, who was in a state of despair, knowing how Richard depended on her. She begged Anutza to do something to solve the situation.

Two days before their departure for Paris, the Wurmbrands were given a party by the Knudsons. At supper, Anutza sat next to a Mr. Olsson. Across from her was Pastor Knudson, to whom, impulsively, she addressed Sabina's problem.

"You know Bintzea can't let Richard go alone to the States. Please try to get her a visa, and the Lord will take care of the fare."

Mr. Olsson butted in, "Bring your friend to the embassy at ten o'clock tomorrow morning, and we'll see what we can do."

Anutza said, "Thank you," wondering who Mr. Olsson was. Next morning at the American embassy she learned that he was the Military Attaché. In less than an hour they left the embassy with the visa in Sabina's pocket.

The Wurmbrands had been in Norway only five weeks when they left for America toward the end of January 1966. On arrival in the States Richard went to work almost immediately, travelling from city to city preaching about the persecuted church and the evils of Communism. This generated much controversy both pro and con. He was soon to discover that the leaders of most evangelical churches, claiming other responsibilities, had no interest.

At times, he took vigorous action. One day in Philadelphia he saw posters calling for a public meeting against the war in Vietnam. It was difficult for him to understand how people could demonstrate against their own government and their army, which, he felt, was fighting a just war against Communism. In a recent (June 1995) newsletter, Richard said, "At that time I did not know what then Secretary of State McNamara has only now admitted in print: that America's leadership did not believe in this cause and were ready to abandon Southeastern Asia to the godless murderers. The soldiers who continued to shed their blood were never given this information."

Richard went to the open-air meeting. The speaker was a Presbyterian pastor, who ranted against the American Army and praised

Communism. Incensed, he jumped to the podium and pushed aside the pastor, whom he described as a little fellow, and grabbed the microphone.

He then issued this challenge: "You speak about Communism without knowing it. I am a doctor in Communism. I will tell you what it is like."

"Go away," the pastor said. "Such a doctorate does not exist."

"I'll show you my doctor's diploma in Communism," Richard replied. At that, he stripped to the waist, revealing scars of deep wounds both front and back. "This is what the Communists did to me along with thousands of other prisoners they tortured."

"Why did they do this to you?"

"The Communists have tortured thousands of clergy and laymen like this simply because they are Christians. And you, a pastor, instead of praising Christ and defending His innocent brethren, praise the Communists. You play the role of Judas."

In the end, the leftist pastor was booed by his own audience. One listener cut the wire to the microphone.

The meeting was over and Richard was picked up by the city police for having disturbed a lawful assembly. They drove him around the block, congratulated him, and then released him.

A newspaper reporter published the incident. Senator Thomas J. Dodd, Vice Chairman of the Senate Internal Security Subcommittee, read the article and called Richard to appear before the subcommittee.

On Friday, 6 May 1966, Richard appeared before the subcommittee in room 318 of the Old Senate Office Building. Senator Dodd of Connecticut presided. Other members of the subcommittee were: James O. Eastland, Mississippi, chairman; John L. McClellan, Arkansas; Sam J. Ervin, Jr. North Carolina; Birch Bayh, Indiana; George A. Smathers, Florida; Roman L. Hruska, Nebraska; Everett McKinley Dirksen, Illinois; and Hugh Scott, Pennsylvania. Others present were J.G. Sourwine, Chief Counsel, and Benjamin Mandel, Director of Research.

On opening the meeting, Senator Dodd remarked, "I must

say, before Mr. Sourwine reads your credentials, that we are grateful for your appearing here. I am familiar with the nature of your testimony—I think I am—to an extent. I feel that you are rendering a real service to the cause of the free world."

Since Richard's credentials had been destroyed by the Communists, Mr. Sourwine read a letter from Dr. Hedenquist, mission director of the Svenska Israelsmissionen. The letter covered Richard's activities from April 1939 to his release from prison on July 1964. Not previously noted in this text, Dr. Hedenquist's letter pointed out that Richard was Professor of the Old Testament in the Seminary of Bucharest.

Richard told of the savage persecution to which he and fellow prisoners were subjected. Senator Dodd asked him if he would be willing to show his scars. While removing his shirt, he said, "I apologize here before the ladies." He turned around when requested to do so. Senator Dodd asked him the source of several of the scars.

"And that it may be very clear," Richard said, "it is not that I boast with these marks. I show to you the tortured body of my country, of my fatherland, and of my church, and they appeal to the American Christians and to all free men of America to think about our tortured body, and we do not ask you to help us. We ask you only one thing. Do not help our oppressors and do not praise them. You cannot be a Christian and praise the inquisitors of Christians. That is what I have to say."

Mr. Sourwine asked this question: "The subcommittee has received substantial information to the effect that the Romanian Communist Government has infiltrated into this country Communist-trained clergy with other missions than those of a spiritual nature. Do you have any information about that?"

Richard replied: "Romanian Communists are very much interested in the fact that you have here in the States something like 300,000 Americans of Romanian origin who speak the Romanian language and are Orthodox.

"The Romanians have a bishop, Bishop Viorel Trifa, who is anti-Communist, and the Communists wish to win these 300,000 on their side. They can't very well win them for communism, but they can win them for a leftwing Christianity which supports communism. They have sent here several men, Moisescu, Liviu Stan, and so on. These don't come with Communist slogans but with the words: 'You must love your Romanian fatherland...You must have connections with the Romanian patriarchy.' When I came out from Romania I saw for the first time a Romanian newspaper which appears in Bucharest, and which nobody in Bucharest has ever seen. *The Voice of the Fatherland* it is called, and in the fatherland nobody sees this newspaper. Only your American Romanians see it, and in France. I have never seen it. My son looked at it, and we have never seen it. In this newspaper you read about priests and churches. In our newspapers you will never have a word about the church. There you have pictures of priests and monasteries and how fine it is and so on. They make this propaganda, surely."

Richard then went on to tell about the Romanian religious services which are beamed to the free world but are jammed in Romania. He ended his testimony with a story about a young priest who was asked by the prison political officer, "Do you still believe in God?" The priest knew that if he said "yes" it meant the end of his life. Yet he answered that he loved Christ with all his heart. He was tortured to death.

"But this is Romania," Richard said. "Romania is a country which is mocked, which is oppressed, but deep in the hearts of the people is a great esteem and a great praise for those who have suffered. The love to God, the love to Christ, the love to fatherland has never ceased. My country will live. With this I finish."

After Senator Dodd told Richard that his testimony had been very impressive, a Mr. L.D. O'Flaherty addressed the chair requesting protection for Richard. Senator Dodd suggested that that should be handled out of session.

"We have a God who protects us," said Richard. "We have the angels around us."

The session had lasted only one hour and thirty minutes but had advanced Richard's cause considerably. During the hearing, Room

318 had been packed with U.S.A. and foreign reporters, as well as TV and radio personnel. The event was published throughout the world with both favorable and unfavorable comments. The minutes of the hearing were printed in a booklet by the Senate and became a bestseller. The *Congressional Record* observed, "Wurmbrand burst like a fireball across the cool complacency of some."

The *New York Times* gave a factual report without editorial comment. The article included a picture of Richard stripped to the waste to show his scars.

The Reverend Michael Bourdeaux, Director of the Institute for the Study of Religion and Communism, London, said: "No contemporary person has meant so much for the opening of the eyes of the West to what is going on in the Communist camp—except the much decried Wurmbrand. Before Wurmbrand came, we spoke to deaf ears."

The Reverend Ingemar Martinson, General Secretary of the Slavic Mission, Sweden: "Wurmbrand irritates, but opens our eyes . . .Wurmbrand has got the world to hearken, even if he has sacrificed himself. He has shouted the cry of the martyrs."

Underground Evangelism: "Wurmbrand is an Iron Curtain Paul. He is the most authoritative voice of the Underground Church, more than a living martyr."

Haratta, Finland: "Since the Sermon on the Mount was delivered, no one has preached with love like Richard Wurmbrand."

Church Times, London: "Wurmbrand has brought to the universal Church a new dimension, reminding it about the martyrs."

Tablet, New Zealand: "We were hit by a hurricane called Wurmbrand."

Christianity Today, USA: "Wurmbrand is a new St. John the Baptist . . .a voice crying in the wilderness."

La Suisse, Switzerland: "Wurmbrand, a fascinating and passionate (some times even excessively so) personality, appears always firm in the fight against the scepticism of occidental Christianity, which with rare exceptions, cannot believe that Communism might be a menace for her."

There were those who thought differently:

Finnish Communist newspaper: "We have checked and can say with almost certainty that there has never been a Pastor Wurmbrand in Romania."

Gerhard Simon in *The Churches in Russia*: "The manifestations of Wurmbrand are determined by high emotions, they are without compromise and often naive His judgements about church politics prove a terrifying narrowness The danger of Wurmbrand's grotesque distortions consists in the fact that he calls Christian groups in Eastern Europe to resistance unto death."

Van de Heuwell, Director of Public Relations, the World Council of Churches: "In the present Communist regimes strong powers for the humanization of society lie hidden . . . Wurmbrand becomes really dangerous."

Arbeiterzeitun , Switzerland: "Wurmbrand is the devil's mouthpiece."

The Pilgrim, USA: "Wurmbrand is a Marxist theologian."

Reformatorisch Dagbladett, Holland: "Wurmbrand completely rejects scholarly objectivity."

Vaderland, South Africa: "Wurmbrand is a red pastor."

Catholic Herald, London: "Wumbrand is intemperate."

Christian Vanguard, USA: "Wurmbrand is a dirty Jew."

Verden Gang, Norway: "Wurmbrand has been pro-Nazi."

Commenting on the results of his Senate hearing, Richard said, "I became a person of international renown who received invitations from both churches and universities. Thus the message of the persecuted churches became known. Soon we were able to organize a mission which spread to some fifty other countries. It was a triumph of the church in chains. We achieved this by speaking before a high political institution."

CHAPTER 22

Following Richard's exposure in the international media, he had a continuous flow of invitations to speak at churches and universities throughout the free world. In spite of the fact that he was traveling from city to city preaching Christ and condemning Communism, he found time to organize The Voice of the Martyrs (originally Jesus to the Communist World, then Christian Missions to the Communist World). This same year, 1967, the new mission published his first monthly newsletter, which hasn't missed an issue since. Also in 1967 he wrote and published *Tortured for Christ*, which became a bestseller, selling over 3,000,000 copies, and has since been translated into some 75 languages. The following year he wrote and published, with the cooperation of Charles Foley, a professional writer, the definitive book about his prison experiences, *In God's Underground*.

Reviews have varied from "incredible" to disbelief. In *Kirkus Reviews*, the reviewer says about *Christ in the Communist Prisons*: "This is a clumsily written record of a Lutheran pastor's fourteen years in a Communist prison in his native Romania. After the first few pages the spell of such a story begins to work and the reader is fascinated by the account of a somewhat naive faith that was strong enough to withstand years of torture, both mental and physical, and, at the same time, to sustain not only Pastor Wurmbrand himself but also many of his fellow prisoners. Even Wurmbrand's emotion-laden attempts to convert his jailers are of interest, not so much because of the pastor's message as because of the Communists' reactions to Christian apologetic. The most informative and stimulating parts of the book describe in some detail the brainwashing techniques of the prison, aimed first at forcing the prisoner to disclaim the value of his non-Communist life and then to accept Communism so as to fill the vacuum."

In a *Times Literary Supplement*, a contributor describes Wurmbrand as "a man who, lifting his soul towards God, never underrated the harsh reality of the world that had imprisoned him."

In the *National Review*, Joseph Sobran states that "Wurmbrand writes with a relentless passion that never falls into simple emotionalism but is always thoughtful and informative. He describes the harrowing tortures, explains his own strategy and tactics, draws Scriptural analogies, philosophizes, tells uplifting anecdotes, reminisces, and gives practical advice. His book is so engrossing because it is so nearly unbearable."

In *Best Sellers*, Paul Kiniery observes that "it is an amazing story." Finding Wurmbrand's account of prisoners in solitary confinement communicating through tapping on the walls somewhat far-fetched, he says, "This seems to be the story of an honest man Perhaps I am merely quibbling. If only one-tenth of the book were factual it would be a devastating indictment of everything communistic."

The United States Congress again became interested in Richard, and he was invited to appear before a subcommittee of the Committee on Un-American Activities of the House of Representatives. On Thursday, August 10, 1967, at 10:20 a.m. in Room 429, Cannon House Office Building, Richard appeared before the subcommittee with Hon. William M. Tuck of Virginia, chairman of the subcommittee, presiding. Other members present were: Edwin E. Willis of Louisiana, chairman of the full committee; and Richard L. Roudebush of Indiana.

Also present were: Representatives John M. Ashbrook of Ohio, and Del Clawson of California. Staff members present were: Francis J. McNamara, director; Chester D. Smith, general counsel; and Alfred M. Nittle, counsel.

The purpose of the hearing was "to determine the extent and character of Communist propaganda and conspiratorial techniques employed within the United States to promote the objectives of the Communist Party in the United States and to advance the purposes of the world Communist movement by the dissemination of false and misleading information concerning Communist doctrine and practice in regard to religion and ethnic and minority groups." The legislative purpose was specifically to provide factual information to aid the Congress in the enactment of any necessary remedial legislation.

Richard provided much information in a hearing lasting two hours and twenty-five minutes. In his opening statement, chairman Tuck noted that as recently as 1964 the Soviet Communist Party had established an Institute of Scientific Atheism to direct an intensified campaign against religious beliefs at every level and in every walk of Soviet life. He then quoted several recent statements which revealed the Communists had ostensibly reversed their position on religion and were now telling Christians that they can and must work together with Communists to obtain what they call a common goal—a better world for mankind.

The chairman then pointed out that these recent statements by Communist officials and publications, if sincere, were certainly earth-shaking. If they were genuine, they reflected a major and fundamental change in basic Communist doctrine, a change that could have far-reaching effects in all parts of the world, a change that could reshape the thinking of millions of people on the subject of communism. He continued, "The Communists, of course, have made many false and treacherous statements in the past to serve their devious purposes. The 50-year history of their dealings with non-Communists on all levels, governmental and otherwise, is filled with examples of this—calculated, cynically and grossly false statements made by Communists and their agents for no other reason than to mislead non-Communists about the real nature and intent of communism."

The highlights of Richard's testimony were: before the Communists came to power in Romania, those who warned what would happen to religion under communism were "besmeared"; Romanian churches had been infiltrated prior to the Communist takeover; he had preached to all religious denominations in the States—the rank and file believe him but the churches' top leaders disbelieve and beg him not to speak against Communism "because this will make men hate the Communists and the Russians"; everywhere, until they have the power, the Communists say that they are the friends of religion; persons had been imprisoned by the Soviet Communists for showing films of a religious nature to children, distributing religious magazines, baptizing children, and teaching religion to children; if parents persist in teaching their children about Christ, the children are removed from their care and placed in state schools away from parental influence; and except perhaps for two or three, all the Catholic bishops have been killed under torture.

Richard's testimony brought out the fact that Communists consider adults lost to religion but that if religious education is denied to children, "in the future all the forms of religion will be thrown on the rubbish heap of history" (from the *Communist of the Armed Forces*, February 1967).

The hearing before the House of Representatives stimulated renewed interest in Richard's campaign but didn't have the impact of the Senate hearing the year before.

Two months later, on October 22, 1967, 60,000 pro-Communists marched to the Pentagon in demonstration. Richard, in a cherry picker, followed the parade, preaching Christ through a megaphone.

With invitations to preach flowing in from all over the world, the Wurmbrands made several tours to Europe, Asia, Africa, Australia, and New Zealand. Not only did they preach, but they organized branches of the Voice of the Martyrs in several locations. Printing presses have since been set up in India, Germany, Australia, Romania, and Albania. Secret presses have been established in several Islamic and Communist countries. The presses print Christian literature, including the Bible and *Tortured for Christ*.

Richard continued to use physical force when necessary. In March 1969 at San Fernando Valley College in California, he struggled with a pro-Communist speaker and wrested the microphone from him. In March 1972, while he was addressing a group of 4,000 in Basle, Switzerland, a left-wing group seized the microphone and started singing revolutionary songs. Richard clapped his hand over the leader's mouth. Pandemonium broke loose. He was attacked but was saved by the police, who dispersed the crowd with tear gas.

Richard ignored warnings of danger. He was advised not to go to Munich in 1970, but he went anyway, saying, "The one hired as my killer might be converted." In 1972 he was threatened with death if he preached in India, but he preached without incident in New Delhi. Richard once wrote, "A man really believes not what he recites in his creed, but only the things he is ready to die for."

When the Wurmbrands visited New Zealand in June-July of 1969, *The Contender* printed in detail Richard's then opinion of the World Council of Churches. It read as follows: "World Council leaders claim to believe that their policies toward Soviet-controlled churches are necessary in order to keep in touch with, and strengthen the Christians behind the Iron Curtain." In relation to the real facts, these threadbare excuses sound sickeningly cynical. Official recognition and honoring of their slave-masters' and tormentors' stooges and puppets does not help the captive Christians! It merely adds bitter insult to injury. The fact is that with few honorable exceptions (like Cardinal Wyszynsky of Poland and Bishop Ordass of Hungary) Iron Curtain church-leaders and their official organizations are the tools of the secret police. Most of the real Christians are not in this show-case church, but in the secret underground church. Consider the following directives from a 1960 circular now in force, of the Committee of the Evangelistic Baptist Christians of the Soviet Union:

"The elder presbyter must not care about preaching" (p. 3, par. 2).
"Less sermons and fulfilling of spiritual works . . .strict fulfilling of the Soviet legislation on cults" (p, 3, par. 5).

"We must strive to reduce the baptism of young ones between 18 and 30 years of age to a minimum" (p. 7, par. 3).

"Children of preschool and school age should not as a rule be allowed to attend religious services" (p. 9, par. 6).

"In the past, not taking into consideration sufficiently the Soviet law on cults...there happened baptisms of men younger than 18. Charities were given from the funds of the churches. Special assemblies for Bible studies and other purposes were organized. It was permitted to recite poems. There have been excursions of believing youth. Illegal relief funds were organized. There have been meetings for instructing preachers and choir leaders...and there have been other violations of Soviet laws. All this must be uprooted now in our churches." (From *The Wurmbrand Letters*, pp. 131-132)

The following excerpts taken from letters written by Pastor Wurmbrand to various ecumenical leaders describe how "real Iron Curtain Christians" felt about World Council of Churches policies:

"I avoided writing to the World Council of Churches in Geneva for a long time, not wishing to put it under a material obligation towards me, but after I managed to secure my daily bread, I did it out of heart full of sorrow.

"This sorrow came when I read an article in the *International Review of Missions*, published by the World Council of Churches in the January 1966 issue, in which it is written that 'the Orthodox Church and Protestantism are growing in Romania in an atmosphere of complete religious liberty.'" Richard then asked Mr. Visser t'Hooft, spokesman for the WCC, if he could give the addresses of the Bible Society in Romania, of the YMCA, of a Sunday School for children in Bucharest, of one charitable Christian organization. He asked him to name one book published by a Protestant during the last 20 years, where he can hear a Christian broadcast in Romania, where are Pastors Vacareanu, Nailesou, and Ghelbegeanu? (According to Richard they are in prison for their faith).

"Why are deliberate lies told," he asked, "which mock the suffering of my fatherland and the suffering of its church?

"I, a Romanian pastor, after 14 years in prison, when one of the main charges against me was that I worked for the World Council of Churches, was asked nothing about my experiences and what I know about the situation in Romania.

"The Archbishop Moisescu . . .a traitor and a man of the secret police, was banqueted in Geneva. I was in prison with 400 Christians denounced by the same Moisescu . . .To me brother Visser t'Hooft sends very kind greetings, but has never asked to speak to me.

"[Prof.] Hromadka, an arch-traitor who went to Moscow and was praised by Mikoyan, the right-hand man of Stalin in the mass murders of Christians, is another one who was banqueted at Geneva. But I was never given a hearing. Nobody asked me how I am living, whether I have enough to eat . . .But what is more important, they did not ask me about what is happening in Romania and how the Christians there are faring.

"The hearts of the Romanian Christians are bleeding, knowing that their traitors and denunciators are embraced in Geneva and yet they are not given a chance to tell what is happening. Very politely I was told, 'Please don't come to Geneva, because the Communists will know and be irked,' just as if the Communists are dictating in Geneva too and not only in the Soviet camp.

"I asked English church leaders, 'Why have you eaten at banquets with our inquisitors?' The answer was: 'We are Christians and must have friendship and fellowship with everybody, including the Communists.' And I was asked if I do not agree with this Christian attitude.

" . . .I faintly remember that it is written in the Bible, 'friendship with the world is hatred towards God.' But even putting aside what the Bible says, I asked again, 'Supposing that we must have friendship and fellowship with everybody, why do you have friendship only with our inquisitors and none with their victims?'

"I speak for those who cannot speak for themselves, because they continue to be kept in chains. I am an unworthy man, but I speak for the worthiest of the Christians of the twentieth century. We have had in Romania saints and heroes like those of the first

Christian centuries. Instead of their names being published everywhere in the publications of the World Council of Churches, I have always found only the names of the traitors and to them were extended words of understanding and friendship—to these, the murderers of Christians.

"At the last Presbyterian convention, as in all the sittings of the WCC, it was decided to build bridges towards the Communist world. Towards the one billion people oppressed by the Communists, leaders of American churches build no bridges.

"Jesus teaches us to love our enemies. The murderer of my family has been converted in my house. I have brought to Christ some of my Communist jailors. I know what love towards enemies means. But how will I love an enemy if I don't love from all my heart my own country and nation?

"Yesterday a Christian leader told me: 'Preach only Christ and don't preach against Communism.' I said, 'Were Niemoeller, Bonhoeffer, and the others right not to preach only Christ, but to take a stand against Hitlerism?' He answered: 'Surely yes, seeing that Hitler killed six millions of Jews.' I said again: 'But Communists have killed 30 millions of Russians and millions of Chinese. Why is it not right to take energetically a stand against them?' His answer was: 'You are mad.'

". . .I know what the Bishops from the East who came to Geneva are worth and who has made them Bishops. It was not the Church. It was the Secret Police. The World Council of Churches believes in speaking with the Church of the East—and speaks with the Secret Police.

"Others don't like that I am not a pacifist. Were these men pacifists when Norway was oppressed or did they like it that the American and British army came to deliver them? They are pacifists when another's fatherland is stolen. No, pacifism is not Christian . . .Jesus taught us to love our enemies, but not only our enemies. We have to love our brethren, too. And if enemies attack the life and liberty of our brethren, if gangsters attack children, if Nazis burn Jews, and Bolsheviks kill Christians, it is a Christian duty to fight."

The Contender writer concluded: "What more is there to be said? Many sincere Christians inside the World Council of Churches no doubt are not aware of these things. But what Christian, knowing the truth, could possibly be a party to such horrors?"

On July 12, 1969, *The Christchurch Star* of New Zealand published the following article: " . . .In Christchurch this week hundreds heard his addresses on the church behind the Iron Curtain. Hundreds were also turned away—from the Civic Theatre, where he spoke last sunday afternoon, and from the Cathedral, where he preached that evening.

"Many have since asked for the establishment of some form of practical assistance for his Underground Church Mission; and a new organization, Jesus to the Communist World, has been formed with interim headquarters in Christchurch.

"Also resulting from Pastor Wurmbrand's visit, some Christians have questioned which is the right attitude towards the official churches of the Soviet bloc countries—to acknowledge and accept them, as does the World Council of Churches, or to reject them because of their persecution of Christians. " . . .the Communists recognize that the Underground Church is the only effective resistance left.

"According to the interim chairman of Jesus to the Communist World, Dr. H. Money: 'Some Western church leaders unfortunately think of Communism as practical Christianity in spite of its basis of hatred rather than love, and force rather than forbearance.'

"As Pastor Wurmbrand said in his Cathedral address, Communist bosses are living in an opulence that would make American millionaires seem poor in comparison, while the peasants have nothing."

"It is no part of Pastor Wurmbrand's program to attack the W.C.C.," commented Dr. Money. "He is not against anyone. His desire is simply to make known as widely as possible the true situation in Communist-dominated countries, to spread the Gospel there, and to support and encourage the Christians who are being murdered for their faith."

The president of the National Council of Churches in New Zealand, the Rev. W. Selwyn Dawson, observed that the basis of membership in the W.C.C. was to be found in the First Article of its constitution: "The W.C.C. is a fellowship of churches which confess the Lord Jesus Christ as God and Savior according to the Scriptures, and therefore seek to fulfill together their common calling to the glory of God, the Father, Son, and Holy Spirit."

"Any church which can fully accept this basis is entitled to belong," said Mr. Dawson. "The churches behind the Iron Curtain which do belong have shown by their life and witness that they are entitled to do so."

CHAPTER 23

Each time Richard greets a friend or perhaps even an enemy, he employs the Romanian method—a light embrace and a kiss on each cheek. But his embrace can be more than light. When he encountered us in the hallway of the ninth floor of our hotel in Tulsa, where we were attending the annual conference of The Voice of the Martyrs, he hugged and kissed my wife, Lynn, saying, "I must make up for the fourteen years I lost in prison."

Later, in the ballroom where the conference meetings were held, Richard sat in a comfortable chair especially placed for him, surrounded by friends and admirers. The air was electric with excitement. A warm-up session of sacred music swelled in volume with a total participation of the assembly. After preliminary remarks by conference leaders, there came a moment of silent anticipation as two young men approached Richard, one on each side, grasped him under the arms, lifted him, and walked with him to the dais.

Part of this is showmanship. Richard has written that a missionary must be an actor to be effective. With one or two present, he has refused assistance and gotten up and walked by himself in spite of his 86 years and tortured body.

A fundamentalist, he preached "Jesus Christ crucified," with little, if any, rhetoric. The smile on his face revealed his sincere love for his Savior. His modulation varied from barely audible to a startling shout. His sermon was interspersed with experiences from his days of harassment by the Communists. With his knuckles rapping on his chair (because of tortured feet, he sits while preaching), he demonstrated the Morse Code with which he converted prisoners in adjacent isolation cells. To a former Boy Scout the code sounded authentic enough.

He has written about the proper use of the hands while speaking. In this he showed his skill. His hands were in almost constant motion, expressing love, hate, urgency, pain, sorrow, joy, and other emotions.

Richard is an intellectual of the first water. He has expressed in his writings that Jews are intellectually superior. He backs this up with the claim that 60% of Nobel awards have been won by Jews.

His formal education was scant. His only degree is an honorary Doctor of Divinity from Indiana Christian University, awarded in 1972. His education came from extensive reading enhanced by an encyclopedic mind. He published several books and articles in Romania and has published over twenty books since his residency in America, at least one of which was a best-seller.

During his hearing with the Senate committee he claimed to speak 14 languages, with fluency in Romanian, English, Russian, and German. His English has a distinct accent but is basically understandable. His large English script is readable with some effort.

His books have been translated into 75 languages. The 72nd one was Dari, also called Farsi, a form of Persian spoken in Afghanistan. I was with him when he received and opened his first copy. His face lit up with a smile as he contemplated the almost impossible task of introducing Christ to the inhabitants of this 100% Islamic country.

He tests his friends to plumb the depth of their commitment to Christ. While having lunch together at the home of Maia Matasaru in New Jersey, he asked me to say grace. After I obliged, it was suggested to him that asking a physician to say grace was like a physician asking a pastor to prescribe medicine. He seemed to take this under advisement.

Later that evening, he requested the ladies to leave the room. After they left, he said that what he had to share was much too horrible for the ladies to hear. He then told us that while he was in prison in Romania, the prison officials trained large dogs to have sexual intercourse with young female prisoners as a means of entertainment for prison personnel. With tears in his eyes he said he never knew any of the girls to survive, as they all committed suicide.

In any gathering, large or small, Sabina defers to Richard. But when he is in another room, she waxes eloquent. Her love for her faith is at least as strong as his. Her eyes sparkle as she speaks of Christ. Approaching her is difficult as she is always surrounded by many people.

When Richard goes to a church to preach, Sabina sets up a bookstore in an anteroom. Willing young men carry the boxes for her. The books consist of those written by the Wurmbrands and other Christian writers. Often Sabina gives the books away if a would-be buyer has insufficient money.

Richard, now 87 (1996) and Sabina, 83, have slowed down considerably physically but remain mentally sharp. They both read extensively and graciously entertain many visitors. He writes an article for the monthly newsletter.

In August 1995, Sabina had surgery for adenocarcinoma of the stomach at St. Mary's Hospital in Hoboken, N.J. Following that she developed pancreatitis which has continued to cause her intense pain. In spite of this, she remains cheerful and solicitous for others.

Although the Wurmbrands have had to put on the brakes, the Voice of the Martyrs, under the able direction of Tom White, moves on with force. The VOM has missions in all the Communistic and Islamic countries. Bibles, *Tortured for Christ*, and other Christian literature, printed in the appropriate language, are smuggled into these countries and distributed to the people. Some of these countries have secret presses. The underground church is active in most. The work is dangerous and can result in severe beatings, imprisonment, and execution, sometimes by crucifixion.

Richard tells the following story: "In Iran, Christian propaganda is forbidden. It was even worse during the rule of Ayatollah

Khomeini. He was not only anti-Christian and anti-Communist, but also fiercely anti-Semitic.

"Somehow he obtained my book *In God's Underground*. As ruler of a state, he was motivated to read the whole book and observed what was written against Communism. This was enough for him. So he ordered that the whole book, which was authored by a Jew and teaches love for Christ, be translated and distributed at the expense of this Muslim state. In the spring of 1996, Iranian radio began announcing that anyone who had this book should turn it in to the police. Now the general population is curious. Khomeini's 'mistake' was God's plan."

In the first days of Richard's Christian life, an old Anglican pastor named Adeney taught him: "Whoever does not pray for China does not pray. The Chinese are a people most beloved by God. The proof is that He made so many of them."

"For over half a century I followed his injunction," said Richard. "When the Jewish messianic congregation in Bucharest was started, we prayed with many tears for China....We also prayed for China in Romanian prisons. Now the prayers of many are being fulfilled."

As proof, Richard referred to the following from *China News and Church Report*: Wei-Hang-Xing, secretary of the Communist Party of Beijing, complains about party members having lost faith in Communism and turning to religion as a spiritual fount. "Our party is facing a challenge from religion, especially Christian. It is as if God is throwing down the gauntlet to Marxism...Party members and cadres take part in illegal religious organizations. The Party has no strength and no faith in itself in its struggle against religion."

The specific contribution of VOM to the growth of Christianity in China has been distribution of Scriptures and books such as *The Answer to the Atheist's Handbook*, *Proofs of God's Existence*, and *Marx and Satan*. These have been translated into the Chinese languages and printed on VOM presses.

Richard trashes the idea that a people must have bread before being exposed to the Bible. "I myself and my wife Sabina have been terribly hungry in Communist prisons," said Richard. "At times, our daily ration was some soup with a few potato peels or cabbage leaves cooked with unwashed intestines, and we received one slice of bread a week. When we shared the Gospel with our fellow prisoners, those who received it entered a new reality in which physical suffering no longer mattered.

"After my liberation, a top leader of the World Council of Churches told me, 'We must first make a social revolution, because the poor cannot accept the Gospel.' He looked like a person who had more than enough to eat. Therefore his mind did not work well. Hungry and tortured prisoners were converted when overfed church leaders were not.

"We cannot give the food needed by hundreds of millions of hungry people, but we can give books that will inspire many of them to see joy in life in spite of its adversities."

When Richard first came to America, he spoke to a Lutheran bishop about the plight of Christians under the Communist regime. He asked the bishop if he would write to his constituents asking them to contribute to their suffering brethren. Richard admits that in his naivete he saw all Americans as rich.

The bishop replied, "We have no money."

"Bishop," Richard said earnestly, "if you were to give half your salary and encourage your pastors to do likewise, all the needs I have mentioned would be taken care of."

Far from being moved, the bishop wrote to all his pastors, "Beware of Richard Wurmbrand, who wants to deprive you of half of your salary."

A story is told by Richard about two Romanian young women who now reside in Pennsylvania. Together with a Romanian brother, Klaus Wagner, these two, Fivi and Mary Delapeta, led for years a clandestine work of distributing at least 100,000 Bibles, plus huge quantities of children's Bibles and various Christian books by men such as Spurgeon and Moody. They also distributed Richard's books printed abroad in Romanian: *Tortured for Christ*, *Answer to the Atheist's Handbook*, and *Marx and Satan*.

The Communist press ranted against these books and against their author, but for years they were not able to discover the "criminals" who spread them.

The Delapetas come from pious parents who belong to the Army of the Lord, an evangelical movement within the Orthodox Church. It was heavily persecuted not only by the Communists, but also by the bishops of the Orthodox Church, who all collaborated with the Reds. The uncle of the women, Valer Ilinca, also of the Army, had been in jail with Richard.

Their enterprise began with small quantities of literature smuggled in by tourists from abroad. They had Gospels in the double bottoms of their luggage and even in the swaddling clothes of their babies. But then the work grew.

Critics have pointed out that in this secret work, the smuggling laws of the state were broken. Richard's response: "Rulers should not make criminal laws."

He asked, "Were lies used in smuggling?" He then answered himself, "Untruths in the defense of innocents, as given under interrogation by Communist and Fascist police, were not lies. They were acts of love toward the innocent. Our assertions in the smuggling work also were not lies, but the means of spreading God's Word. We use such means in our smuggling work in other Communist and in Muslim countries.

"Once many packages of books were unloaded and transported by big cars to houses, God worked together with us. Often snow or heavy rain fell, destroying all the muddy tracks of cars and human feet on the roads traversed. The passengers in our cars looked like ordinary youth, out for a good time. They were not stopped at checkpoints. Inside the car, over the Bibles lay great quantities of cucumbers, onions, and food for pigs."

According to Richard, this went on for two years. In 1981, Fivi, Mary, and Klaus were arrested. Under interrogation by the police, they pretended to be just stupid. They resisted betraying secrets for 48 hours under uninterrupted interrogation. Klaus was severely beaten but maintained silence.

In court, lighter sentences were promised if they would ask forgiveness. They refused. They replied with dignity to the judge, who shouted at them, "You cows! Animals!" In the end, each one was sentenced to six years in prison. The judge's parting shot was, "You will rot in jail."

The story was published abroad by Christians. Strong interventions resulted. The USA ambassador to Romania, O. Rudolph Aggrey, a Christian, induced the Romanian government to free them after only 18 months in prison.

Immediately after liberation, the Delapetas brought gladiolus to the judge and spoke to him about Christ. They visited him again after the overthrow of Communism. Now they are good friends. The judge is studying the Bible and gives Bibles to others.

In the December 1993 issue of the newsletter, Richard wrote: "Madelyn O'Hare won her battle. Not only prayer but also hymns, Christian literature, and pictures have disappeared in schools.

"Years ago when I debated Mrs. O'Hare on TV, she told about her life. Her parents and grandparents had been godless and evil. She was brought up a Communist from an early age. She told her children, 'There is no God. There is no right or wrong. Homosexuality is better than Christianity. Life consists of physical pleasures such as sex and drinking.' Her sin had not started with her. Much of it was inherited, as with many of us.

"Later, her son William, who had followed in her footsteps until the age of thirty, realized that a man need not remain poor or illiterate just because his parents are; neither should he be an atheist or follow a false religion simply to please his parents.

"William read the Bible, even though his mother forbade it, and found Jesus. His mother would no longer talk with him, but he had found his heavenly Father. He now spreads the Bible in Russia, which had been his mother's idol."

Richard has much confidence in miracles. He cited several incidents in which he disobeyed doctor's orders so that he would be able to carry on his evangelism. He told the following story:

"One of the greatest gifts from God to our mission was the fact that we were able to hold our international board meeting in Albania's capital, Tirana. We met in the very conference room in Dictator Hoxha's villa where his government used to gather and where the abolition of all religion had been decreed. There we consulted about methods to use to bring religion back into Albania and other countries.

"God then performed a miracle. On that day, in my hotel room in Tirana, I suffered severe chest pain, the result of an ongoing heart condition. I took a nitroglycerin tablet, as prescribed. The pain continued. I took a second. The pain continued. Doctor's orders in such a case were to take a third pill and call the ambulance, because persistent pain may signal another heart attack.

"Just at that point, Brother Neureder from our German mission stormed into my room. 'Come quickly! Our meeting in Hoxha's villa will take place just where he had decreed the destruction of all religion.'

"I had to choose between this triumph of Jesus or heading for the emergency room of the hospital. I chose to go to the meeting. After the meeting, I felt much improved and was able to preach that same evening."

He told of another event in his life and in the life of a Buddhist:

"In 1951, I was in a Romanian jail, in a cell reserved for dying prisoners A person might last a week or two, no more. I had tuberculosis of both lungs, as well as of the bones, a weak heart, and a battered body.

"All waited for my death. I decided to use my last days to compose a book which I would write if—against all odds—I would survive and be freed.

"Well, the miracle happened. I lived and I was freed. I even wrote the book, *Tortured for Christ*, which contains essentially what I thought on my deathbed. It was translated into 66 (now 75) languages It was the springboard for our international mission.

"Now I have received news from Burma. A Buddhist was doomed to die of tuberculosis as I had been. On his deathbed he was saved and read *Tortured for Christ*. Afterwards, the doctors could not believe their eyes. The tuberculosis disappeared as it had from me.

"I know this story is incredible, but it is also incredible that I should have left a death cell and written the book.

"Ben Gurion, late president of Israel, said, 'Whoever does not believe in miracles is not a realist.'"

On June 2, 1994, Father John Caton was offering Mass at the main altar of St. Patrick's Cathedral in New York City. It was the feast of Marcellinus and Peter, two martyrs who were beheaded at the beginning of the fourth century, simply for being Christians.

As he was preaching about the sufferings of Christ and the holy martyrs, a tall, somewhat feeble old man, supported by a young man and a young woman, went down the center aisle. The Father pretended not to notice and continued his sermon on the idea that "the more one participates in the suffering of Christ, the more one shares in His consolation," a direct quote from St. Paul.

At communion time, the young woman gestured toward the elderly gentleman, explaining he was tortured for many years in prison behind the Iron Curtain. Father Caton assumed that she wanted him to bring Holy Communion over to her elderly friend because he was weak. He did so immediately. The old gentleman received it reverently, thanking the priest many times.

"Later, before the final prayer," Father Caton said, "I did something I've never done before. I spoke to the congregation about a man in their midst who had spent many years confined in a Communist prison. Then I directed a question to him, 'What country are you from, sir?'"

"Romania," he replied in broken English. "I spent fourteen years in prison there, three of them in solitary."

The priest noticed for the first time that he was wearing what looked like a gray clerical shirt but without the white collar. "Are you by any chance a priest?"

"No," he said. "I was confined with many brave Catholic priests and bishops, but I am a Lutheran pastor."

"I was taken aback. I had just given Communion to a Lutheran minister in St. Patrick's Cathedral. I had to smile at God's wonderful sense of humor. Quickly recovering, I said, 'You are all the more welcome here, my friend.'"

After Mass, the young escorts went back to Father Caton to thank him for making their friend feel welcome. They told him his name was Richard Wurmbrand, the author of *Tortured for Christ*.

A week later, they sent six of Richard's books to the priest. In the one entitled *100 Prison Meditations, Cries of Truth from Behind the Iron Curtain*, Richard had written, "Christians are meant to have the same vocation as their King, namely that of cross bearers. To be conscious of a high calling and a partnership with Jesus brings gladness in tribulation. It makes Christians enter prisons for their faith with the joy of a bridegroom entering the bridal room."

"Reflecting on this whole experience some months later," said Father Caton, "I feel privileged to have encountered this great Christian gentleman who suffered so much for Christ. I think the Lord wanted him to be treated as an honored guest at St. Patrick's Cathedral that day, and happily, I was His unwitting instrument, canon law notwithstanding."

CHAPTER 24

Without pen or paper, in a Bucharest prison, on Christmas 1948, Richard composed and memorized a poem, "Rejoice, Emmanuel the Child King Is with Us." Out of prison, he wrote it in rhymed verse in Romanian and then translated it into free verse in English.

He describes his thoughts that Christmas day:

When I was in solitary confinement, I felt much longing for my mother, who had had a difficult life and now, in her old age, had the added suffering of knowing that her youngest son was in prison. After my liberation, I heard that she had written innumerable times to the Romanian president asking him to release me. She never received a reply.

My thoughts went also to the many other mothers of sufferers. Then I remembered the Virgin Mary, whom the evangelist Luke describes as the lady with the pierced heart. Looking upon her with different eyes, I composed a lullaby that I imagined she might have sung to the Baby Jesus, lying in the manger.

> In tears, I sing to You a lullaby.
> Gabriel supposed he could hide the truth from me.
> He promised victory, but You, my Child, will be defeated.
> You will have not a throne, but a cross.
>
> Gabriel was considerate. He would not say

Richard and Sabina

What fate awaits You in the world.
Another angel, too, brought a joyful message
To the shepherds. He said You'll have renown.

But today, my little Child, may
You sleep quietly. You are small and don't know what follows.
But I feel as if a knife were piercing
My heart, which is full of You.

Your whole delicate body I see lacerated by the whip.
You have nails in both hands and feet.
I see Your hair in disorder and spittle on your face.
Yet I hear the wind blow softly round the stable.

Has there ever been a mother with so much pain,
Set apart to bring up a Man of Sorrows?
Lord, I would gladly give You all You ask
That the storm may come and beat upon me instead.

Gladly would I bear Your cross and mine
While whispering an honest prayer:
"Give Your love to Your tormentors;
Show them love in this dark night."

I pray You might have a throne after the cross—
But not a small one, like King David's.
May not the slightest rumor trouble it
With wrong intent and greed, like Absalom's.

May Your throne be beauty, with all forgiven.
May Your eyelids be closed in heaven, too,
That even Your enemies will appear clean.
And may hell-fire be quenched with love's strange ice.

Sleep quietly, my sleepless Babe.

Soon they will come to kill You.
But You'll arise as Lord with healing in Your wings,
The Sun of righteousness for all the worlds.

CHAPTER 25

After 25 years of exile, the Wurmbrands returned to their native land. This was made possible by the execution of Nicolae Ceausescu and his wife on Christmas Day, 1989, ending Communist control of Romania.

On May 14, 1990 they arrived at Otopeni airport in Bucharest, where they were met by a throng of friends. After embraces and Romanian kisses, prayers were said and hymns were sung. One of the singers was Nicolae Moldoveanu who had written many of the hymns. He sang lustily the one he had composed while forced to lie on his back on the cold damp stones of his prison cell. During his years in prison with Richard he composed over 180 hymns.

The Wurmbrands spent much time at the Stephanus Bookstore established by the Voice of the Martyrs. It was the only Christian bookstore and library in Romania. Well stocked with Bibles and other Christian literature in several languages, it was a popular place to browse, read, and buy. Twenty thousand books were sold the first day and 300,000 Bibles had been sold before the Wurmbrands' visit.

Thus far, the books had been printed by VOM presses in Australia and Germany. In September 1990, it was learned that an auction of a printing press was to be held in Germany. VOM got the press at a considerable discount and it was taken to Bucharest and set up in a Stephanus annex. On January 1991, the press was put into operation.

An interesting sidelight to the story of the printing press is that it had belonged to the East Germany Communist Party to produce, among other things, atheistic propaganda. Now it is producing Christian literature.

The Stephanus Press was turning out so many books that a storage area was needed. When Ceaucescu was in power, he built a magnificent palace requiring the razing of several buildings, including the Secret Police headquarters under which was the prison that held Richard in solitary for three years. His cell is still there. Richard cried when he entered it, but later, he and Sabina danced with joy. Ironically, the cell became part of the storage area for Stephanus Christian books.

At Constanta, beside the Danube canal, Sabina relived her slave-labor days with Mr. Caraiman, a fellow slave, who demonstrated the days of labor by heaving large rocks. They were two of the rare survivors of those rigorous days.

Tirgusor prison, in which Sabina had been incarcerated, now held female criminals (political prisoners were released with the demise of Communism). In the packed auditorium, Sabina climbed onto a bench, saying she wanted to see them all while she spoke to them. She preached a sermon about Christ and his forgiving nature. She emphasized it with a story about a mother who kept her front door open and a light on for many years while she waited for the return of a wayward daughter. When the daughter finally returned and asked why, the mother told her of her love for her and how she never lost faith.

Many faces registered remorse and several women sobbed. Sabina comforted them individually as they filed out. New Testaments, food, and toiletries were given to them.

While in Romania Richard preached in many churches, especially Lutheran, Baptist, and Pentecostal.

The Wurmbrands noted the severe post-Communism poverty of the people. Unemployment was high. Those fortunate enough to have employment were making about 20 to 30 US dollars per month. The black market was active and police bribery was rampant.

Those who suffered the most were the children. Richard said

that thousands fled abusive homes and state-run institutions, where food was in short supply and compassion even shorter. At night, they lived in sewers and subway stations. During the day they begged for money to buy food or drugs.

According to a syndicated wire in May 1996, the situation of Romania's orphans is one of the world's ongoing tragedies. There are now more than 100,000 institutionalized children in Romania, and their living conditions are often primitive.

Tens of thousands of babies have been abandoned on doorsteps and at state facilities. As before, healthcare workers and orphanage employees routinely steal goods—for use by their own scarcely surviving families or to sell on the black market. And many parents are still abandoning children they can't afford.

Despite these sobering statistics, national pride still prevents the adoption of these tragic orphans into comfortable homes in the West. "We won't sell our heritage," one Romanian official defiantly proclaimed, thus sentencing another generation of children to a life of psychological torture and abuse.

Although it's only a tiny fix for a chronic situation, the VOM founded an orphanage at Pascani, in eastern Romania. They named it Agape Children's Home, *agape* being quite appropriate, as it means "love."

Often, several children come from one family, allowing them to grow up together. Here the children experience more than just three meals a day, clean clothes, and a warm bed. They experience life in a home as a family. "They learn what it means to be a child of God," Richard said. "They are taught Bible stories, learn to pray, and read Christian books. Through the demonstration of the love of Christ, these children can grow up in a stable, loving environment."

Although slowed down by age and illness, Richard and Sabina, through the Voice of the Martyrs, continue to preach Christ throughout the world.

EPILOGUE

Twelve days ago on August 11, 2000 Sabina left this earth to join her beloved Jesus. Those present said her eyes turned a brilliant blue as she gazed into the distance. Her physician, Dr. Donato Garcia said, "I felt as though the Lord came into the room and took her with Him. I did not dare intervene."

Sabina had been brought by her son Michael to a Catholic hospital in Tijuana, Mexico to receive a controversial method of chemotherapy in which insulin is used in conjunction with smaller doses of chemicals. She was in much pain and physically wasted by an adenocarcinoma of the stomach which had metastasized. Her original surgery had been in a hospital in New Jersey five years previously. The recurrence was rapidly progressive. Nine days before it was discovered she had been pronounced free of cancer.

Those who were with her in Tijuana felt that the treatment gave Sabina a few extra weeks of meaningful life. It lessened her pain, made her able to take nourishment and made her alert, at least enough to teach bible lessens and comfort those around her.

Sabina's memorial service and interment were at Sky Rose Chapel and Rose Hills Cemetery in Whittier, California. Reverend Daniel Brinzei of Romania conducted the service. It is estimated 1500 people participated. All continents except Antartica and all major islands were represented.

Over 250 newspapers throughout the world published Sabina's

death and burial. A New Delhi paper gave her full front page coverage. Churches throughout the world held memorial services for her. Surely she was universally beloved.

Right up until shortly before her death, Sabina asked about the status of her biography which this author had hoped would be in her living hands. An elegy, which was read at her graveside, was thus written. It follows:

Elegy for Sabina Wurmbrand

Sabina dear, I let you down,
You wished to see your warmth
Spread on cold pages of a book
So others may find their way
Amidst the jungles of the world.

Have no fear, you wrote
Your own biography
On hearts of those who passed your way.
Idle words—fear was not a part of you,
Danube slave, orphan of the Holocaust,
Converter of your torturers.

Your smile masked your pain
And eased the pain of those
Touched by your magnetic presence.

Resting beside a Cape Cod pond
A continent separates me from your bier.
While birds sing a lullaby,
The only sound except
A breeze among the trees
Bringing Bintzea to my ear,
A name reserved for closest friends
Including me.

I salute you Bintzea,
Lover of mankind and our God.

In April of this year Sabina addressed the Voice of the Martyrs Mission Volunteers at a Volunteer Appreciation Dinner. She ended her sermon with the following personal story.

"I would like to close with a personal story. I would like to tell you of just one of the experiences which we had in Communist prisons. At a certain moment, I was a slave worker in a Communist prison-camp and worked at building a huge canal. Altogether thousands of women we were sad. But we had among us a young Jewish lady who was a doctor. She was sadder than all the others. Nobody could speak with her. One day I was on my straw mattress. Near me was this Jewish lady, the doctor, and I tried to comfort her sad heart. I said, 'You as a Jewish lady should not be so in despair. For God has promised to our forefather Abraham, that the Jewish people will have a bright future. That they will be like the sand on the seashore and like the stars in the sky.' She lifted up to me her beautiful sad eyes, tears ran down her cheeks. She said, 'Surely, like the sand on the seashore, trodden under the feet of everyone as we are trodden here under the feet of the Communist guards. But like the stars in the sky? Don't speak to me anymore about your God.' She went away. Nobody could speak with her. A very few days after this, I awoke one morning deathly sick. I say deathly sick, that means near, near to death. So in order not to die in this cell, I was thrown in a van of the Communist police and taken to another prison which they called the hospital.

Many women dying were here. Two or even three in a small bed. Everyone waiting just a day or two or three to be taken out to the nearby cemetery. There we were. It was before a Communist holiday. So in the evening the director of the prison entered together with some ten of his officers. He looked around among the dying women. Altogether we looked like ghosts. Remember thousands and thousands like them today in Communist prisons and slave labor camps in Communist China, Vietnam, North Korea.

Your sisters. He looked around to the dying women and delivered a speech. 'Now you see, we the Communists have all the power. We prevailed. We are stronger than your God. We have hospitals. We have medicine. We have doctors and we don't need your God anymore, your Christ. In here, in our hospital, you are not meant even to mention the name of God or Christ.' Silence, big silence followed. Nobody dared to answer nor did any of the women have strength to speak even. But the Holy Spirit was there. He gave me strength. He gave the right words. I said, 'Mr. Officer, as long as death and sickness will be on earth, and you see how near death we are all together. As long as death and sickness will be on earth, we need absolutely God. We need Jesus Christ the son of God, the only giver of life.' The director went into a rage and answered. I answered. When he didn't know anymore what to say, he went out and banged the door. The women were so happy. It was the most beautiful event which happened in their sad prison life. They embraced each other on the beds of happiness that someone had stood up to this Communist brute. Early the next morning when it was still dark, a guard entered with a list of three names—women who were fit to go back to work. The first of the three names was mine. No question about going. I was dying. I was thrown again into the van and brought back to the prison cell. When the prisoners saw me they started to cry. They banged at the door calling for help. Nobody came. The next morning when the thousands were gathered in order to be taken to the field, I had to go with them. No question about going, standing. The other prisoners took me on their arms, walking miles and miles. Who could ever, who could ever describe what it meant—marching, hungry, sick, marching, marching, marching to the fields day by day, surrounded by the many Communist guards with their rifles. Surrounded by big, big dogs. When you only saw them, your heart was frozen. So they walked, having also to carry me on their arms. When we arrived, they had to put me down on the ground. Nobody was allowed to stand near me. Everyone had to work. There I was. Many of the Christians worked and wept, being convinced that they had put me there in my grave forever. While nobody was allowed to come near me, in a second, Jesus stood before me. He had passed the guards. Jesus touched my dying body and in the evening, when the thousands of prisoners were brought to the prison cell, I was with them. Like a fire, it spread all over the prison. Late in the evening, I was on my straw mattress, on the concrete when this Jewish lady doctor came and confessed that seeing such a miraculous healing she acknowledged now her belief in the true prophet, the Messiah who had touched my body and had healed me.

Sabina, as well as Richard, not only claims to have experienced miracles but has utmost faith in them.

Richard, at the age of 91, is in a precarious state of health and was unable to attend his wife's funeral. He has 18 deep torture scars on his body as well as other torture residuals such as painful feet and a stenosed esophagus which requires feeding through a tube penetrating his abdomen. For years he has had cervical and lumbar stenosis and peripheral neuropathy. He is in and out of lucidity. This past week my son Chris sat by his bedside for two hours talking about Sabina's life and death and he appeared to be completely lucid. But then he forgets she is dead. For the past couple of years he has spent hours screaming as though reliving his years of torture.

Son Michael is happily remarried to a lady by the name of Mi who has a six-year-old daughter Mimi. Michael's children by his first wife Judy are doing well. Daughter Amy, age 28, is a talented painter. Son Alex, age 22, is a concert violinist.

The Voice of the Martyrs, founded by Richard and Sabina, is a highly successful organization under the able direction of Tom White, a devout Christian who was imprisoned in Cuba because of his religious activities. The VOM serves the persecuted church, working in over fifty countries through its own International Christian Association of mission offices.

VOM's main purpose is:

1. To encourage and empower Christians to fulfill the Great Commission in areas of the world where they are persecuted for their involvement in propagating the gospel of Jesus Christ. They accomplish this by providing Bibles, literature, radio broadcasts, and other forms of aid.
2. To give relief to the families of Christian Martyrs in these areas of the world.
3. To equip local Christians to win to Christ those who are opposed to the gospel in countries where believers are actively persecuted for their Christian faith.
4. To undertake projects of encouragement, helping believers rebuild their lives and Christian witness in countries that have formerly suffered Communist oppression.
5. To emphasize the fellowship of all believers by informing the world of atrocities committed against Christians and by remembering their courage and faith.

The Voice of the Martyrs is alive and well. It has over 98,000 regular contributors, some of whom also volunteer their time and services.

CHRONOLOGY

1. March 24, 1909—Richard Wurmbrand born.

2. July 10, 1913—Sabina Wurmbrand born.

3. 1919—Greater Romania born of Versailles Treaty.

Bessarabia and Northern Bukovina, under Russian rule from 1812 to 1918, given to Romania because populated by mainly Romanians. This not recognized by new Soviet government.

4. Oct.23, 1935—Richard and Sabina married.

5. 1937—Richard and Sabina converted to Christianity.

6. 1938—King Carol II institutes a personal dictatorship because of widespread disillusionment with parliamentary government which in turn caused increased support for the Fascist Iron Guard.

7. March 23, 1939—German-Romanian economic agreement guaranteed German predominance in Romanian economy.

8. Aug.1939—Nazi-Soviet pact forced Romania to cede Bessarabia and N. Bukovina to Soviets and northern Transylvania to Hungary.

9. Sept. 1939—treaty of Craiova caused Romania to cede S. Dobruja to Bulgaria.

10. 1939—Richard becomes Secretary to Anglican Church Mission to the Jews.

11. May 27, 1940—Carol shifts toward Germany after Germany's sweep to the Channel.

12. June 26, 1940—Romania accedes to Soviet ultimatum demanding cession of Bessarabia and N. Bukovina to them.

13. Aug. 2, 1940—Bessarabia and N. Bukovina and some other territory became Moldavia, S.S.R. Romanians deported to Central Asia as laborers to replace Soviets drafted into army. It is estimated about 300,000 deported.

14. Sept. 6, 1940—By popular demand, Carol abdicated his throne to his son Michael, age 19.

15. Oct. 12, 1940—German military mission entered Romania to rebuild Romanian army. German economic mission arrived to direct Romanian economy toward Germany's military needs. Iron Guard unleashed reign of terror against its opponents and against Jews. Hitler supported Prime Minister Antonescu's disarming Iron Guard.

16. Dec. 4, 1940—Germany, by economic maneuvers, achieved both direct and indirect control of Romania's economy.

17. 1941—Richard becomes a member of Swedish Israel Mission.

18. Jan. 21, 1941—Antonescu with Hitler's approval crushed rebellion of Iron Guard because Hitler needed a stable Romania as a springboard for invasion of U.S.S.R.

19. Jan. 27, 1941—Iron Guard dissolved. Antonescu formed new cabinet almost entirely of military officers. Military dictatorship established which remained in power until Aug. 1944.

20. June 22, 1941—Deportation of Romanians interrupted by German attack on Soviet Union. Germans were joined by Romania under General Antonescu in order to recover Bessarabia and N. Bukovina.

21. July 27, 1941—Bessarabia and N. Bukovina regained by Romania at a cost of over 10,000 soldiers.

22. Oct. 16, 1941—Odessa captured at a cost of almost 42,000 Romanian soldiers killed or missing and almost 90,000 wounded. In addition to desire to annex lost territories, Antonescu considered it a holy war against Bolshevism.

23. Nov. 28, 1941—under pressure from Stalin. Britain sent ultimatum to Romania to cease military operations in the U.S.S.R. by Dec. 5.

24. Dec. 7, 1941—United Kingdom declared war on Romania.

25. Dec. 12, 1941—Romania declared war on U.S.A.

26. Winter of 1941-2—Romania deported Jews and Gypsies from Bessarabia to camps in Transnistria which Antonescu had annexed from the Ukraine in Aug. '41. 108,000 resettled. Many deportees, packed in railway cars without food and water, arrived dead. Many survivors were shot or starved to death by German and Romanian units.

27. Jan. 7, 1943—Soviets victorious at Stalingrad. Antonescu received peace feelers from within his own government and from the enemy. Romania attempted to convince Italy to make a

joint proposal to Allies to withdraw from war. Mussolini said no. Romania attempted to withdraw from war but foundered on Anglo-American insistence on unconditional surrender. Antonescu required a guarantee of post-war independence from U.S.S.R.

28. 1944—Richard becomes member of Norwegian Israel Mission.

29. April 1944—Romania reached agreement on armistice terms with U.K. and U.S.A.

30. June 1944—Armistice confirmed by Soviet. No Romanian empowered by Antonescu to sign agreement because of his reluctance to abandon German ally.

31. Aug. 23, 1944—Because of rapid Soviet advance on Romania, King Michael arrested Antonescu. Romanian forces opposing Soviet army surrendered. Romanian army turns on German army in Romania. Romanian casualties in German-Soviet war were 625,000. More than 100,000 taken prisoner by Soviets the week after Michael's coup although Molotov promised Romanian forces would keep their arms to fight Germany and Hungary.

32. Sept. 12, 1944—Soviet-Romanian armistice signed. Stalin fashioned legal framework to secure dominant political and economic interest in Romania. U.K. and U.S.A. were mere observers. Bessarabia is now part of Moldavia and Ukraine.

33. Oct. 1944—above agreement conceded by Churchill.

34. 1945—Romanians fought along with Red Army to drive Germans from Hungary and Czechoslovakia at a loss of 160,000 men. In terms of troops engaged in W.W.II, Romania was fourth after U.S.S.R., U.S.A., and U.K..

35. March 1945—Stalin ordered Romanian forces demobilized and installed puppet government under Petru Groza.

36. 1947—Peace treaty between U.S.S.R. and Romania signed.

37. Feb. 29, 1948—Richard arrested and imprisoned.

38. Aug. 1948—Sabina arrested and imprisoned.

39. 1951—Sabina released.

40. March 5, 1953—Stalin died.

41. 1956—Richard released from prison. Studied theology Univ. of Cluj. Ordained Lutheran minister.

42. 1959—Richard rearrested and imprisoned.

43. 1964—Richard released.

44. Dec. 6, 1965—Wurmbrands left Romania. Arrive in Norway on Christmas day.

45. Jan. 1966—Arrive in U.S.A.

46. May 1966—testified before U.S. Senate Committee of the Judiciary.

47. Sept. 1966—warned by Romanian government he would be assassinated if he continued his present exposures.

48. Aug. 10, 1967—testified before House of Representatives committee on Un-American Activities.

49. Oct. 1967—Wurmbrands founded Voice of Martyrs.

50. 1971—Wurmbrands naturalized.

51. 1972—Richard given honorary D.D. degree at Indiana Christian Univ.

52. May 26, 1984—Danube-Black Sea Canal opened by Romanian president Ceausescu.

53. Nov. 19, 1984—Ceausescu reelected president

54. Dec. 25, 1989—Ceausescu assassinated.

55. May 14, 1990—Wurmbrands visit Romania.

BIBLIOGRAPHY

Drewery, Mary, *Richard Wurmbrand: The Man Who Came Back*. Hodder & Stoughton, 1974.

Moise, Anutza, *A Ransom for Wurmbrand*. Grand Rapids: Zondervan, 1973.

Hanks, Geoffrey, *70 Great Christians*. Scotland: Christian Focus Publications Ltd, 1992.

Wurmbrand, Richard, *Tortured for Christ*. Bartlesville: Living Sacrifice Book Company, 1967.

Wurmbrand, Richard, *In God's Underground*. Bartlesville: Living Sacrifice Book Company, 1968.

Wurmbrand, Richard, *Christ on the Jewish Road*. Bartlesville: Living Sacrifice Book Company, 1970.

Wurmbrand, Richard, *From Suffering to Triumph*. Grand Rapids: Kregel Publications, 1993.

Wurmbrand, Sabina, *The Pastor's Wife*. Middlebury: Living Sacrifice Books, 1970.

Dear & Foot, *The Oxford Companion to World War II*. Oxford New York: Oxford University Press, 1995.

Monthly Newsletters of The Voice of the Martyrs.

Personal communications and interviews.

Senseless Love   4/24/11

[Em] Bloodied hands
[G] bloodied feet
[D] A chosen suffering just for me [A] A mess of pain
all to make me clean.

[Em] Why such misery
for my [D] victory?
Doesn't make sense to [A] me.

Chorus
[G/Em] Senseless love - that's what you [D] gave
For [A] your creation that turned away [Em]
Senseless [G] love - that what you did [D]
When you gave your life [A] away [Em]
for [G] me.

Tongues that cursed
hands that bruised
and so much more that we did to you.
How could you bear to take the blame
Take on our sin when we trashed your name

Chorus.

Bridge

C
Yet while we were still sinners.
    Em   A
An innocent man was slain
C
Yet while we were still sinners
   Em   A
The father gave His only son away.

Chorus.